SOCIAL JUSTICE IN HUMAN RELATIONS
VOLUME 2
Societal and Psychological
Consequences of
Justice and Injustice

CRITICAL ISSUES IN SOCIAL JUSTICE

Published in association with the International Center for Social Justice Research, Faculty of Social Sciences, ISOR, University of Utrecht, The Netherlands.

Series Editors: **MELVIN J. LERNER** AND **RIËL VERMUNT**
University of Waterloo *University of Leiden*
Waterloo, Ontario, Canada *Leiden, The Netherlands*

Recent volumes in this series

A Continuation Order Plan is available for this series. A continuation order will bring delivery of each new volume immediately upon publication. Volumes are billed only upon actual shipment. For further information please contact the publisher.

SOCIAL JUSTICE IN HUMAN RELATIONS VOLUME 2
Societal and Psychological Consequences of Justice and Injustice

Edited by
Herman Steensma
and
Riël Vermunt
University of Leiden
Leiden, The Netherlands

PLENUM PRESS • NEW YORK AND LONDON

Library of Congress Cataloging-in-Publication Data

Social justice in human relations.
        p.   cm. -- (Critical issues in social justice)
    Includes bibliographical references and indexes.
    Contents: v. 1. Societal and psychological origins of justice /
edited by Riel Vermunt and Herman Steensma -- v. 2. Societal and
psychological consequences of justice and injustice / edited by
Herman Steensma and Riel Vermunt.
    ISBN 0-306-43625-6 (v. 1). -- ISBN 0-306-43626-4 (v. 2)
    1. Social justice.   I. Vermunt, Riël.   II. Steensma, Herman.
III. Series.
HM216.S556   1991
303.3'72--dc20   90-25382
                                                               CIP

ISBN 0-306-43626-4

© 1991 Plenum Press, New York
A Division of Plenum Publishing Corporation
233 Spring Street, New York, N.Y. 10013

Printed in the United States of America

Contributors

Jacques Allegro, Department of Psychology, University of Leiden, P.O. Box 9555, 2312 KM Leiden, The Netherlands

Piet Hermkens, Department of Planning Organization and Policy Studies, Faculty of Social Sciences, University of Utrecht, P.O. Box 80.140, 3508 TC Utrecht, The Netherlands

Guillermina Jasso, Department of Sociology, University of Iowa, Iowa City, Iowa 52242

Louise H. Kidder, Department of Psychology, Temple University, Philadelphia, Pennsylvania 19122

David van Kreveld, Institute of Social Psychology, University of Utrecht, P.O. Box 80.140, 3508 TC Utrecht, The Netherlands

Henk Kruidenier, Dutch Institute for the Working Environment, Amsterdam, The Netherlands

E. Allan Lind, The American Bar Foundation, 750 North Lake Shore Drive, Chicago, Illinois 60611

Sally Lloyd-Bostock, Centre for Socio-Legal Studies, Wolfson College, University of Oxford, Oxford OX2 6UD, England

David M. Messick, Department of Psychology, University of California, Santa Barbara, California 93106

Leo Montada, Department of Psychology, Trier University, FB1–Psychologie, D-5500, Trier, West Germany

Susan Muller, Department of Psychology, Temple University, Philadelphia, Pennsylvania 19122

Bert Overlaet, Department of Psychology, K. U. Leuven, 3000 Leuven, Belgium

Bernard M. S. van Praag, Econometric Institute, Erasmus University, P.O. Box 1738, 3000 DR Rotterdam, The Netherlands

Nico L. van der Sar, Department of Business Finance, Erasmus University, P.O. Box 1738, 3000 DR Rotterdam, The Netherlands

Erik Schokkaert, Center for Economic Studies and Center for Economics and Ethics, K. U. Leuven, 3000 Leuven, Belgium

Herman Steensma, Department of Social and Organizational Psychology, University of Leiden, P.O. Box 9555, 2333 AK Leiden, The Netherlands

A. Szirmai, Department of Economics, University of Groningen, P.O. Box 800, 9700 AV Groningen, The Netherlands

Tom R. Tyler, Departments of Psychology and Political Science, Northwestern University, Evanston, Illinois, 60208, and The American Bar Foundation, 750 North Lake Shore Drive, Chicago, Illinois 60611

Riël Vermunt, Department of Social and Organizational Psychology, University of Leiden, P.O. Box 9555, 2333 AK Leiden, The Netherlands

Preface

Justice plays an important role in our culture. The topic of justice has attracted the attention of scholars all over the world. Beginning in 1985, a continuing series of international conferences on social justice started in The Netherlands at which scientists present and discuss papers, exchange information, and choose new roads to theory building.

In this volume, a selection of papers, presented at the International Conference on Social Justice in Human Relations (Leiden, 1986) is published. There has been some refinement and improvement, thanks to the comments made by experts in the field. The chapters in this volume represent second (and, in some cases, even third or fourth) versions of the papers.

As organizers of the conference and editors of this volume, we hope that the reader will be pleased by the content and the high quality of the chapters. There is some diversity, but there also are some common themes. We have organized the chapters with respect to what we think are two important themes: (1) behavioral and attitudinal reactions to (in)justice and (2) macrojustice. These categories are not mutually exclusive, for some chapters could have been placed in both categories. Still, we think the distinction between these themes has value.

The volume's contributors are all well known for their commitment to the study of justice. This book demonstrates that such commitment can take many forms. We believe that all these forms are necessary for finding solutions to what we think is the most important problem for human beings: finding just procedures to allocate outcomes in a way that give rise to feelings of justice.

This book could not have been published without the efforts of many persons, who deserve our sincere acknowledgment. We wish to thank the Royal Dutch Academy of Sciences and the Department of

Social and Organizational Psychology of Leiden University for their financial support, which made the conference possible. We wish to acknowledge the support of the "Dienst Sociaal Wotenschappelijk Onderzoek" of Leiden University for the valuable assistance in running the conference, and our secretary Maja Metselaar for her help in preparing this book.

Eliot Werner, of Plenum Press, and Melvin J. Lerner, editor of the Critical Issues in Social Justice series, have been very kind, patient, and most of all very helpful in the process of preparing this volume. We must also mention the help of Faye Crosby, who reviewed the manuscript. And, of course, we wish to thank all the contributors to the Social Justice in Human Relations conference. Without their contribution neither the conference nor this book would have been possible.

Herman Steensma
Riël Vermunt

Contents

**Chapter 5   Aspects of Distributive and Procedural Justice
in Quality of Working Life 99**

Jacques Allegro, Henk Kruidenier, and Herman Steensma

PART II   MACROJUSTICE

**Chapter 6   Social Justice, Income Distribution, and
Social Stratification in The Netherlands:
A Review 119**

Piet Hermkens and David van Kreveld

Introduction

Herman Steensma and Riël Vermunt

At our request, several experts in the field have written chapters on social justice in human relations, which are published in two volumes. As in Volume 1, *Societal and Psychological Origins of Justice*, the chapters in this volume are organized in two parts: "Behavioral and Attitudinal Reactions to (In)justice" and "Macrojustice." In this Introduction, we shall briefly summarize the several chapters of the two parts.

Behavioral and Attitudinal Reactions to (In)justice

People are interested in promoting justice. Now sometimes things happen that violate their well-being. Can we say more about the nature of these stressful events and about their effects?

Sometimes the events come rather unexpectedly: People are robbed or they are involved in an accident. These events are so stressful that they create a personal crisis for the victim. But, in general, victims are not the only persons involved. Sometimes other persons are responsible for the fate of the victim. And sometimes professional assistance is offered to victims (e.g., by police officers).

Professional assistance is frequently sought in other kinds of stressful events: conflicts that have escalated in such a way that legal institutions have to find a solution. Quite often, we cannot speak of a

Herman Steensma and Riël Vermunt • Department of Social and Organizational Psychology, University of Leiden, P.O. Box 9555, 2333 AK Leiden, The Netherlands.

victim in this case but of two (or more) different "parties" with different interests in outcome distributions.

Escalation of conflicts may create a crisis for society. Therefore, we must know more about the effectiveness of the institutions that have been created to solve these problems and the mechanisms that make these institutions work. In this part of the volume, the focus is on the different responses of several persons and parties involved in stressful events: victims, perpetrators of the events, professionals, and the parties, both with and—in the case of the presence of third parties— without a personal interest in the distribution.

Montada (Chapter 1) pays attention to the complex relationship between life stress and injustice. Not every stressful life event is experienced as unjust by the victim. Montada discusses several factors that may influence the experience of injustice. In that respect, the question "who is responsible" has to be answered first. Personal control seems to be very important (e.g., feelings of control over outcomes and feelings of injustice are incompatible). In his review, Montada notes that two questions have guided most research: the aspect of blaming the victim and the aspect of (reduction of) self-blame. Several hypotheses are presented to explain the research evidence.

Victims differ in coping ability and in their responses to events. In our society, some people specialize in taking care of victims and/or in removing the causes of stressful life events. Actions of these "professionals" may differ sharply from reactions of victims. This result is shown very clearly in the research by Lloyd-Bostock (Chapter 2). Victims of occupational accidents take a lot of time before an understanding of the causes and implications of the accident crystallizes, whereas factory inspectors respond comparatively rapidly, and more or less automatically. Categorization of events (e.g., accidents) may have important consequences for the judged appropriateness of particular outcomes and procedures. In this respect, the interesting observation has been made that categorization will be at least partly a function of the social context.

In his contribution, Messick (Chapter 3) states that social dilemmas are situations in which individuals or groups, through their behaviors, create undesirable consequences and try to realize desirable consequences. Solutions of the social dilemma may be realized at the individual level or at the structural level. Messick mentions the appointment of a leader as one of the possible structural solutions. Another structural solution is changing the rules of the game; in this way, Messick relates solutions of social dilemmas to the topic of procedural justice. Distributive justice is, in his view, related to individual solutions of social dilemmas. Individual solutions are also related to concepts of efficiency and equality.

In the contribution of Tyler and Lind, (Chapter 4), the results of the past decade of procedural justice research are summarized, and new developments in that field are identified. The focus is mainly on procedural justice in legal institutions. Results from several studies show clearly that fairness judgments are more than simple reflections of the favorability of outcomes. Fair procedures have a positive effect on law abidingness, on political behavior, and—in work settings—on turnover intentions. In the literature, these effects are explained in terms of the possibility of "controlling" outcomes. Tyler and Lind defend the so-called "expression-orientation" position: expression or "voice" seems to be the key factor in procedural fairness. The question Tyler and Lind raise is whether these findings can be generalized to nonlegal settings, for example, work settings.

Allegro, Kruidenier, and Steensma (Chapter 5) present shocking data about the uneven distribution of quality of working life (QWL). Blue-collar workers as a group have a much lower QWL than white-collar workers have. They also suffer more from health problems and job disabilities, a major problem in terms of macrojustice. The authors present a strategy for improvement, based on a model of humanization of work. A central concept in this model is that of participation of workers. To have a voice is a very important aspect of procedural justice, as has been indicated by Tyler and Lind in this volume. Participation is conceived in this perspective by the authors.

Macrojustice

Principles of macrojustice apply to the perception of the overall distribution of rewards in a social system. People have preferences for the overall shape of the outcome distribution per se. It is quite possible that a conflict exists between micro- and macrojustice: A series of fair microdecisions may work out into an overall distribution that is considered unfair by most people involved (Brickman, Folger, Goode, & Schul, 1981). Principles of macrojustice specify constraints on the allowable characteristics of an overall distribution of resources, that is, the range should not be too large, there is a minimum standard, and so forth. In general, preferences for the shape of an overall outcome distribution are rather egalitarian. However, this egalitarianism varies with the kind of outcomes and with situations.

Macrojustice gets more attention in the contribution of Hermkens and van Kreveld (Chapter 6). These authors review studies on social

justice, income distribution, and social stratification in The Netherlands. As for the nature of income distribution, they conclude that this
distribution is fairly stable as far as it concerns the rank order of
positions. It turned out that the distribution is mainly affected by
educational level, age, and sex, as well as by job level. The authors
conclude the discussion by noting that two contradictory principles
seem to have governed the development of income distribution: a
microjustice principle, leading to a preference for equity, and a
macrojustice principle of social concern, leading to leveling of income
differences.

Although every human society has to solve the problems with
respect to authority, division of labor, and allocation of resources, each
society solves these problems in its own way. According to Kidder and
Muller (Chapter 7), Japan is a good example to study opinions of justice
because its historical development is different from that of the Western
countries. Kidder shows us a society in which the terms *just* or *fair* are
hardly applied in human interaction. Terms like *polite* and *honor* are
more important in human interaction than the term *fair* and reflect the
hierarchical nature of Japanese society.

Jasso (Chapter 8) describes how the basic sense of distributive
justice leads to the emergence and maintenance of social welfare
institutions. Welfare institutions increase the average well-being of (a
majority of) the population. Social welfare seems to increase with the
geometric mean of the actual holdings of a valued good, but it
decreases with the geometric mean of the just or expected holdings. By
mathematical manipulation, Jasso obtains a more refined expression
for social welfare.

Problems concerning societal gender inequalities and the social
welfare effects of monastic institutions are used in a very creative way
to illustrate the utility of this approach.

Overlaet and Schokkaert's chapter (Chapter 9) demonstrates the
importance of questionnaire research on ethical institutions predomi-
nant in society and its subgroups. It is found that seniority, educational
level, and hierarchical position are under some conditions viewed as
legitimate justifications for income differences. One of the main
conditions under which these claims are made is that the efforts are
comparable. Needs and tastes are viewed as important components of
justice evaluations. Finally, it was found that people react differently
toward distribution of a profit compared to distribution of a loss.

The main virtue of the chapter "Social Distance on the Income
Distribution Dimension" by Van Praag and van der Sar (Chapter 10) is
its methodological contribution. The concept of social distance is
defined by a measurement method. This concept is asymmetric, that is,
the distance between Morton and Melvin is not necessarily equal to

that between Melvin and Morton. The social distance concept is measured in terms of influence: the more influence, the smaller the social distance. Operationalization is based on the social-filter function that translates the objective income distribution into the subjective norms on incomes, as reflected by the Income-Evaluation-Question response. Empirical evaluation of an American data set gives promising results.

Szirmai (Chapter 11) presents some results of a study on attitudes toward income inequality in The Netherlands. From the results it can be concluded, among other things, that a considerable part of the variation of attitudes toward inequality can be explained by respondent characteristics. The tendency to equalize incomes is strongly associated with self-interest in relative terms. Subjects who favor equality of income generally believe that equality will improve their relative income position. These results may be important in setting standards for income policy.

References

Brickman, P., Folger, R., Goode, E., & Schul, Y. (1981). Microjustice and Macrojustice. In M. J. Lerner & S. C. Lerner (Eds.), *The justice motive in social behavior* (pp. 173–202). New York: Plenum Press.

I

Behavioral and Attitudinal Reactions to (In)justice

1

Coping with Life Stress
Injustice and the Question "Who Is Responsible?"

Leo Montada

Justice and the Responsibility for Harmful Events

When analyzing victimization by stressful life events, we must answer questions: Who is responsible for the stressful event? What rights have been infringed? Is someone to blame? Who is responsible for restitution or compensation?

Answers to these questions are seldom given unanimously (they often change intraindividually, too, either as a function of external information or of coping strategies). People have different and conflicting perspectives, beliefs, attitudes, value systems, ideologies. There are formal and informal negotiations about the answers, formal ones in trials, informal ones in everyday communication and interaction. The participants in these negotiations are victims, harmdoers, and observers (Steil & Slochower, 1985).

Until now, research on this topic has pointed out some puzzling phenomena, such as blaming the victim or denying being victimized. Theoretical accounts have brought forth some fascinating hypotheses, such as belief in a just world where everybody gets what he/she deserves (Lerner, 1977, 1980) or belief in a controllable world (Shaver, 1970; Walster, 1966).

However, these concepts and hypotheses are often used *post hoc*

Leo Montada • Department of Psychology, Trier University, Fb I–Psychologie, D-5500 Trier, West Germany.

for interpretations of the observed phenomena. Perceived entitlements and responsibilities, as well as the needs for a just and controllable world, are not independently assessed. In many cases, it is open to question whether persons, after stressful events, perceive themselves as victims of a blind fate, as victims of actions and decisions of others (persons or institutions), or as losers in a fair play or a risky enterprise.

The racing driver who suffers an accident, the gambler in Monte Carlo who loses all his money, the AIDS patient—they need not necessarily experience any injustice. Whether they feel victimized or not depends on their perceived entitlements, which are established with reference to various rules of justice such as the rules of proportionality, of equality, of need; those of legal, political, and social rights; or those of procedural justice. Certainly, there are situational and individual differences in selecting and applying rules of justice when appraising a situation (Deutsch, 1975; Leventhal, 1976; Schmitt & Montada, 1982). And the selection, in turn, depends on the perceived responsibilities for the disadvantaged or for the victims.

Not every disadvantage or loss is judged as unjust, not necessarily because of repression of feelings or denial of injustice but because of a reasonable application of that very concept of justice. Some examples may illustrate this point. Bad events may be seen (1) as a just punishment for moral or legal offenses in the past (e.g., failure in an examination that was not carefully prepared for or breaking a traffic law), (2) as just compensation for lucky (undeserved) advantages in the past (e.g., paying an extra tax when the owner's house was not destroyed in the war), (3) as a retribution provoked by the person's own behavior, (4) as a consequence of a freely chosen commitment to a dangerous and risky enterprise motivated by the expectancy of highly valued gains, and (5) as generally imposed by social norms, obligatory for all similar members of the society (e.g., retirement or examinations that are of great stress).

Causality, Responsibility, and Liability to Blame: Some Distinctions

The designation of responsibility is at the core of the experience of injustice. This point needs to be clarified. The problems caused by stressful events may be great; yet they will only be perceived as unjust when a person or institution is held responsible and liable to blame. The impact of the concepts causality, responsibility, and blameworthiness, which unfortunately are often used interchangeably, were analyzed by Heart (1968), Fincham and Jaspars (1980), Shaver (1985), and Semin and Manstead (1983) among others.

Let us start with a real-life example. A truck with steel pipes drove through a village at high speed. In a curve, some of the heavy pipes fell off the truck. A bystander saw that a small child on the sidewalk was in deadly danger. He ran to the child and saved it by throwing it over a hedge into a garden. He himself was badly injured by the pipes. For months he was in the hospital. His legs and feet remained crippled. Who is to blame? The first candidate for blame is the driver of the truck. He caused the accident by driving too fast. Is he responsible? The driver has excuses. Surely, he did not wish or intend to cause the accident. He drove at his usual speed. He did not foresee the outcome. The truck had been overloaded. This was done by other people. (Putting the blame on other people might not be accepted by everyone. The driver is responsible for his truck. According to Hart [1968], this is a case of strict [or role] responsibility.)

Excuses do not deny any casual contribution to the outcome, but they deny responsibility, and if they are accepted, they cancel it. Semin and Manstead (1983), following Tedeschi and Riess (1981), mentioned as excuses (1) denial of agency (It wasn't me. It was not me alone. I was under hypnosis. I was forced), (2) denial of foreseeability, (3) denial of intent or denial of volition (with reference to physical causes, fatigue, drugs, paralysis, lack of competence, lack of authority), (4) claim of mitigating circumstances (behavior was an automated response to behavior of others, e.g., a provocation or reference to a dismal past).

Maybe the driver does not deny his responsibility. Is he to blame in this case? Blameworthiness is not implied in responsibility. The driver may have justifications. Justifications do not deny responsibility; they deny or reduce blameworthiness. We must consider several possibilities of a justification in this case:

1. The driver has a role responsibility only for the loading of the truck. In fact, he has no control over the weight or the stability of the load.
2. He was given the order to drive fast and, in general, he would risk his job if he observed all speed limits.
3. In this special case the load was urgently needed to repair a pipeline.

Semin and Manstead (1983) distinguished eight categories of justifications (see also Tedeschi & Riess 1981): (1) the claim that the effect has been misrepresented or misinterpreted (denial or minimization of injury). (2) reference to a principle of retribution (e.g., the victim deserves the injury because of his or her actions or qualities). This is a typical justification for blaming or derogating the victim; (3) reference to equality (others do the same or worse but go unnoticed or unpunished or even praised); (4) reference to higher authority (other persons commanded, institutional rules stipulated); (5) self-fulfillment (self-maintenance, self-development, action in accordance with one's own conscience); (6) reference to principles of utilitarianism (law and order, self-defense, or benefits outweigh losses); (7) reference to values (political, moral, religious values with which the action was in accordance); and (8) reference to a need for face (face-saving and building reputation).

These justifications do not deny responsibility; they rather offer reasons to reduce or cancel blameworthiness and liability for blame. Liability for blame is one aspect of the affair; liability for compensation is another. Let us go back to the example. Legally, the driver is not liable for compensation, but the insurance company is. And ultimately, it turned out that the offer for compensation by the company was considered unfairly low by the victim, who was very upset and felt victimized a second time. He found relief only in the knowledge that he saved the life of a child.

What are the reasons for this lengthy discussion? When turning to empirical studies, we find statements about attributions of responsibility to oneself, to an inflictor of pain or losses, to bystanders, to victims, to society, and so on. There are hypotheses connecting these attributions of responsibility to emotional and behavioral outcomes or to the health status of the victim. In many cases, it remains unclear what is meant or assessed: causal attributions, attributions of responsibility, liability for blame or blameworthiness? The implications of these various cognitions for coping with life stresses differ. Thus it is not surprising that the empirical evidence is not consistent.

Factors Affecting Perceived Injustice of Critical Life Events

Critical life events can be described by several attributes. Filipp (1981) offers a taxonomical scheme for analysis. There are several attributes of the event (as well as of the victim) that determine the outcome. Important attributes of the events are unforeseeability, controllability, or developmental aspects such as in-time—that is, whether an event such as pregnancy, retirement, or physically disability occurs within the normative age period—or off-time. Which attributes are relevant for the evaluation of the justice of life crises? Life crises caused by catastrophes, illness, crimes, changes in job requirements, social environments, and so forth imply losses of material goods, status,

health, loved ones, securities, self-esteem, and so forth. Often, losses are perceived as unjust. Why? I would like to refer to Moore (1984). Trying to answer the old question, why there is social peace despite enormous inequalities in wealth or power, Moore argues that people tend to justify given life circumstances, including given inequalities. When, however, things are changing for the worse, especially when this happens rapidly and unexpectedly, the same justifications will lead to feelings of injustice and to social conflicts because one's own justified entitlements are now hurt. Moore gives many historical examples, based primarily on the analysis of documents from nineteenth-century German.

Many critical life events are characterized by a sudden, unexpected worsening of a person's life circumstances. The entitlements so far existing are not (or have not yet been) given up. There was no opportunity for the construction or internalization of justifications for this new reality. Successful coping with stressful changes can be conceived of as finding justifications for the new situation. Age normative events or transitions such as initiation rites, leaving the parental home for college or marriage, becoming a parent, or reaching retirement are all expected in advance and anticipatory coping is possible. If events were foreseeable, for example, the death of a relative or friend after a long illness, anticipatory coping would be possible, such as focusing on the gains associated with the event. When a loved one dies after a severe illness, it may mean relief from pain for the loved one and also relief from experienced helplessness for the caregiver. Empirically, foreseeability of stressful events is a potent predictor of better coping and adjustment (Filipp, 1981; Filipp & Gräser, 1982).

Equity theory postulates that people experience justice or injustice in comparison with similar others. Critical life events often lead to deprivation in comparison with similar others, who are not equally affected. The distinction between normative and nonnormative stressful events bears on this point. Aside from age-normative (age-graded) events, there are history-normative (graded) events: natural, manmade, technical, or economic catastrophes (wars, for example) affect a large proportion of the population and one's own comparison group. In such cases, the experience of injustice is less probable than it is in the case of nonnormative events (e.g., crimes, accidents, diseases), which usually happen to single or a few individuals only.

However, this must not be true when one group of people is deprived unequally or inequitably. Shared fate as compared to single fate does not always prevent feelings of injustice. For example, when unemployment is unequally frequent among black people in the United States, Turkish people in Germany, women in all nations, then fraternal deprivation (Martin 1984; Runciman 1966) is not unusual and may motivate collective actions.

Reviews of the literature suggest that people usually cope more successfully with normative than with nonnormative events (Filipp & Gräser 1982). There are several hypotheses related to justice that explain this observation:

1. Injustice is not obvious, if one compares oneself with similar others sharing one's own fate.
2. There are more similar others with an even worse fate to be selected for downward comparisons (see Taylor et al., 1983, on cancer patients).
3. According to Kelley's analysis of causal attributions (Kelley 1973), the observation of shared fate (which is a case of what Kelley called "consensus") does not suggest personal (internal) explanations. Compared with the observation of a single, individual fate, situational (external) explanations, which do not effect self-esteem, are more probable. Derogative internal explanations are unusual after normative events. Thus, a secondary victimization by others' attributions is less probable.
4. Frequently, more public empathy, concern, and support are offered when there are numerous victims. Thus, compensation or restitution is socially managed. However, the overall effect of normative events will not always be less problematic. High unemployment rates may ease coping with unemployment, yet they may also reduce the chance of getting a new job.

Critical events may change one's reference group; hence, the similar others must be redefined. After separation, a spouse may become a single. Losing the job may imply change of neighborhoods and friends. Suffering an accident may turn a great sportsman into a handicapped person.

Critical life events per se are not just or unjust. The very concept of justice implies that some agent or agency is responsible for experienced losses or hardships. The experience of injustice is associated with resentment toward an agent, whose freely chosen actions or omissions lead to "unjust" consequences (the freedom to make decisions is a crucial prerequisite for the attribution of responsibility). Resentment is directed toward those persons (or institutions) who are perceived as being responsible for disadvantages that are not convincingly justified, and, as Mark and Folger (1984) add, have a "low likelihood" to improve in the near future.

A person who suffers disadvantages caused by his or her own

decisions (actions, omissions) does not have a target for complaints about injustice. The racing driver who survives an accident as a handicapped person does not complain about injustice. If he perceives other persons (another driver or mechanic) to be responsible, he may feel victimized. The donor of a kidney does not perceive himself as a victim but as a moral hero as long as he feels free to decide or not that he will donate his kidney. But if someone feels compelled by others, he/she is prone to reproaches. One's own decisional control over actions and outcomes seems to be incompatible with feelings of injustice. Successful coping with emotions of injustice is possible by choosing attributions that discharge the others of responsibility.

But even if another person is seen as responsible for one's losses or disadvantages, justice must not be doubted. One might accept the losses as did Abraham, who did not doubt the justice of his God. He was willing to obey the command to sacrifice his own son. Without understanding the reason of that demand, he seemed to take it for granted that his God had a reason. This is one of several ways in which feelings of injustice are avoided.

Paths to Subjective Justice

The need for justice can be satisfied in several ways: (1) by the assertion and carrying through of one's entitlements, (2) by an adequate compensation for disadvantages, (3) by blaming and punishing the responsible harmdoer, and (4) by apologies of the harmdoer to the sufferer. In research on critical life events, these—let us say—"normal" ways to achieve the restitution of justice have been rather neglected. I am not aware of studies on the effect of success or failure in lawsuits. Research was focused on the question: How do victims avoid perceiving themselves as victims and consequently, perceiving injustice?

Coping Strategies of Victims to Avoid the Perception of Injustice

According to Taylor, Wood, and Lichtman (1983), subjects' reports of stressful events may lead to the impression that there are no victims at all. They argue that victimization is aversive and that therefore, victims may tend to minimize their experience of injustice. Not only the primary effects of stressful events are harmful but also the implied loss of control, self-esteem, and normality. Some victims intuitively fear becoming stigmatized when they make their fate public, and hence they ignore their problems. Indeed, criminologists believe that a large proportion, if not a majority, of rape victims do not file a lawsuit (Schneider 1979).

What are the paths to avoid the feeling of being victimized? Taylor *et al.* (1983) mention several strategies apt to reduce feelings of being victimized: downward comparisons, imagination that it could even be worse, seeking some benefits or a meaning in the harmful event, self-enhancing evaluation of one's own coping. Self-blame may serve to reduce feelings of injustice. Certainly, not all victims accept the disadvantages imposed on them through actions and decisions of others, or the state and its institutions, and not all appease their feelings of injustice, but they rather resent them. Quite a few victims of crimes, or accidents, of unemployment, of illnesses caused by their job conditions, victims of pollution or of noise or of nuclear disaster fight for their entitlements. They might bring their complaints to trial, they might engage in political actions, they might organize civil protests, or they might accuse their God. But surprisingly often, people try to avoid feelings of injustice.

Downward Comparisons. Downward comparisons with people still worse off are frequently observed. Only two of 78 breast cancer patients, interviewed by Taylor *et al.* (1983), conceded that they had more problems than other patients. Burgess and Holmstrom (1979) reported that rape victims drew comparisons to other victims who suffered a greater loss of status or who died being raped. Wills (1981) reviewed the experimental evidence on downward comparisons and pointed to several signs of the preference frightened subjects have for downward comparisons, including seeking contacts with fellow sufferers.

Imagination of a Hypothetical Still Worse World. Downward comparisons are effected not only by the selection of adequate reference groups or people but also by the selection of adequate referent attributes. One patient stated after a mastectomy: "Sometimes I tell myself, it could be worse. I don't see it as if I have lost a hand." (Taylor *et al.*, 1983).

This may be an example for what Taylor (1982) called the strategy of building up functional illusions, for example, imagination of a hypothetical still worse world. Further examples of this strategy are as follows: A traffic victim states that he could have died in the accident; an elderly woman with cancer asserts that she is still lucky having cancer herself and not her daughter; or a patient after apoplexia with left side paralysis says: "If I imagine that I could have lost my speech, I feel that I am still well off."

Seeking Benefits in the Harmful Event. Some benefit can be found in the (victimizing) event itself. Sixty percent of the breast cancer patients in the Taylor *et al.* study reported positive changes in their lives as a side effect of their disease. Respondents listed, among other things, a reorganizing of priorities; they gave the relationship with spouse, children, and friends a higher value. In his study on victims of concentration camps, Frankl (1963) assumed that those survivors who were able to use their experience to find meaning in their lives were better adjusted. Similarly, cases may be subsumed to this category where the victimization happened on the occasion of an action or enterprise of which the actor is proud or which he/she perceives as an obligation, for example, intervention in crimes, accidents, or catastrophes. Wounded soldiers may feel like heroes if the war is perceived as a just one. Battered women often do not try to escape because of ethical responsibilities to help their victimizing husband or to take care of the children (Ferraro & Johnson 1983).

Self-Enhancing Evaluations of One's Own Coping. A positive evaluation of one's coping with stress and one's adaptive abilities and efforts may lead to satisfaction and even pride. Here, too, downward comparisons may be helpful because one's own coping efforts are put in a more favorable light. Twenty-one percent of the cancer patients in the Taylor *et al.* study made such comparisons. A similar tendency was found in partners of the patients. Some of the husbands were proud of not having abandoned their wife "like some guys would do in comparable situations".

Self-Blame for Stressful Life Events. In several reviews, evidence is reported that victims blame themselves for the occurrence of the stressful event even if there is no objective reason to do this. In some of the studies, self-blame was associated with indexes of better adjustment, for example the studies by Chodoff *et al.* (1964) on parents who lost a child, by Rappaport (1971) on relatives of Nazi victims in concentration camps, by Medea and Thompson (1974), Burgess and Holmstrom (1979) on rape victims, by Frieze (1979), and Ferraro and Johnson (1983) on battered women. However, the implications and consequences of self-blame are not homogenous with respect to the success of coping. Therefore, this strategy must be considered in more detail.

Excursus: Adaptive and Nonadaptive Aspects of Self-Blame

There is growing evidence that self-blame may have nonadaptive consequences. In a well-controlled German study on accident victims, Frey (1985) found that rehabilitation was retarded in patients who perceived the accidents as avoidable and self-inflicted. Meyer and Taylor (1986) found self-blame by rape victims associated with poor adjustment (sexual dissatisfaction, depression, fear). Studies on the effects of unemployment suggest that self-blame was not adaptive compared with external and societal explanations (Jaspars *et al.*, 1983).

Whenever there is contradictory evidence, one should think about differentiation within concepts. The core of the argument, that self-blame may be adaptive, is the following: Self-blame is thought to include beliefs of controllability. Victims who blame themselves seem to believe that they would have been able to avoid the event. They take responsibility for the event retrospectively. Does this imply that they will be able to avoid or to prevent a reoccurrence of the stressful event in the future, meaning they have prospective-control beliefs? Maybe some victims make such (logically doubtful) inferences: Perceived responsibility for the occurrence of an event and controllability beliefs with respect to future events do not imply each other. Some studies show that at least a significant proportion of the subjects distinguish between responsibility for past events and controllability of future events, but perhaps not all of them do. In an early study on rape victims, Libov and Doty (1979) did not find a correlation between self-responsibility and the belief in not being raped a second time.

Taylor (1982), in her study on cancer patients, points to another distinction between contributions to the causation and the control over the further development. Only 17% of the patients thought they contributed to the causation of the disease (see also Linn *et al.*, 1982), but a majority believed they had some control over the cure.

Janoff-Bulman (1979) introduced another useful distinction between characterological self-blame (with reference to stable attributes, which are not controllable) and behavioral self-blame. Characterological self-blame is seen as a symptom of depression and thus as dysfunctional, whereas behavioral self-blame may be functional and reduce perceived vulnerability. In other words, if a student attributes his or her failure in an examination to a lack of effort, he or she is neither helpless nor hopeless and may believe in succeeding in a second try. The attribution to extreme test anxiety or lack of ability leads to more pessimistic expectancies, as studies on the self-concept of ability prove (Meyer, 1984). Characterological self-blame may be interpreted as a case of helplessness: The outcome is believed to be objectively controllable, but one is not able to control it. However, there is also contradictory evidence. In the Meyer and Taylor study on rape (1986), both kinds of self-blame were associated with poor adjustment, whereas external and societal explanation were uncorrelated with adjustment scores.

So far coping with feelings of injustice has not yet been considered in theories of self-blame and in interpretations of empirical data on the effects of self-blame. Justice comes into play, however, when different effects of controllability beliefs are analyzed. Controllability may reduce feelings of injustice: If a student who has failed an exam thinks he or she was unfairly treated by the professor, feelings of injustice will arise that can be avoided or reduced by attributing responsibility for the outcome to himself or herself. The decrease in aversive feelings of injustice is expected to have positive emotional and behavioral effects. But it may also be that the decrease is equalized by a proportional increase in aversive feelings such as anger about an avoidable error, or shame about a lack of knowledge, or guilt about the careless preparation for the examination.

Consequently, controllability may increase negative feelings. The very concept of blame implies controllability of the outcome. Without control over the outcome, responsibility and blame are not to be attributed. Believing one has control may have positive effects, but it does not necessarily have to: The accused person, for example, may deny controllability as an excuse. The controllability component implied in self-blame may have positive effects on adjustment, provided it is generalized to the future, thus leading to hopes of being able to avoid the recurrence of the stressful event. If this is not the case, however, controllability beliefs may have negative effects, such as guilt and anger about an avoidable fault. In this regard, it is necessary to assess the different emotions that might be associated with controllability (Montada, 1989). Besides this, different levels of responsibility attribution should be observed. Heider distinguished five levels (association, causation, foreseeability, intention, denial of justification) with only the last of these implying blameworthiness (in the logical sense of the concept). One should be cautious in speaking of "self-blame" if one's causal contributions to an outcome, foreseeability of the outcome, or even volitional control over the outcome are admitted. These beliefs do not necessarily imply self-blame (Shaver, 1985).

One example should illustrate this point. At times, when we did not have knowledge of the transmission of the AIDS virus, responsibility for an infection could not be attributed reasonably. However, retrospectively, a patient may admit objective causal contributions of his own to becoming ill. Because we have now a great deal of knowledge on the transmission of the AIDS virus, homosexual AIDS patients, for example, may feel responsible for the infection. Some may regret their careless behavior and blame themselves (if they do not prefer to blame their mate, e.g., for not having disclosed being infected by a third person); others may accept the disease as a risk of their sexual life that they do not wish to change. That means that even if responsibility is not denied, there must not necessarily be self-blame.

In empirical studies, views of victims concerning their own causal contributions are usually assessed under the label *self-blame*. Often, it is not assessed whether or not the effects of these contributions could have been foreseen, whether or not they are perceived as avoidable, whether or not the victims feel responsible, whether or not the victim feels blameworthy. So-called self-blame may often be indicated by this kind of statement: "If I had not done this or that, it would not have happened." Someone had an accident driving from his home to place X. Now he imagines that this might not have happened if he had not gone there or if he had not chosen this very route. Mark and Folger (1984) argued that the amount of dissatisfaction with the outcome increases with the growing ease of imagining a hedonically better (or "high referent") outcome. Concerning one's own responsibility for the outcome, several different possibilities should be distinguished. It is reasonable to deny responsibility if the actor had no freedom of choice to behave in another way. That is, if the driver was on his usual way to work or if he was on the way to the pharmacy because his wife was ill, he had less freedom of choice than if he had deliberately decided to go to a pub: Carrying out duties reduces one's freedom (Montada and Albs, 1990).

Finally, another totally different adaptive function of self-blame should only be mentioned. Self-blame may be a strategy used to avoid social blame. The confessing child who demonstrates signs of remorse is seldom punished by his or her parents (Aronfreed, 1968). Analogous to this is the idea that self-blame often helps to prevent being blamed by others. Of course in this strategic function, remorse or real self-blame is not necessarily implied. The mere demonstration of self-blame may prevent victimization.

Victimization after Critical Life Events: Coping Strategy of Observers to Avoid the Preception of Injustice

People in crises, people with fears, pain, or grief, and the like need support: material, emotional, and appraisal support. Broad evidence on different critical events corroborates the view that in general social support is very useful (Dunkel-Schetter & Wortman, 1981). However, people in crises do not always receive the support they need. Instead, many victims of crimes are derogated, the handicapped, severely ill, or the dying are avoided, people after bereavement are given the advice not to show their grief, not to complain, but to look forward in a positive way.

Categories of Secondary Victimization. We call "secondary victimization" a second deprivation of a disadvantaged person that is inflicted by others (individuals or institutions). Several categories can be distinguished.

1. *Refusal of victim's view of who is responsible.* The victim blames a perpetrator, but the judge or other significant people come to a different attribution of responsibility. Especially if the victim feels that principles of procedural justice are not observed, for instance, that his or her claims are not considered objectively, resentment may arise because of supposed biases (Tyler, 1984).

2. *Ignoring claims for blame and punishment.* The victim answers with resentment when obvious violations of the law are not prosecuted. A referee who does not punish violations of rules provokes hostility and resentment. There are legitimate claims that laws and rules must be enforced and that the guilty are punished. If this is not done, it may be viewed as a kind of structural victimization (Nagel, 1979) that has been identified as one of the precipitating events leading to riots (Lieberson & Silverman, 1965). Michael Kohlhaas in Kleist's drama became a terrorist, fighting for a trial that was unjustly withheld. When there are rules and laws, there is an entitlement to have them enforced. The victim of a crime especially will call for law enforcement and restitution.

Nagel (1979) reported that in 1973 the Dutch psychiatrist Bastiaans founded a hospital for victims of the Nazi occupation in The Netherlands. He had observed that many of the victims who seemed to have overcome their traumatic experiences developed psychic problems again. Many of them reported enormous (emotional) problems because of two facts that they had perceived as very unjust: (1) All former collaborators with the Nazis, judges, policemen, clerks, politicians, who had participated in the persecution and degradation of the victims now held their former positions again; (2) there was a collective denial of the crimes during that time and, therefore, a denial of the victimization. Phrases like "One must be able to make an end" or "One must be able to forgive" represent this attitude. The victims suffered from being cheated of their status as victims. Forgiving the harmdoers by society may hurt the victims and their claim for restitution by punishment. The victims may also ask: "Who is entitled to forgive?" The observer? Society? Many victims feel that only they are entitled to forgive.

Victims are more likely to forgive when the harmdoer has confessed his or her guilt and accepted blame or punishment as just. Goffman (1971) analyzed apologies by the harmdoer and their effect on the victim and society. A complete apology is characterized by the following components: (1) emotional distress, (2) knowledge of the moral codes, (3) acceptance of own responsibility for actions or omissions, (4) acceptance of liability for blame, and (5) willingness to observe the transgressed moral or legal rules in the future.

There are several resocialization programs in North America and Australia trying to bring together the harmdoer and the victim in order to negotiate an adequate restitution or compensation by the harmdoer (Schneider, 1979). If the mentioned components of apologies are acknowledged by the victim, these interactions can help to reduce the victimization. Indifference of society, including that of police, toward the victim's plight is a very common phenomenon (Symonds, 1975). Being the victim of a crime such as mugging and rape is an extraordinarily traumatic experience. For the police, this is daily routine work with low probability of apprehending and convicting the perpetrator. Statements like "You are not the only one who has been mugged. We got plenty of other calls" are denying the very status of being a victim.

In general, society is much more preoccupied with the perpetrator than with the victim, with a fair and objective trial, with the question of how to ensure that he or she will be treated justly, will not be stigmatized, and so forth. The victim and his entitlements receive much less attention. In court, the victim's role is that of a witness. In order to guarantee fairness to the defendant, the witness may be treated with skepticism, and doubts about his/her honesty are permitted.

O'Hara's (1970) widely accepted book on criminal investigation techniques reflects this skepticism toward the victim/witness. Correspondingly, the victim may develop doubts about the justice in society and about the state who not only neglected to protect him or her against crime, but now fails to side with him or her.

3. *Ignoring and refusing victim's claims for compensation.* Refusal of a victim's claim for restitution or compensation is a second victimization, provided that the victim is convinced that he or she is entitled to them. His or her claims for compensation will probably be refused if the disadvantages are perceived as self-inflicted. Judgments of responsibility may have tangible consequences.

4. *Stigmatization by attribution of responsibility to the victim.* By bringing the rapist to trial, the rape victim not only risks the sentence "not guilty" and subsequently her belief in a just society, but she also

risks losing her reputation and eventually her attractiveness (for a review, see Krahé, 1985). The longer people are without employment, the more they will be stigmatized (as unable or lazy) (Hayes & Nutman, 1981), a tendency seemingly dependent on political attitudes and ideological convictions (Furnham, 1982). (Left-wing voters tend to attribute more importance to societal factors, right-wing voters more to internal individual factors, which is the typical observer bias for internal personal explanations; Ross, 1977). Stigmatization leads to social isolation and exclusion through notoriety. Some rape victims who did experience stigmatization had to move from their neighborhood (Symonds, 1975).

5. *Blame and punishment of the victim.* Not only may support and help be withheld because of attribution of responsibility, the victim may even be punished. In World War II, Soviet soldiers with frozen feet were executed with the unproven assumption that they actively let their feet freeze hoping to become able to quit the army. A mother whose preschool child dies in an accident is usually blamed for negligence.

Excursus: Blaming the Victim or Pointing to Control against Victimization

There is much systematic and everyday experience for a widespread tendency to blame the victim (Ryan, 1971). Phenomena such as these can be observed in cases of catastrophes, crimes, accidents, and illnesses, loss of jobs, and other categories of bad fate (Lerner, 1971; Walster, 1966). They can also be observed in the laboratory when some participants are seemingly allocated to a more unfavorable experimental treatment than others (Lerner & Simmons, 1966). There is an impressive amount of research describing and analyzing phenomena of blaming the victim (Lerner, 1980; Shaver, 1985).

There is no doubt that these phenomena often occur, yet there is no doubt either that possibly a majority of victims get sufficient support from the family, their spouse, friends, neighbors, and social services. Therefore we have cases of indifference, of supporting, and of blaming the victim. The scientifically and practically important questions are who reacts with support; who reacts indifferently; who reacts with blame, to what victim in what situation, in which case of victimization. To answer these questions, research has been focused on two hypotheses: belief in a just world (Lerner, 1977) and belief in a controllable world (defensive attribution, Shaver, 1970; Walster, 1966). But before explaining the phenomenon of blaming the victim, the actual fact of blaming should be validly evidenced. Perusing the literature one can have doubts whether all that is called blaming really is blaming.

If blameworthiness is stated merely on the basis of causal contributions to an outcome, blaming will be very probable. Viewed in this way, all rape victims contributed causally to the crime: They walked alone through a street, they smiled to a colleague, they wore nice clothes, or they opened the door when the bell rang and let their acquaintance enter, and so forth. Many diseases, as social medicine tells us, are contingent on behavior (Schäfer, 1979), on too much eating, drinking, smoking, jogging, working, worrying, or on too little of all these. As stated, causal contributions are not an adequate reason for blame. At least, foreseeability of consequences must have been perceived when responsibility is to be attributed reasonably, and again, responsibility is not a sufficient reason for blame, but justifications should be considered also.

Thus, it is doubtful whether all reports of blaming the victim have validly identified a tendency or an intention to blame. Sometimes causal attributions are not meant to blame the victim but to prevent further victimization. Kidder and Cohn (1979) make the point very clearly in exploring everyday opinions on crime prevention. Asked for the causes for criminality, people mention distal causes such as ineffective laws, unemployment, poverty, lax parental control of the children. Asked how to prevent crimes, they seldom propose changing these distal causes, probably because these distal causes are not easy to change. Instead they focus on proximal causes, which are much easier to control and to change: escort services, avoidance of careless behavior, raising the number of police controls, and the like. Asked for crime prevention measures, people answer with victimization prevention measures that are not directed at the delinquents (actual or future) but at the potential victims. The latter have the advantage that they are controllable by potential victims. In line with this important distinction, we should be cautious not to misinterpret statements concerning causality, controllability, and responsibility. Mentioning causal contributions of the victim, mentioning victimization prevention measures does not necessarily imply blaming the victim and discharging other causal agents, society, or fate.

Motivational Biases in Interactions with Disadvantaged People. Research and models of prosocial behavior offer many reasons why someone does not help another one who is in need (Bierhoff, 1980; Schwartz, 1977; Staub, 1979). A person may not feel able to help or may be convinced that other people are responsible for providing help or may be empathically too distressed to give any support or may have doubts whether the person in need of help wishes support from him or her or may fear the costs of helping (Bierhoff, 1988). The reasons to give or not to give help touch on the question of justice. Helping is more probable if the helper feels indebted to the needy, or if the needy one seems to have a title for receiving help. Helping is less likely if the needy himself or herself is seen as responsible for his or her problems.

Being confronted with people in need, a helper must decide whether they are entitled to get support and who is responsible for giving support. There are biases that influence the answers to these questions. The two favorite hypotheses explaining these biases are (1) belief in a just world (Lerner 1970, 1977, 1980) and (2) belief in a controllable world (Shaver, 1970; Walster, 1966). Empirical evidence corroborating Lerner's hypothesis is steadily growing, whereas there are contradictory data and some conceptual problems concerning the defensive attribution hypothesis (see Burger, 1981; also Semin & Manstead for a discussion of these problems).

1. *Belief in a just and controllable world.* If there are doubts as to whether the observed disadvantages or losses are just or not, blaming the victim (Ryan, 1971) as being responsible for his or her fate is a suitable way of denying injustice. There are many suitable arguments for denying one's own responsibility for supporting the disadvantaged, and there are many suitable arguments justifying the given inequalities as well. Belief in a just world seems to be a powerful predictor for justifications of inequalities if they cannot be changed easily (Montada et al., 1986). Attributing responsibility to the victim may also have the function of defending one's view that the world and one's own fate are controllable, stabilizing the belief that one is personally able to avoid bad luck. The worse the harm or the loss (Chaikin & Darley, 1973) and the less clear its objective causation (Lowe & Medway, 1976), the more probable it will be that responsibility is attributed to the victim. These hypothese are fascinating and many counterintuitive phenomena become understandable in the light of them.

2. *Models of attribution of responsibility.* Brickman et al.(1982) propose an interesting taxonomy of biases based on the distinction between the responsibility (1) for the occurrence of a problem (Who is responsible for a past event?) and (2) for the solution (Who is responsible for future development?). They distinguish four models of helping and coping with different biases concerning the attribution of these two kinds of responsibilities. (It is open to question whether the preference of one of these models is mediated by a more basic motive for justice such as belief in a just world).

In the first model, called the moral model, actors are held responsible for both kinds of responsibilities. Other persons only have to point out this self-responsibility to the actor. The second model is called the compensatory model: People are seen as not responsible for the occurrence of a negative event but as responsible for the solution. People are not derogated for their problems but are encouraged to make efforts in finding solutions.

In the third, the medical model, individuals are neither seen as responsible for the occurrence nor for the solutions of problems. They are believed to need support and treatment. In a sense, the person is put under the tutelage of professional experts. The fourth model is called the enlightment model: Actors are seen to be responsible for problems but unable or unwilling to provide solutions. They are believed to need discipline provided by authoritative guidance. The Alcoholic Anonymous groups are considered prototypical for that model.

These models have different normative implications. On the basis of the compensatory and the medical model, needy people are entitled to get support and help. On the basis of the moral model, such entitlement is denied. The enlightment model neither offers support nor help. Instead, it is assumed that authority is needed to provide strict guidance. Concerning the origin of the problems, the moral and the enlightment model attribute responsibility to the needy person. The needy is answerable; maybe he or she is to blame. He or she is not ill, not a victim of external forces or blind fate. Instead, he or she is perceived as liable to blame because of avoidable faults. From the perspective of needy people, the attribution of responsibility for their own disadvantage may be perceived as unjustified. The needy may perceive himself or herself to be the victim of an informal sentence, a biased sentence. Because there is no formal negotiation in line with principles of procedural justice, there is perhaps no opportunity to correct this sentence. The disappointment over denial of help from others, because of questionable attributions of responsibility to the needy, can be seen as a case of secondary victimization.

Normative Implications of Research on Life Stress and Justice

Empirical research is descriptive, but it has normative implications. Which ones could these be? It is not the task of social psychology to decide what is a just or an unjust claim or what is a just or an unjust treatment of a victim. Looking back on the previous sections of this chapter, one may discover a bias in favor of needy people. The mere use of the term *victim* may mirror this bias. Is the term *victim* only appropriate if a person suffers from an unjust disadvantage for which another person or institution is responsible? Or may the term also be used if a person is hurt by his/her own misbehavior? Of course, not every claim of every person in a stressful situation or with a handicap is just, and not every need justifies a claim for help and support. And of course following every accusation the question, "Who is responsible and who is to blame," is to be answered in a fair trial.

There are seldom clear-cut answers to questions about what is just and who is responsible. As stated, people have different and conflicting perspectives, beliefs, values, and options. There are formal and informal negotiations about the answers, formal ones in trials and informal ones in everyday communications and interactions. Social psychology can contribute to making negotiations possible and fair. This requires information about possible biases. They may be personal as, for example the belief in a just world or the tendency to defensive attributions; they may be institutional as are the different models of helping as described by Brickman *et al.*, or they may be societal such as the preoccupation with the fairness against the perpetrator (and thereby neglecting fairness against the victim). Empirical research can point to those biases and to further personal and social barriers against fair negotiations. Thus it may help to come closer to an ideal where everybody has a fair chance to express his or her claims or options and to convince the other parties concerned. Philosophers such as Habermas (1983) have proposed ideal concepts that are free from biases and prejudices, that are open to consider the perspectives, claims, and options of all parties concerned, and that are willing to contribute to a rational and fair solution. Empirical research describes the participants as they are and not as they should be. Doing this offers useful information for those who are aiming at changing the world toward some ideal.

References

Aronfreed, J. (1968). *Conduct and conscience.* New York: Academic Press.
Bierhoff, H. W. (1980). *Hilfreiches Verhalten: Soziale Einflüsse und pädagogische Implikationen.* Darmstadt: Steinkopff.
Bierhoff, H. W. (1988). *Sozialpsychologie.* Stuttgart: Kohlhammer.
Brickman, P., Rabinowitz, R. C., Karuza, J., Coates, D., Cohn, E., & Kidder, L. (1982). Models of helping and coping. *American Psychologist, 37,* 368–384.
Burger, J. M. (1981). Motivational biases in the attibution of responsibility for an accident: A meta-analysis of the defensive-attribution hypothesis. *Psychological Bulletin, 90,* 496–512.

Burgess, A. W., & Holstrom, L. L. (1979). Adaptive strategies and recovery from rape. American Journal of Psychiatry, 136, 1278–1282.

Chaikin, A., & Darley, J. (1973). Victim or porpotrator: Defensive attribution of responsibility and the need for order and justice. Journal of Personality and Social Psychology, 25, 268–275.

Chodoff, P., Friedman, S. B., & Hamburg, D. A. (1964). Stress, defense, and coping behavior: Observations in parents of children with malignant diseases. American Journal of Psychiatry, 120, 743–749.

Coates, D., Wortman, C. B., & Abbey, A. (1979). Reactions to victims. In I. H. Frieze, D. Bar-Tal, & J. S. Carroll (Eds.), New approaches to social problems: Applications of attribution theory (pp. 21–52). San Francisco, CA: Jossey-Bass.

Deutsch, M. (1975). Equity, equality, and need: What determines which value will be used as the basis of distributive justice? Journal of Social Issues, 31, 137–149.

Dunkel-Schetter, C., & Wortman, C. B. (1981). Dilemmas of social support: Parallels between victimization and aging. In S. B. Kiesler, J. N. Morgan, & V. K Oppenheimer (Eds.). Aging: Social change (pp. 349–381). New York: Academic Press.

Ferraro, K. J., & Johnson, J. M. (1983). How women experience battering: The process of victimization. Social Problems, 30, 325–339.

Filipp, S.-H. (Ed.). (1981). Kritische Lebensereignisse. München: Urban & Schwarzenberg.

Filipp, S.-H., & Gräser, H. (1982). In J. Brandtstädter, & A. von Eye (Eds.), Psychologische Prävention (pp. 155–195). Bern: Huber.

Fincham, F. D., & Jaspars, J. M. (1980). Attribution of responsibility: From man the scientist to man as lawyer. In L. Berkowitz (Ed.), Advances in Experimental Social Psychology, 13, 81–138.

Frankl, U. E. (1963). Man's search for meaning. New York: Washington Square Press.

Frey, D. (1985). Ursachenattribution und Rehabilitationsverlauf bei Unfallopfern. Universität Kiel, unveröffentlichtes Manuskript.

Frieze, I. H. (1979). Perceptions of battered wives. In I. H. Frieze, D. Bar-Tal, & J. S. Carroll (Eds.), New approaches to social problems: Applications of attribution theory (pp. 79–108). San Francisco, CA: Jossey-Bass.

Furnham, A. (1982). Explanations for unemployment in Britain. European Journal of Social Psychology, 12, 335–346.

Goffman, E. (1971). Relations in public: Micro-studies of the public order. Harmondsworth: Penguin.

Habermas, J. (1983). Moralbewusstsein und kommunikatives Handeln. Frankfurt/Main: Suhrkamp.

Hart, H. L. A. (1968). Punishment and responsibility. Oxford: Varendon Press.

Hayes, J., & Nutman, P. (1981). Understanding the unemployed. London: Tavistock.

Heider, F. (1958). The psychology of interpersonal relations. New York: Wiley.

Janoff-Bulman, R. (1979). Characterological vs. behavioral self-blame: Inquiries into depression and rape. Journal of Personality and Social Psychology, 37, 1798–1809.

Jaspars, J., Fincham, F., & Hewstone, M. (1983). Attribution theory and research: Conceptual, developmental, and social dimensions. London: Academic Press.

Kelley, H. H. (1973). The process of casual attribution. American Psychologist, 28, 107–128.

Kidder, L. H., & Cohn, E. S. (1979). Public views of crime and crime prevention. In I. H. Frieze, D. Bar-Tal, & J. S. Carroll (Eds.), New approaches to social problems: Applications of attribution theory (pp. 237–264). San Francisco, CA: Jossey-Bass.

Krahé, B. (1985). Die Zuschreibung von Verantwortlichkeit nach Vergewaltigungen: Opfer und Täter im Dickicht der attributions-theoretischen Forschung. Psychologische Rundschau, 36, 67–82.

Lerner, M. J. (1970). The desire for justice and reactions to victims. In J. Macaulay & L. Berkowitz, (Eds.) Altruism and helping behavior (pp. 205–229). New York: Academic Press.

Lerner, M. J. (1971). Observer's evaluation of a victim: Justice, guilt, and veridical perception. Journal of Personality and Social Psychology, 20, 127–135.

Lerner, M. J. (1977). The justice motive: Some hypotheses as to its origins and forms. Journal of Personality, 45, 1–52.

Lerner, M. J. (1980). The belief in a just world: A fundamental delusion. New York: Plenum Press.

Lerner, M. J., & Simmons, C. H. (1966). Observer's reaction to the innocent victim: Compassion or rejection. Journal of Personality and Social Psychology, 4, 203–210.

Leventhal, G. S. (1976). The distribution of rewards and resources in groups and organizations. In L. Berkowitz & E. Walster (Eds.), Advances in experimental social psychology (vol. 9, pp. 91–131). New York: Academic Press.

Libov, J. A., & Doty, D. W. (1979). An exploratory approach to self-blame and self-derogation by rape victims. American Journal of Orthopsychiatry, 49, 670–679.

Lieberson, S., & Silverman, R. A. (1965). The precipitants and underlying conditions of race riots. American Sociological Review, 30, 887–898.

Linn, M. W., Linn, B. S., & Stein, S. R. (1982). Beliefs about causes of cancer in cancer patients. Social Science and Medicine, 16, 835–839.

Lowe, C. A., & Medway, F. J. (1976). Effects of valence, severity, and relevance on responsibility and dispositional attribution. Journal of Personality, 44, 518–539.

Mark, M. M., & Folger, R. (1984). Responses to relative deprivation: A conceptual framework. In P. Shaver (Ed.), Review of personality and social psychology (Vol.5, pp. 192–218).

Martin, J. (1984). The tolerance of injustice. In J. Olson & M. Zanna (Eds.), Relative deprivation and assertive action: The Ontario Symposium. Hillsdale, NJ: Erlbaum.

Medea, A., & Thompson, K. (1974). Against rape. New York: Famar, Straus, Giroux.

Meyer, C. B., & Taylor, S. E. (1986). Adjustment to rape. Journal of Personality and Social Psychology, 50, 1226–1234.

Meyer, W.- U. (1984.). Das Konzept von der eigenen Begabung: Auswirkungen, Stabilität und vorauslaufende Bedingungen. Psychologische Rundschau, 35, 136–150.

Montada, L. (1989). Attribution of responsibility for losses and perceived injustice. Paper presented at the First International Conference on "Life Crises and Experiences of Loss in Adulthood" in Trier Federal Republic of Germany, Summer 1989.

Montada, L., Schmitt, M., & Dalbert, C. (1986). Thinking about justice and dealing with one's own privileges: A study of existential guilt. In H. W. Bierhoff, R. Cohen, & J. Greenberg (Eds.), Justice in social relations (pp. 125–143). New York: Plenum Press.

Montada, L. & A lbs, B. (1990). Emotionale Bewertung von Verlusten und erfolgreiche Bewältigung bei Unfallopfern. Berichte aus der Arbeitsgruppe "Verantwortung, Gerechtigkeit, Moral" Nr. 57, Trier: Universität Trier.

Moore, B. (1984). Ungerechtigkeit: Die sozialen Ursachen von Unterordnung und Widerstand. Frankfurt: Suhrkamp.

Nagel, W. H. (1979). Strukturelle Viktimisation. In G. F. Kirchhoff & K. Sessar (Eds.), Das Verbrechensopfer (pp. 61–83). Bochum: Studienverlag Dr. Norbert Brockmeyer.

O'Hara, C. E. (1970). Fundamentals of criminal investigation. Springfield IL: Charles Thomas.

Rappaport, E. A. (1971). Survivor guilt. Midstream, August/September, pp. 41–47.

Ross, L. (1977). The intuitive psychologist and his shortcomings: Distortions in the attibution process. In L. Berkowitz (Ed.), Advances in experimental social psychology (Vol. 10, pp. 173–220). New York: Academic Press.

Runciman, W. G. (1966). *Relative deprivation and social justice: A study of attitudes to social inoquality in twenthieth century England*. Berkeley, CA: University of California Press.

Ryan, W. (1971). *Blaming the victim*. New York: Random House.

Schäfer, H. (1979). Aspekte einer sozialen Medizin. In Deutsches Institut für Fernstudien (Ed.), *Funkkolleg Umwelt und Gesundheit*. Weinheim: Beltz.

Schmitt, M., & Montada, L. (1982). Determinanten erlebter Gerechtigkeit. Zeitschrift für Sozialpsychologie, 13, 32–44.

Schneider, H. J. (1979). Opferschaden, Wiedergutmachung und Opferbehandlung. In G. F. Kirchhoff, & K. Sessar (Eds.), *Das Verbrechensopfer* (pp. 365–378). Bochum: Studienverlag Dr. Norbert Brockmeyer.

Schwartz, S. H. (1979). Normative influences on altruism. In L. Berkowitz (Ed.), *Advances in Experimental Social Psychology, 10*, 221–279.

Semin, G. R., & Manstead, A. S. R. (1983). *The accountability of conduct. A social psychological analysis*. New York: Academic Press.

Shaver, K. G. (1970). Defensive attribution: Effects of severity and relevance on the responsibility assigned for an accident. *Journal of Personality and Social Psychology, 14*, 101–113.

Shaver, K. G. (1985). *The attribution of blame: Causality, responsibility, and blameworthiness*. New York: Springer.

Staub, E. (1979). *Positive social behavior and morality. Socialization and development*. New York: Academic Press.

Steil, J. M..& Slochower, J. (1985). The experience of injustice: Social psychological and clinical perspectives. In G. Stricker & R. H. Keisner (Eds.), *From research to clinical practice* (pp. 217–242). New York: Plenum Press.

Symonds, M. (1975). Victims of violence. *The American Journal of Psychoanalysis, 35*, 19–26.

Taylor, S. E. (1982). Social cognition and health. *Personality and Social Psychology Bulletin, 8*, 549–562.

Taylor, S. E. (1983). Adjustment to threatening events. A theory of cognitive adaptation. *Amearican Psychologist, 38*, 1161–1173.

Taylor, S. E., Wood, J. V. & Lichtman, R. R. (1983). It could be worse: Selective evaluation as a response to victimization. *Journal of Social Issues, 39*, 19–40.

Tedeschi, J. T., & Riess, M. (1981). Verbal strategies in impression management. In C. Antaki (Ed.), *The psychology of ordinary explanations of social behavior (pp. 271–309)*. London: Academic Press.

Tyler, T. R. (1984). The role of perceived injustice in defendants' evaluations of their courtroom experience. *Law & Society Review, 18*, 51–74.

Walster, E. (1966). Assignment of responsibility for an accident .*Journal of Personality and Social Psychology, 3*, 73–79.

Wills, T. A. (1981). Downward comparison principles in social psychology. *Psychological Bulletin, 90*, 245–271.

Wortman, C. B. (1983). Coping with victimization: Conclusions and implications for future research. *Journal of Social Issues, 39*, 195–221.

2

Interactions between Law and Everyday Thinking in the Social Categorization of Events

Sally Lloyd-Bostock

The question behind this chapter is, very broadly, how do events come to be understood and defined such that particular legal responses are perceived to be appropriate? I shall be looking at this as a process of social categorization. By that, I mean the process whereby events or cases are classified as examples of a class, where the categorization carries social, perhaps legal, consequences or implications.

This focus on process raises questions not so much about *what* is perceived as fair or just, but rather about *how* this type of decision or judgment is made. How do differing perceptions of objectively of very similar events occur? To what extent are judgments of this kind automatic and rapid, and to what extent reflective and time consuming? How do legal and nonlegal factors mix and link to produce these responses? It raises questions also about the interface between the individual and society. How do societal norms structure individual perceptions and responses to a particular event? Do there in fact exist extralegal, everyday perceptions of fairness (etc.) that may be compared with legal procedures and outcomes? Although reference is often made to "everyday thinking," "common sense," and so on in discussions of legal processes, very little work has been done analyzing exactly what is meant by these terms, and how legal and extralegal elements in ordinary thinking interrelate.

Sally Lloyd-Bostock • Centre for Socio-Legal Studies, Wolfson College, University of Oxford, Oxford OX2 6UD, England.

This Chapter, which is somewhat speculative, is in three sections. First I would like to expand on what I mean by "interactions between law and everyday thinking," and second on what I mean by "social categorization of events." Third, as illustration of how these two areas are related, I shall consider the question of deciding the legal consequences of accidents. In particular I shall be concerned here with decisions about pursuing civil damages claims and decisions about the enforcement of health and safety regulations, comparing the responses of factory inspectors with those of accident victims.

Law and Everyday Thinking

The idea of ordinary, everyday extralegal thinking, or common sense, as distinct from legal norms, concepts, and definitions, crops up in some form in a great many discussions of law and legal processes. In the area of legal procedures, discussion by researchers has frequently involved the idea of a legal and an everyday version of disputes and settlement processes that may be compared and contrasted. Abel (1979), for example, describes a pendulum swing between "legalization" and "delegalization" in dispute resolution, where delegalization is a move toward mechanisms outside the legal system. These mechanisms depend on a high degree of consensus on substantive nonlegal norms of behavior. Abel sees evidence of an assumption of this consensus in proposals for decriminalization of behavior, and for the use of mediation in place of adjudication, thereby resolving disputes with reference to what he calls "a common, if implicit, normative framework." (Abel himself is sceptical about this "consensus".)

More generally in the literature on dispute resolution, legal procedures for dispute resolution have often been analyzed as alien to ordinary thinking. The more similar the legal can be made to the ordinary and everyday, the more accessible, and hence fair it will be. Legal formality and legalism should be minimized, and legal remedies thus made more available to ordinary people. This is of course a great oversimplification and rather a caricature. But the idea is nevertheless there that there are extralegal ways of dealing with many disputes and that these often contrast with legal procedures, especially in degree of formality. And that taking a dispute to law involves some kind of translation process from everyday, commonsense definitions and perceptions to legal ones—a process that will very likely need the help of a lawyer.

There are also discussions of legal decision-making procedures that make more implicit use of this concept (or cluster of concepts). Many examples arise in the area of discretion, and discussions of how discretion is or should be exercised in legal contexts. Here the idea often is that discretion is used or should be used in a way that reflects extralegal moral norms. For example, the sociologist Keith Hawkins has analyzed parole board decisions and argued that these are frequently "just deserts" decisions, as to whether the amount of time served in prison matches the moral heinousness of the crime (Hawkins, 1983). He draws on similar ideas in his study of the use of discretion in the enforcement of regulations about water pollution (Hawkins, 1984). In this study, his analysis relies extensively on the notion of the water pollution inspector making an assessment of the moral blameworthiness of the rule-breaker. Pollution inspectors have and use very wide discretion over whether or not to take legal action against a rule-breaker and routinely tolerate technical breaches of standards. A factory might be discharging 5 or even 10 times the formally permitted amount of a chemical into a river, and this is ignored by the pollution inspector. The decision whether to do something about it, Hawkins argues, is infused with moral judgments about the wickedness of the rule-breaker (though this is not of course the only consideration) and the inspector's commonsense reasoning about the deliberateness, recklessness, and so forth of the action, factors, strictly speaking, that are legally irrelevant.

Extralegal, commonsense reasoning is also relied on in official guidelines as to how discretion ought to be used. To take another example from discretion in the enforcement of regulation—in the United States, health and safety regulations are enforced in a highly legalistic, "by-the-book" way. Inspectors' discretion is closely hedged about with rules. All violations of health or safety standards are supposed to be cited, and the fines imposed are to be calculated according to a complex formula. Yet, in the manual setting out of this formula in elaborate detail, a rider is added to several of the components to the effect that if the application of the formula seems to result in too high a fine, then the particular factor may be discounted. Thus even within a set of legal rules apparently designed to minimize inspectors' discretion, a commonsense source, external to the rules, is invoked as an ultimate check.

So far I have given examples where common sense has been invoked by social scientists. There are also many instances where common sense has been explicitly evoked by lawyers, either in dealing with particular cases, or in discussion of law. One example is in the area of civil claims for damages, where questions about the causes of an injury need to be decided. In this context, appeals have been made to common sense as a legal standard, or part of a legal standard. The legal test of what constitutes "a cause" involves "what common sense tells us is 'a cause'." The English courts have frequently stated that questions of causation are to be decided by the application of common sense and have claimed that this is what they are doing. Because common sense is frequently invoked by lawyers, it has been analyzed by such writers as Hart and Honoré (1959) in analytical jurisprudence. Another context in which common sense has been invoked is in discussions of the definition of mental illness. Thus the American lawyer, Michael Moore, in his book, *Law and Psychiatry: Rethinking the Relationship* (Moore, 1984), discusses the insanity defense. He argues that the legal definition of mental illness should draw on the "popular moral notion" of mental illness and offers an analysis of what this popular moral notion is.

The examples I have given are rather varied, and one may question whether they are in fact examples of a single thing or are a loosely related ragbag. I believe they do include several different things that need to be differentiated. However, I believe they do have some general features in common. All are contexts in which principles of reasoning, or moral rules or norms, are located in "ordinary" thinking. They may perhaps be thought of as nonlegal social rules, often with a moral flavor. In the examples I have given, these are about attributing cause and fault; about when mental illness excuses actions; how the wickedness of crimes, intention, and blameworthiness ought to relate to sanctions or other consequences; and what constitutes justice in social relationships. All also involve the idea that common sense, ordinary principles, norms, modes of reasoning, and the like have a life of their own, not necessarily independent of law, but in some sense separate and distinguishable from law, so that they may act as a resource for law; as a basis for justification for, or explanation of, legal decisions; or be compared with or translated to a legal counterpart.

I would argue also that all involve empirical claims about how ordinary people in fact think, reason, and/or respond to events. In other articles I have looked more closely at the question of exactly what empirical claims might be involved in lawyers' references to common sense in the context of tort liability (e.g., Lloyd-Bostock, 1979, 1981), and suggested that these are usually claims that certain social rules are actually being used or followed. However, in order to decide what, if any, empirical claims are being made, it is necessary to examine closely the particular context in which the appeal to common sense is being made. This varies and is not always clear. I do not wish to go more deeply into this here. Instead, I want to move on to discuss what I mean by "social categorization of event," before relating this to the contexts I have used as examples.

Social Categorization of Events

The process whereby outcomes and procedures come to be seen as fair and appropriate in response to a given event can be looked at as a categorization process—that is, a process of classifying events, and possibly mapping them onto prototypes, with implications for appropriate action or response. An analogy might be drawn with medical diagnosis, where clusters and patterns of symptoms and other information are classified as examples of a type; and the diagnosis carries with it implications about what procedures, treatment, etc. are relevant and appropriate. My central interest is thus in a psychological rather than a social process: what is going on in people's heads rather than, say, sociolinguistic processes of accounting. However, these two must certainly be closely related. The way we describe and explain things or hear them described or explained must affect how we perceive them, and vice versa. In looking at this categorization, I wish to draw on approaches in cognitive psychology that see decision making as falling on a continuum of automaticity, depending on how automatic the process is. Thus, at the automatic end of the continuum, slamming on the brakes can be an action chosen very quickly and automatically. At the other end lies a more reflective and time-consuming evaluation.

Rasmussen (1980) developed a model that distinguished three levels on this continuum: "skill based," "rule based," and "knowledge based" behavior. The approach is summarized by Wickens (1984). The skill-based level is the most automatic. Responding to a red traffic light falls at this level, as might a skilled doctor's classification of a syndrome into a category that triggers automatic action. At the rule-based level, action is selected more as a trainee medical student might do. Here a response is selected by bringing into working memory a hierarchy of rules, of the "If-x-then-do-y" form. The situation may be familiar, but the processing is considerably less automatic and rapid. The final category of knowledge-based behavior is invoked when entirely new problems are encountered. Neither automatic mappings, nor rules, exist. Choice of action involves integrating information and more general knowledge in a novel way. This level is typical of troubleshooting strategies when diagnosing an unfamiliar malfunction in a complex system. It is also often typical of corporate or government decision making. Decision latencies at the skill-based level are of the order of seconds and milliseconds, while for rule- and knowledge-based decisions, they are of the order of minutes, hours, days, or even longer.

Drawing on this notion of a continuum from automatic to more reflective decisions, I would like to apply it to the categorization of events where a legal or social response may be at issue. The specific type of event I shall use as illustration is accidental injury. My general points, however, apply more widely. There are two general points I wish to make, and which I shall develop more fully later (1) The ways in which events are perceived and categorized is a function not only of characteristics of the event itself but also of the social and legal context. Referring back to Rasmussen's levels, the rules used at the rule-based level, or the categories that became established at the skill-based level, reflect the legal and social context of the event and of the decision or judgment being made. (2) Those individuals who have the experience of repeatedly taking a particular kind of decision will do it differently from those who are less experienced. I referred before to the difference between the experienced doctor and the trainee in the level of automaticity that they diagnose and act. This difference, I suggest, applies also to participants in the legal process. Thus the experienced judge will perceive a case differently from an inexperienced juror. The whole process of categorizing the event in question will be carried out differently because the judge has seen similar cases before and has established a repertoire of responses. The juror has not. Allied to this, the skill-based level is likely to involve comparatively specific responses to repeated configurations of information, whereas the rule-based level may be more fluid until a response has crystallized.

The process of categorization can be looked at as a particular type of decision making in which a social response or course of social action is to be decided on. In this case, the decision-making task involves a choice of action, diagnosis, or prediction that is in some way social in nature. What I am calling social categorization thus mediates between an event and responses to that event. Very similar models have been used in attribution research, for example, by Kelley and Michela (1980) (see Figure 1). The response to an event is thus viewed as a response,

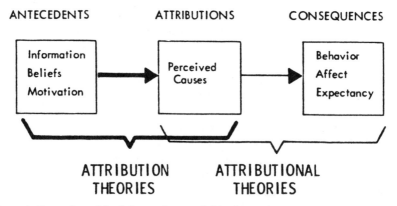

Figure 1. General model of the attribution field. (From H. H. Kelley & J. L. Michela, Attribution theory and research. *Annual Review of Psychology*, 1980.)

not directly to the event but to attributions made about it, or constructions put on it.

However, in talking about social categorization rather than attribution, I am going somewhat beyond causal judgments. For example, it would include a sentencer's categorization of a case as typical of a category of cases of, say, car theft, burglary in a dwelling, or whatever, or a parole board member's perception of a case as a "typical drugs case."

The broad decision-making model underlying this can be represented very simply as follows:

lb
Need to decide
on response

la	2	3
Receive information about event	Social categorization	Social response to event

This, of course, does not break down many different stages or factors that could be elaborated. However, it provides a framework for developing the two points outlined before.

The Social Context

First the process is not self-generating nor self-contained. This fact is not allowed for in Kelley and Michela's model, but it is of great importance in the model I propose. The event (1a) does not necessarily give rise to a process of categorization. Whether this happens and what form it takes will be a function of the need to decide whether to make some kind of response or take action (1b), and what, from a range of possibilities, that action is to be (3). For example, in the illustrations I shall be coming to, I shall be looking at responses to accidents by factory inspectors. Factory inspectors need to respond to initial, usually very scanty, accident reports with a decision whether to carry out an accident investigation that might in turn lead to further action. The action or response to be decided on initially is thus whether to investigate or not to investigate. The kinds of categories inspectors use are geared to this purpose (e.g., a potential prosecution, an apparent breach of regulations, a typical woodworking accident, etc.). These are very different from the categorizations used by the victims of the accidents.

The need to make a response not only gives rise to the process but also sets parameters for it. The categorization made will thus be at least partly a function of the social context. The initial event does not "give off'' its own explanation, which in turn leads to social consequences. The potential social consequences are themselves a factor affecting the categorization process. Thus, to use Kelley and Michela's (1980) terminology, *attribution theories* cannot sensibly be divorced from *attributional theories.*

The well-known "contextual levels" distinguished by Heider illustrate this interdependence between the appropriate grounds for an attribution of responsibility and the potential social consequences. Heider (1958) distinguished five levels:

1. *Association*—A person is held responsible for the outcome of an event with which he is associated in any way (e.g., a person is blamed for the harmful actions of his friends).
2. *Commission*—A person is held responsible for an outcome of his own actions even though he could not have foreseen the outcome. Motive does not enter the judgment.
3. *Foreseeability*—A person is held responsible for any foreseeable effect of his actions, even though the effect was not part of his goal or intentions.
4. *Intentionality*—A person is held responsible for any effect of his actions that he foresaw and intended. Motives are the central issue.
5. *Justification*—A person is held responsible for any effect that he intentionally produced unless the circumstances were such that most people would have acted as he did.

These five levels imply that there are different kinds of grounds for attributing responsibility, ranging from merely being associated with an event to being unjustified in one's actions. Heider suggests that the level at which a judgment is made is a function of the maturity and sophistication of the person making the judgment. However, clearly it is also a function of the context in which the judgment is made and the anticipated consequences of assigning responsibility. In law the context (perhaps the charge being brought) sometimes explicitly prescribes response level, so that responsibility, guilt, and the line are defined with reference to intention, foreseeability(murder, manslaughter, justifiable homicide, malicious damage, negligence, strict liability).

In much less formal and less explicit ways, the social context can be a major factor defining responsibility. An acceptable attribution of responsibility for an accident paving the way to compensation might look very different from one anticipating some other consequence—such as striking someone off a professional register or modifying safety rules—or a hunt for a scapegoat after a disaster. Knowledge that one's judgment will lead to compensation or sanctions, as, in varying degrees is the case for a jury or judge, may mean that the attribution becomes a judgment of the appropriateness of these consequences. A jury may be unwilling to find fault or guilt if it is aware that the sentence or other sanction would be in its view too severe.

Automaticity

The foregoing has emphasized comparatively overt sociolinguistic processes. However, the social context does not only define the everyday and/or legal rules within which responsibility and the line are to be negotiated. I would suggest that it also contributes to the process of building up cognitive categories into which events can comparatively rapidly and automatically be placed. The extent to which this process can be rapid and automatic will be a function of experience. Thus, in the medical context drawn on earlier, it is generally thought that more experienced doctors arrive at a diagnosis by a rather more rapid, cognitively economical, automatic process than do inexperienced junior doctors, who have not yet built up through experience the same sort of categories of recurring configurations of symptoms and other information that more experienced doctors have.

There has been very little research on legal decision making that explicitly takes this approach. Most has treated decisions as characteristically reflective and largely done from scratch. Little emphasis has been given to the frameworks built up through experience that differentiate the experienced "regular" from the newcomer, occasional, or one-off decision maker. Nor has enough attention been given to the cognitive demands of the task, the strategies of simplification that may be used, and the limitations and sources of bias as well as advantages that lie in these strategies. There are a few examples of research moving in this direction. Personal construct theory would seem to provide one approach to mapping out the categories people use, and Cliff McKnight, looking at magistrates' sentencing, developed a model of choice behavior based on a combination of personal construct theory and multiattribute utility theory (McKnight, 1981). The study thus does go some way toward this approach, but only three case histories were used. A much larger scale study over a large number of cases would be needed to examine fully how constructs and cases cluster into repeated correlated patterns.

Fitzmaurice and Pease's book on judicial sentencing (Fitzmaurice Pease, 1986) is the first attempt to synthesize in a systematic way recent research in cognitive psychology on the "shortcomings" of human judgment and the literature on sentencing. Their conclusions are inevitably speculative because the research specifically in this area simply has not been done, but their suggestions are to a large extent, persuasive. Payne (1980) has noted that the parolee who shares some but not all of the attributes of a "typical" drug offender is likely to get categorized as one for parole purposes, often to his detriment. This is exactly the process of mapping or categorization to which I wish to draw attention.

Before I attempt to link all this with what I have said about everyday thinking, let me summarize what I have said about social categorization of events. This is a process interposed between receiving information about an event and responding to it, whereby an event is classified as an example of a class of events that carry certain social implications. The categorization is not generated by the event itself but by social factors and is to a greater or lesser extent a function of the social (perhaps legal) context. It may be more or less automatic, depending on constraints on the alternatives and on the experience of the individual. It is subject not only to social influences but also the effects of cognitive strategies in coping with the type of decision concerned. Examples of the kind of thing I mean include sentencing, parole decisions, and responses to accidents, where social and legal issues of punishment, compensation, and prevention arise.

How does this relate to questions about commonsense, everyday thinking? First I have emphasized that social categorization is a function of the context. There is no "pure" interpretation of events. Where there are laws and legal rules or norms relevant to the event, law forms part of that context. In many contexts, therefore, everyday thinking already embraces legal thinking and legal rules, sometimes to the extent that the law provides the whole framework for thinking about events. Road accidents are an example. Here, the ways in which causes and blame for accidents are ascribed are very largely a function of the rules of the road. So my first point is that the relationship between everyday, commonsense thinking and law is reflexive, and common sense can in some settings be structured very largely by law and legal institutions. Second, commonsense processes of social categorization depend on the building up of mental categories by the individual. Both the structure and content of these will vary according to the individual's experience. Therefore an important contrast may sometimes be between those individuals who repeatedly make certain types of decisions and build up categories through experience and those who do not have this experience.

Victims and Inspectors Compared

The differing responses of accident victims and factory inspectors to similar events illustrate these points. Victims and factory inspectors have different reasons and purposes in arriving at an understanding of what happened after an accident. The social and legal consequences they are concerned with differ. And they differ greatly in the extent to which categorizing accidents is an oft-repeated task. For accident victims, the social factors affecting their perceptions of what happened include the prospect of damages and their social relationships with other people involved (such as coworkers, friends, family, employers). Because they are unlikely themselves to have suffered similar previous accidents, they could be expected often not to have a ready repertoire of categories into which the event can be placed. In contrast, factory inspectors are not concerned with compensation but with prevention and possibly prosecution. They are concerned also with public expectations, so that their response may have a symbolic element, such as making an extended investigation of a fatal accident where there is really little to be achieved from the safety point of view, but where there is an expectation that a thorough investigation will be made, and perhaps a prosecution brought. They work within a framework of legal rules and regulations and organizational constraints and incentives. And they see accident reports and carry out investigations as a repeated and integral aspect of their work. They would thus be expected to have developed categories of types of accidents that occur and are responded to in repeated patterns. These categories would be expected to discriminate accidents according to those aspects that are salient for deciding on a response—their public impact; whether they involve an apparent breach of regulations; and so forth.

The data I have on victims and inspectors are indicative rather than definitive. The data on inspectors, in particular, are not yet fully analyzed. However, a pattern emerges that is consistent with the above analysis. For accident victims, the data were obtained through interviews; and for inspectors, through open-ended interviews, observation, and analysis of files.

Injured Victims

Approximately 1,000 victims of serious accidents were interviewed. All had suffered from their injury (or its continuing physical effects) within the previous 2 years. To qualify for an interview, the victim must have been unable to carry on a normal life for at least 2 weeks. This criterion meant that the accidents or illness were nonminor and the victim was likely to have needed to rely on some form of compensation or support. Statistically an accident or illness this serious can be expected to occur roughly once every 10 years in an individual's life. The accident victims were asked (among many other things): How did the accident happen? Was it anyone's fault in any way? (If so, in what way?) Did you feel anyone should pay you compensation? (If so, why and who?).

The study and results are described in full elsewhere (e.g., Lloyd-Bostock, 1984). A brief summary of some of the results is offered here. Looking first at the question of the influence of the social context, I suggested that the prospect of *compensation* is one important factor. There are indications in the data that this is indeed so. Accident victims attribute fault to someone else where there is a prospect of damages and what is more, in a way that would justify the most promising claim.

First, many accidents are described as "just accidents," or as the victim's own fault. Fault is attributed to others most often for those accidents where the possibility of a damages claim is most likely to occur to the victim. Table 1 shows that there are very marked differences in the blaming rates for different types of accidents—that is, according to where the accident happened. "Objective" differences in fault based on the causes of accidents cannot explain such large differences. Very similar accidents often occur at work and at home, for example. But if someone falls off a ladder or scalds him/herself at home, they see that as no one else's fault. If it happens at work, they probably blame their employer. In practice, road and work accidents account for the vast majority of legal claims to damages in the United Kingdom. In this sample, 19% of work-accident victims obtained damages; and 29% of road-accident victims. Only 2% of all other categories did so, and those who did were mostly claiming against the

Table 1. Whether Fault or Liability Attributed by Type of Accident

	Someone else at fault	Someone should compensate	Number
Road	67%	54%	246
Work	38%	53%	409
Leisure/sport	24%	19%	184
Domestic	4%	0%	142
Assault	90%	62%	21
Industrial illness	25%	42%	12
Total			1,074

local authority for falls on an uneven pavement. No one in the entire sample claimed damages for a domestic accident. So there is a remarkable fit between the pattern of whether or not someone is said to be at fault and the general pattern of successful damages claims. There is an even more marked difference between accident types in the numbers who said they thought someone should pay them compensation. The numbers of work-accident victims who said they felt someone should compensate them is in fact higher than the number of those who said someone else was at fault. This again illustrates the effects of various rule systems on people's perceptions of just outcomes. There are many different systems of compensation and support operating in relation to work accidents as well as the fault-based tort system. Work-accident victims are likely to feel they should be compensated simply because the accident was a work accident. They are also often confused about the criteria for compensation under the different systems and sometimes say that they should be compensated simply because they have paid their national insurance. This entitled them to sick pay and other benefits but not compensation.

Second, there are striking differences between work and road accidents in the way in which someone else is said to be at fault. Table 2 shows a breakdown of responses to the question, "In what way was it (so and so)'s fault?" for work and road accidents. The breakdown is in two general categories. The first is in terms of the immediate causes of the accident, for example, "He pulled out in front of me without looking"; "he tipped the oil all over the floor." The second is where fault is attributed in more background, less proximate terms, such as poor management practice—for example "there were two men on a three man job"; "the building was in poor repair." Table 2 shows that in road accidents the first type overwhelming predominates, whereas in work accidents the second predominates.

Of course it is true that work accidents often are the result of poor management or inadequate safety standards, whereas road accidents

Table 2. Type of Fault by Type of Accident (Road and Work Only)

Type of fault	Road accidents		Work accidents	
	n	Percentage	n	Percentage
Careless/negligent act at the time	149	90	31	20
Negligence at another time or place; background conditions	12	7	122	79
Not stated/not codeable	4		2	
Total where someone else at fault	165		155	

often are the result of someone doing something careless at the time. But this does not account for these differences. The same accident can often be explained with reference either to an immediate cause or to a more background one. For example, if someone falls through a roof, this might be said to be caused either by the victim's failure to use crawling boards or by the company's failure to enforce regulations requiring their use. The question is, which , out of the range of possible factors, gets the label *fault* attached. I am suggesting that here again the prospect of damages is an important factor. The insured other driver's contribution to the accident is likely to be an immediate one. The insured employer's is likely to be more remote.

Although accident victims are not likely to be dealing with accidents as a matter of routine in the way that factory inspectors do, they are not responding from scratch either. Indeed, at some workplaces, certain types of accidents recur and are regarded as "part of the job." Even quite serious injuries such as amputations of fingers at woodworking machines are regarded in this way. Cuts to the hands while filleting fish (a process employing extremely sharp knives and carried out at high speed) are scarcely regarded as "accidents" in the usual sense. More generally, there are familiar, customary ways of responding to work accidents and to road accidents. What an accident victim sees as the rights and wrongs of the situation is going to be a function of the rules and norms he or she is used to applying in that sort of context. In other words, accident victims will to some extent have developed ready-made categories into which accidents may fall. As mentioned, driving is governed by rules of the road with which the victim of a road accident is likely to be familiar and that provide a framework for deciding who was in the wrong. At work there are various rule systems that place responsibility on an employer for ensuring that accidents do not happen, correspondingly moving emphasis away from the more immediate causes of accidents in the actions of employees and toward more background conditions for which the employer is responsible.

The effects of those rule systems is, however, rather weak and confused and mediated by the contacts that an accident victim has with others following the accident (such as the police; trade union officials; fellow workers) who may be looking for certain kinds of account such as any possibility of a breach of the law; or a compensation claim. Victims, for instance, were often unclear about the rules governing entitlement to compensation and often confuse criminal with civil law.

The general unpleasantness of being caught up in making a legal claim is very clear in a victim's responses to questions about his or her claims, or about why he or she did not try to claim. Claiming is seen as a rather nasty, vindictive thing to do. Blaming and embarking on a legal action against a work colleague, friend, or family member, in particular, carries social costs. The picture one gets from victims who did bring a claim for compensation is that they find it an upsetting process, were bewildered, and felt buffeted and anxious.

To summarize, accident victims' perceptions of their accidents are not only affected by the objective facts of the accident itself; they are also affected by (1) the prospect of compensation, (2) customary/legal frameworks and rule systems, (3) personal relationships with others involved in the accident, and (4) subsequently contacts with others.

These various factors interact and over time a story crystallizes and becomes what the accident victim tells and believes. That the process often occurs over an extended period of time and is affected by the possibility of a compensation claim is confirmed by factory inspectors, who say that for their purposes the injured person is often not a good source of information about the causes of the accident. Too soon after the accident they have not worked out what happened. And by the time they have, their "story" is colored by their interests in a compensation claim, or other vested interest.

Factory Inspectors

I shall discuss inspectors quite briefly, to bring out some contrasts with accident victims. The main sources of differences in perceptions of accidents are:

1. The social and legal context within which inspectors work as compared with victims
2. The possible action they might take (such as bringing a prosecution, offering advice, or issuing an improvement notice, as compared with claiming compensation, or taking no action
3. Their experience in categorizing accidents and hence degree to which the process is rapid and automatic.

A fourth factor, the personal salience of the accident to the victim, must also surely be important but is not dealt with in detail here.

Responses to accidents by factory inspectors are very highly routinized. They have ready categories and repeated patterns of responses. The major source of these categories and responses is the legal framework of regulations, standards, and sanctions that define what is a breach of law and their powers to take enforcement action. This is not to say that what inspectors are doing is "mindless" in a pejorative sense. They are a very impressive and committed profession. It is simply that they have seen many of these accidents before. They have a certain repertoire of possible responses and categories into which accidents repeatedly fall. Unlike accident victims, they are not confused about the law, much influenced by others' interpretations and suggestions, or slow to arrive at a categorization. They know what the range of actions open to them is and have the experience on which to base a swift response—often on the basis of very meager information. The inspector often knows from a very brief initial report that, for example, a prosecution is likely. In contrast, an accident victim may not know that, for example, there may be a possibility of claiming compensation and is therefore uncertain about the possibility of taking any action. This, combined with the comparative lack of experience, and perhaps also the personal salience of the accident, results in a much more uncertain and lengthy process open to the influence of others. The contrasting routinization of the process for factory inspectors is encapsulated in what is said to be the shortest (and probably apocryphal) prosecution case ever brought by an inspector. It was in six words: "Power press, no guard, fingers off"; to which the magistrate replied "Done."

The rapid process of categorization is most clearly seen in the stage of selecting accidents for investigation. At the time of the study (the system has recently been altered), a principal inspector might scan around 30 brief written accident reports in 10 minutes. The reports contain very brief information on how the accident occurred: where, type of injury, age and sex of the victim, and other summary background information. In a matter often of a few seconds, the inspector would decide whether or not on-the-site investigation was needed. (Around 5% were investigated.)

Conclusion

In broad terms, the subject of this chapter has been how events come to be understood and defined in certain ways, so that particular legal outcomes or procedures are perceived to be appropriate. When these perceptions and understandings differ from one person to another, there is potential for perceived injustice in social relations. The Chapter has suggested how, even with a community with shared values, such divergences may arise; and how the perceptions of those who rarely meet the need to catergorize a particular type of event can be greatly influenced by the law or other rule system and the responses of others. Once an understanding of an event and its just outcome have been reached, however, this appears to crystallize and deviations from it are viewed as unjust. One illustration of this is accident victims views about how much compensation they should receive. All respondents in the Oxford survey said they had had no idea what their claim was worth until they spoke to a lawyer. But once they had a figure in mind, they viewed this as what they deserved and felt dissatisfied if they eventually had to settle for less.

I have suggested that the process of categorizing a given event, and hence appropriate responses to it, may vary along a continuum. At the one end there is a comparatively automatic, skill-based mapping onto prototypical events. At the other is a much more reflective and time-consuming working out on the basis of more general rules and norms. An illustration of this is found in the differing responses of accident victims and factory inspectors to objectively similar events, where factory inspectors tend to respond comparatively rapidly and automatically to repeated accident types, whereas victims tend to take much longer and puzzle more over the event before an understanding of how it happened and its implications crystallizes.

These effects of context and experience have implications for the way we talk about everyday thinking, common sense and so on. Where there are legal rules or norms relevant to the event, law forms part of the context. Common sense can therefore in some settings be structured very largely by the law and legal institutions. The data on accident victims illustrate how their attributions of fault and liability reflect (often in a rather diluted or distorted way) the law concerning personal injury compensation. There is no reason why similar effects would not be found in other dispute resolution contexts. What Abel (1979) describes as a pendulum swing between legalization and delegalization may describe changes in formal procedures, but the idea of nonlegal norms of behavior that can be used instead of legal ones, or that may survive independently of law and be returned to and revived, makes little sense when ordinary ideas are influenced and structured by legal rules.

In addition, the commonsense reasoning of an individual who repeatedly takes similar decisions may be very different, both in form and content, from that of someone less familiar with the decision task. This was illustrated by the data on factory inspectors as compared with accident victims. The formal legal rules, regulations, and habits of administration and management are inextricably mixed in the repertoire of categories and responses from which an inspector learns with experience, to select very quickly. In Hawkins' (1983, 1984) studies of parole board decisions and of pollution inspectors, referred to before, he is looking at groups of people who, in varying degrees, have had experience of making the same sort of decision before. In exercising their common sense they therefore use categories of typical events (or prisoners, managers, etc.) that nonexperienced decision makers do not have. Their common sense is in this sense, while distinguishable from formal legal rules, not all that common.

References

Abel, R. (1979). Delegalization. A critical review of its ideology manifestations, and social consequences.
Fitzmaurice, C. Pease, K. (1986). *The psychology of judicial sentencing*. Manchester: Manchester University Press.
Hart, H. L. A., Honoré, A. M. (1959). *Causation in the law*.Oxford: Clarendon Press.
Hawkins, K. (1983), Assessing evil: Decision behaviour and parole board justice. *British Journal of Criminology, 23* (2) 101-127.
Hawkins, K. (1984). *Environment and enforcement*. Oxford: Oxford University Press.
Heider, F. (1958).*The psychology of interpersonal relations* New York: Wiley.
Kelley, H. H. & Michela, J. L. (1980). Attribution theory and research. *Annual Review of Psychology, 31,* 457-501.
Lloyd-Bostock, S. M. A. (1979). The ordinary man and the psychology of attributing causes and responsibility *Modern Law Review. 1,* 143-168
Lloyd-Bostock, S. M. A. (1981). Do lawyers' references to"common sense" have anything to do with what ordinary people think? *British Journal of Social Psychology. 20,* 161-163.
Lloyd-Bostock, S. M. A. (1984) Fault and liability for accidents: The accident victim's perspective. In D. Harris et al. (Eds.),*Compensation and support for illness and injury* (pp. 139-163). Oxford: Oxford University Press.
McKnight, C. (1981). Subjectivity in sentencing. *Law and Human Behaviour 5,* 213, 141-147.
Moore, M. S. (1984). *Law and psychiatry: Rethinking the relationship*. Cambridge: Cambridge University Press.
Payne, J. W. (1980). Information processing theory: Some concepts and methods applied to decision research. In T. S. Wallsten (Ed.), *Cognitive processes in choice and decision behavior*. Hillsdale, NJ: Erlbaum.
Rasmussen, J. (1981). Models of mental strategies in process control. In J. Rasmussen & W. Rouse (Eds.), *Human detection and diagnosis of system failures*. New York: Plenum Press.
Wickens, C. D. (1984). *Engineering psychology and human performance*. Columbus, OH: Charles E. Merrill.

3

Social Dilemmas, Shared Resources, and Social Justice

David M. Messick

Introduction

Social dilemmas are pernicious interpersonal situations in which undesirable consequences are created by a group of people each of whom is sensibly trying to bring about desirable consequences. Why should secretaries or faculty members pay the dues to join labor unions the benefits of which they would enjoy whether they become members or not (Messick, 1973)? But, of course, if no one joins, there will be no union and no benefits to enjoy.

In the United States, a crisis is developing about what to do with the nation's nuclear waste (Marshall, 1986). Fifteen thousand metric tons of radioactive garbage are awaiting a safe, permanent home, and everyone agrees that finding a suitable site for this mess is terribly important. But everybody also believes that the only suitable sites are those found in someone else's neighborhood.

Social dilemmas are often created when people share renewable resources to which all have free access. This problem has been eloquently described by Hardin (1968) in his famous essay on the tragedy of the commons. When a group of herdsmen share a common pasture, it is to the advantage of each to increase his herd size because the profit from the animals is collected by the herdsmen, whereas the cost, measured in terms of damage to the common pasturage, is shared

David M. Messick • Department of Psychology, University of California, Santa Barbara, California 93106.

by all. When all of the herdsmen respond to this incentive, calamitous overgrazing is the result, and the pasturage is destroyed and lost to all.

Hardin's pessimistic conclusion may be avoidod if the rate at which the resource is being consumed can be reduced. The rate of consumption can be factored into two separate components—the average rate of consumption per person and the total number of people using the resource. This fact highlights a distinction that lies at the center of the research that will be reviewed here, namely that to control the rate of consumption of a resource, one can proceed by attempting to reduce voluntary individual consumption, or one can attack the problem by structurally limiting people's access to the resource. In California, the total demand for water during the drought years of the mid-1970s might not have been affected at all by the sacrifices made by individual water users if the total number of water consumers had been permitted to increase. Thus in many parts of the state, the water authorities imposed a moratorium on new water hookups, thereby depriving a large number of prospective water consumers of access to the common resource.

What is important about this distinction is that it underscores the existence of at least two different routes that can be taken to solve a problem with shared resources. The first concerns an individual's rates of consumption and the factors that can influence it, whereas the second concerns the individual's willingness to institute changes in the procedures that are used to allocate the resource. Citizens of California could not only decide what kinds of personal sacrifices they would make to reduce their water use, they could also express their preferences for systematic changes in allocation procedures by voting for people to be members of the water regulatory agency. People could not only decide how to use the resource, they also had preferences for the rules that would govern the allocation of the resource. Messick and Brewer (1983) have referred to the first class of decisions as *individual* efforts to solve the problem, whereas the second type illustrates decisions to make *structural* changes. These decisions about structural changes are metadecisions in the sense that they are decisions about the kind of environment in which one wants individual decisions to be made.

The research that will be discussed in this chapter is an inquiry into the psychological processes that are involved when members of a group share renewable resources. Although the research is not con-cerned with a particular type of resource, our interest in the problem was sparked by the drought in southern California in 1976–1977. People share not only water, however, they share clean air and healthy environments; they share naturally renewing resources like forests, pheasants, and fish; and people in organizations ranging from governments to families share budgets that are periodically renewed.

I will first describe our general experimental setup. Then I will summarize some of our major research findings regarding factors that influence both individual self-restraint and preferences for structural solutions. I will conclude by noting some parallels between our research and research on social justice.

Experimental Task

Most of the experiments that we will review were conducted in the computer-controlled laboratory described by Parker, Lui, Messick, Messick, Brewer, Kramer, Samuelson, and Wilke (1983). Subjects participated in groups of six. Upon arrival at the laboratory, the subjects were seated in one of six shielded cubicles that prevented them from seeing each other. Each subject was seated in front of a keyboard and a visual display that was used to present all of the experimental information to the subject.

The instructions stressed that the experiment involved decision making in an environment involving shared resources. The analogy to the use of real natural resources was highlighted and the conflict between short-term use and the long-term health of the resource was pointed out. The subjects were told that their job was to try to accumulate as much of the available resource as they could, while at the same time preserving the resource so that it would be available for a longer period.

The subjects were told that they would share a renewable resource with five other subjects. On each of a series of trials, they would be given the opportunity to "harvest" from this resource, and the amount harvested would become the private property of the subject. There was a possibility that this private resource could be exchanged for a considerable sum of money at the termination of the experiment, and subjects typically seemed motivated to perform well.

The instructions further explained that the resource was capable of replenishing itself. After all group members had made their harvests, a new pool size was calculated that was proportional to the size of the postharvest pool. The rate at which the pool was replenished could be varied.

At the end of each of these trials, the subjects were given feedback about the purported harvests of the five other subjects for that trial and about the amount of the resource remaining in the pool. In many of our experiments, this information was preprogrammed and did not reflect the actual decisions of the others.

This part of the experiment typically lasted for 10 trials. On each of these trials we recorded the harvest made by the subject. This was the first set of dependent variables that we recorded.

After this first set of trials, we told the subjects that they were going to be given the chance to do the experiment a second time. We told them that some groups in the past had expressed a preference for changing the way the experiment was done. Although the details of how this was accomplished varied from study to study, the general goal was to give the subjects a chance to state whether they wanted to perform the second session of the experiment according to the same rules that they had used in the first session—with each member of the group being permitted to harvest as much as he or she wanted—or whether they wanted to change to a different system. This expression of a preference for either the status quo or for a structural change was the second dependent variable of importance in our research.

Individual Self-Restraint

In this section I will summarize our findings with regard to the factors that influence self-restraint in individual decision making. The general theoretical picture that has emerged is that subjects harvest decisions reflect three underlying motives that may or may not be in conflict with each other. These three motives are, first, a desire to do as well as possible in the short term; second, a concern with prolonging the life of the pool; and, finally, a desire not to depart too dramatically from the observed behavior of the other group members.

The basic pattern of results that led to this conceptualization was reported by Messick, Wilke, Brewer, Kramer, Zemke, and Lui (1983) and by Samuelson, Messick, Rutte, and Wilke (1984). The pattern has been replicated by Samuelson (1986) and Samuelson and Messick (1986a, 1986b). All of these studies have examined the effects of two factors on individual decisions and on preferences for structural change. The first of these factors pertains to the perceived "health" of the resource pool. Some of the subjects in all of these studies received (false) feedback that the pool was being overused and that the pool size was dropping dramatically. Other subjects, however, were led to believe that the pool size was not being depleted. Within each of these groups, roughly half of the subjects saw that the other group members were rather similar in the size of their harvests, whereas the other half witnessed great variation in these harvests. Although the total amount taken from the pool was the same, the subjects experienced either intragroup homogeneity or heterogeneity among the other five members. These different experiences were created by means of false feedback.

When the subjects believe that the pool is being depleted, all things being equal, they should reduce their harvests to permit the pool to be replenished. However, if the pool is not being depleted, then the subjects are free to increase their harvest size in order to try to increase their personal returns from the pool. The major restraining force on them should be their desire not to drift too far above the norm established by the harvests of the others. This tendency to conform, moreover, should be stronger when the norm is clearer than when it is more obscure, and we hypothesized therefore that it would exert greater influence when the harvests of the others were more rather than less homogeneous. Our basic prediction therefore was that subjects would harvest less when the pool was being depleted than when it was not, but that in this latter case, subjects seeing the homogeneous harvests of their fellow group members would take less than subjects who witnessed heterogeneous harvests. This is the general pattern of results that we have found over and over again.

There is a slightly different way to view this effect. When the purported harvests of the others are heterogeneous, the subject witnesses two of the others who are taking extremely large harvests, harvests that are very close to the maximum. These bogus others provide a reference point in comparison to whom the subjects are doing rather poorly. If these large harvests are particularly salient they could be expected to raise the *comparison level* (Thibaut & Kelley, 1959) of the subjects, making them more dissatisfied with their outcomes and prompting them to increase their own harvests. This interpretation implies that heterogeneous subjects should be more dissatisfied than the homogeneous subjects, an implication for which we have sound empirical support. It also implies that the process that reduces the influence of the group norm is upward outcome comparisons The average harvest is made less salient by the extremely large harvests.

This interpretation is important because it provides an explanation for an interesting exception to our normal pattern of results. Samuelson *et al.* (1984) performed essentially the same experiment in the United States and in The Netherlands. The pattern of results described characterized the data from the American subjects but not from the Dutch subjects. Like the American subjects, these latter individuals took smaller harvest when the pool was seen to be dropping, but unlike the Americans, there was no difference between the heterogeneous and homogeneous groups who saw that the pool was not dropping. The Dutch subjects appear to have made upward outcome comparisons because the heterogeneous group reported itself more dissatisfied than the homogeneous group, but what they did about it was quite different. As we shall see, they opted for structural change, whereas the Americans increased the size of their personal harvests.

The three processes that we have focused on in our conceptualization of the determinants of harvest behavior have been analyzed in a number of other experiments, some done in our laboratory and some done by others. I will briefly review some of these.

Self-Interest or Group Interest

In our experiments, we ask subjects to try to accumulate as many points for themselves as they can. By so doing, we try to focus or simplify their goals. However, even under these and similar experimental circumstances, we find that people display a rich variety of interests in addition to simply accumulating points. We know on purely theoretical grounds that if subjects define their "self-interest" as including some concern for the outcomes of fellow group members, then the dilemma in some social dilemmas disappears (Messick, 1973–1974). Experimental research has also found systematic individual differences in the way people respond to diminishing resources. Messick et al. (1983) found that people who were high on a measure of reciprocal trust displayed more self-restraint in the face of a diminishing pool than people who were lower on this measure. Kramer, McClintock, and Messick (1986) found a similar pattern of results differentiating cooperators, subjects who in a previous decision-making task had shown systematic concern for the outcomes of others, from noncooperators. When the pool was perceived as being depleted, cooperators decreased their harvests, whereas noncooperators did not. Other experiments showing similar outcomes have been reported by Liebrand (1986), Kuhlman and Marshello (1975), and Samuelson (1986).

Self-interest not only manifests itself differently in different people, but different circumstances can lead people to take more or less account of the outcomes of others. One of these factors has to do with the extent to which one identifies with the group and perceives him or herself to be a group member as opposed to an independent individual. In one study investigating the effects of group identification on the use of a shared resource, Kramer and Brewer (1984) made the common group membership salient for groups of six subjects, or they made salient categories that divided the group into two subgroups of three subjects each. When the common group category was salient, the subjects, especially the men, were more cooperatively restrained than when the categories that divided the group were salient. Brewer and Kramer (1986) have reported other results that are in general agreement with their first study, and Kramer and Brewer (1986) have provided a conceptual overview of these research findings.

The research summarized by Kramer and Brewer (1986) has shown, among other things, that a willingness to exercise self-restraint for the good of the group can be induced by varying the salience of group boundaries. If we see each other as members of the same group, we are more likely to think of self-interest as involving group interest than if we view ourselves as a collection of independent, unrelated individuals. Having a group discussion of the problem may have a similar impact. Dawes, McTavish, and Shaklee (1977) showed that groups that were able to discuss a social dilemma were much more cooperative in their choices than groups that could not discuss anything or groups that could discuss only irrelevant topics. The question created by this dramatic finding is to determine just how it is that discussion increases cooperativeness. Although Messick and Brewer (1983) discuss four different ways that this might happen, van de Kragt, Dawes, Orbell, Braver, and Wilson (1986) describe a series of studies that suggest that the mechanism has to do with the arousal of what they call "group-regarding motives." This conclusion is supported by a series of experiments in which the authors systematically eliminate explanations based on the assumption that the subjects think that they will be better off personally by cooperating. The inference then is that subjects must be cooperating after discussion because it matters to them that the group do well even if they personally do not. An experiment reported by Orbell, van de Kragt, and Dawes (1986), in which subjects know that there is absolutely no way in which they personally can be benefited by a self-sacrificial cooperative decision, leaves little room for doubt about this interpretation. A very high fraction of the subjects in groups that could discuss the problem made self-sacrificial cooperative decisions, whereas a small proportion of the subjects did in groups that could not discuss it.

Maintaining the Pool

Using a shared resource pool wisely implies that the members of a group have some knowledge of the way in which the pool behaves. Such knowledge would allow people to devise optimal strategies for using the resource. Much of the ecological debate about whale fishing, harvesting of harp seals, or the maintenance of clean air concerns the definition of "safe" levels of use of the resource. What are the levels of exploitation of a resource that do not endanger future access to it? In the real world of biology and environmental chemistry, questions like these are complicated and rarely have simple answers.

Even in simple experimental simulations of the sort we have used, gaining a knowledge of the optimal strategy is not trivial. In an experiment reported by Messick and McClelland (1983), we found that groups of three or six subjects did a much poorer job in maintaining a replenishable pool than subjects who had exclusive private access to such a resource. The inferiority of the group performance could have been the result of a number of factors. Allison and Messick (1985) performed an experiment to evaluate the hypothesis that the performance loss was a result of the fact that the more people who share a resource, the less clear the relationship becomes between one's decision and the subsequent level of the pool. A person with a private pool can use trial and error to determine the maximum harvest size that does not begin to deplete the pool. However, when several people are trying independently to do the same thing with a shared pool, they get in each other's way.

To evaluate the importance of this mutual interference, Allison and Messick (1985) gave some subjects private experience with the pool before putting them into groups to share the pool. The result was that groups containing experienced individuals were nearly as good as individuals in their ability to maintain the pool. The group performance decrement did not seem to be caused by motivational losses or diffusion of responsibility (Kerr, 1986; Latane, Williams, Harkins, 1979) but rather by the inability of group members to learn the optimal harvest size before it was too late.

Normative Influences

The third factor that we think is important in determining harvest size is a tendency to adhere to perceived group norms or standards. One reason why people might imitate the responses of others is because they think this information is useful in determining the optimal harvest size. An experiment by Schroeder, Jensen, Reed, Sullivan, and Schwab (1983) provides some support for this interpretation. Schroeder et al. showed that this tendency to imitate others was sharply reduced when the subjects were told what the optimal strategy was. This makes sense if subjects were using the others' harvests as "guesses" about the best harvest size.

Although this kind of simple informational process is undoubtedly important, there are probably other types of influence as well. Kramer and Brewer (1986) point out that the simple use of others' harvests to estimate an optimal response will not account for patterns of influence that they find in their experiments. They point out that subjects may use the behavior of others to rationalize or to justify decisions that have been made for other reasons. From their own experiments, they suggest that what subjects extract from witnessing the behavior of others is some sense of what the appropriate orientation to the task might be. Should they try to maintain the pool, or should they try to get as much as possible before the pool disappears? The situation is an unusual and ambiguous one, and the behavior of the others sheds light on what values should be paramount rather than what numerical harvest size is best.

A study by Rutte, Wilke, and Messick (1987) supports this idea that what subjects learn from the behavior of others concerns the appropriateness of different ways of interpreting the task. In the task used by Rutte et al. (1987), subjects were told that they would be taking money from a shared pool of cash that the experimenter had made available to them. They were told that they would do so in an sequential order that would be randomly determined. In fact, all subjects were told that they had been assigned to the fifth of six positions so that their turn would be next to the last. The subjects were also told that each subject would be able to keep the amount of cash that he or she claimed so long as the total amount claimed did not exceed the amount in the pool. If the total claimed was more than the amount in the pool, all subjects got nothing.

The experimental variables that were manipulated were first, the total amount of money in the pool, and, second, whether the subjects thought that the four subjects whose decisions preceded the subjects knew how much money was in the pool when they made their claims. All subjects were told that the amount of money in the pool would be between 5 and 55 Dutch guilders (the experiment was conducted in The Netherlands) and that the exact amount would be determined by chance. Half of the subjects were told that the selected amount was fl.25, whereas the other half were told that the amount was fl.35 (At the time this study was done, the exchange was approximately 3 guilders to $1 U.S.) In addition, half of the subjects in each of these groups were told that the first four decision makers would have to make their claims without knowing what the group total was. The other half was told that all decision makers knew the group total before making their claims. All subjects then saw (through false feedback) the first four subjects claim 6, 5, 4, and 5 guilders respectively, leaving either 5 or 15 guilders for the final two group members to share.

Rutte et al. hypothesized that when subjects believed that their predecessors had made their decisions in ignorance of the pool size, there would be no normative influence because the behavior of the others could not be informative about what was appropriate. They further hypothesized that subjects in this condition would not blindly imitate the average claim of the first 4 and request 5 guilders but would rather chose to divide the remaining money equally. Subjects who believed that the first four did know the pool size, on the other hand, were expected to be influenced by their claims. When the first four took 20 out of 25 of the guilders, they were displaying greed; when they took 20 out of 35 guilders they were manifesting generosity. Thus we hypothesized that subjects having 5 guilders left would take more than half, imitating the greed of the predecessors, whereas those having 15 guilders left would take less than half. This is precisely what happened.

Thus it seems that subjects scrutinize the behavior of others in order to clarify the appropriate stance or orientation to take. The research that I have summarized suggests that this is not a process of mindless imitation but rather an active process of interpretation or inference that deserves to be better understood.

Structural Solutions

We have known for a long time that changes in the structure of the group decision task can improve performance. One of the earliest experimental studies of social dilemmas showed that levels of cooperation could be altered by changing the payoffs in rather predictable ways (Kelley Grzelak, 1972). Komorita, Sweeney, and Kravitz (1980) have systematically explored the effects on cooperative choice of varying the payoff structure. Other changes might include permitting the group members to communicate. As I noted in the previous section, this change also tends to increase cooperative responding (Dawes et al., 1977; van de Kragt et al., 1986). The size of the group sharing a resource, another structural property of the task, has also been shown to influence the amount of cooperative behavior that will be observed (Cass Edney, 1978; Kramer Brewer, 1986; Messick & McClelland, 1983). Komorita and Lapworth (1982) have shown that providing an additional choice alternative does so as well. Yamagishi (1986) has described an ingenious system that tends to elicit high levels of cooperation, especially from those least likely to cooperate. There is no doubt that structural properties are important.

The research question that we have asked, however, is not whether structural properties can improve a group's use of a shared resource. The question that we have asked is: Under what circumstances will people want to bring about a structural change in the way they share resources, and what kinds of change will they want? Yamagishi's (1986) system, which works by punishing the most greedy member of a group, may be effective, but when would people chose to live under that system rather than one that does not have the punitive component?

Our initial answer to the question of when people would want to change the rules was that they would do so when they were dissatisfied with the status quo (Messick et al., 1983). This answer turned out to be as incorrect as it was simplistic. We hypothesized that subjects would feel dissatisfied if they saw (1) that the resource was being poorly used, resulting in its depletion, or (2) that there were large inequalities in the way that the resource was getting distributed among the group members. In our first test of these hypotheses, Messick et al. (1983) exposed some of the subjects to a pool that was shrinking whereas others dealt with a pool that stayed at or close to the maximum. The subjects who witnessed their pool dropping did express more dissatisfaction than the others, and they did vote for a structural change for the second session more frequently than the others.

The only alternative that the subjects in this study had to the free access that characterized the first part was to elect a leader from among the group members. The role of this leader would be to make a single harvest for the entire group and then to allocate the total to the group members. Thus the leader would have not only exclusive access to the resource but also the right to determine how much of it each group member would receive.

Our second hypothesis was that subjects witnessing great inequalities in the harvests of the others, some of them taking a great deal on every trial and others taking very little, would experience dissatisfaction because of the perceived inequity in the allocation of the resources. We expected that these subjects, relative to others who saw a more equalitarian distribution of the resources, would express their dissatisfaction by opting to elect a leader for the second session. This did not occur. Although the heterogeneous subjects did display more dissatisfaction than the homogeneous ones, they did not vote in favor of electing a leader significantly more often.

Samuelson et al. (1984) made another try to obtain this effect and, with American subjects, failed to do so. As I mentioned earlier, the article by Samuelson et al. (1984) reported two essentially identical studies, one conducted in the United States and the other in The Netherlands. Although the American subjects failed to show the predicted preference for structural change in response to perceived inequity, the Dutch subjects did display it. The Dutch subjects, like the Americans, also voted for a leader when they saw the declining pool. These studies, considered together with that of Messick et al. (1983), suggest two conclusions that we have not had to alter as a result of subsequent studies.

First, people want to change the rules, to bring about structural change when they see that the pool is being depleted. It is better to give up one's private access to the pool and to have to depend on someone else—a leader—than to give up the pool completely and forever because it has been overexploited.

Second, the effects of perceived inequity in harvest outcomes are much more subtle and fragile than the effects of resource overuse. In these two studies, we find no inequity effect with American subjects, but we do find such an effect with Dutch subjects, suggesting a cultural difference in subjects' response to the inequality. This suggestion is reinforced by the finding that I mentioned earlier to the effect that Dutch and American subjects harvest were influenced differently by the manipulation of perceived inequality. Thus Dutch and American students appear to respond differently to inequality on both of our dependent measures.

The results of Messick et al. (1983) and Samuelson et al. (1984) clearly show that dissatisfaction is not a sufficient condition to promote change. Our subsequent studies (Samuelson & Messick, 1986a, 1986b) examining the relationship between harvests harvest equality or inequality and peoples' preferences for structural change force the conclusion that the process is much more complicated than we originally had thought.

This discovery should not be surprising. One of the major conceptual contributions of Thibaut and Kelley (1959) was the distinction between the comparison level (CL) and the comparison level for alternatives (CLalt). The comparison level is the neutral point on the affective or hedonic scale on which we evaluate experiences. Unpleasant or affectively negative outcomes fall below this zero point, whereas pleasant outcomes fall above it. In deciding whether to remain in a relationship or to leave it in favor of a different relationship, Thibaut and Kelley claim, people do not simply ask themselves whether or not they are satisfied or dissatisfied, whether their outcomes are above or below their CL. Instead they compare their outcomes to the CLalt that is the outcome level they could anticipate in their most attractive alternative relationship. If the outcome level of the status quo exceeds the CIalt, people will remain in their current situation; if the outcome level is below the CLalt, people will exit for the more attractive alternative. Thus there is no necessary connection between satisfaction and dissatisfaction, which depends on the relative positions of the outcomes and the CL, and whether people will remain in or leave a relationship. This depends on the relationship between the outcome level and the CLalt.

This analysis may explain why subjects who are dissatisfied with the result of allowing everyone free access to a resource may not want to give up the free access. The alternative, electing a leader to do the job, might be even worse. The person who gets elected, for instance, might be one of the most extreme abusers of the resource, and this risk may be magnified in the inequality conditions where there are a couple of exceptionally greedy group members. So the need for change may be perceived to be greater with more unequal outcomes, but the risk of electing a leader may also be seen as greater. The general question raised by this way of thinking is how do people make the evaluations that permit them to compare the attractiveness of one allocation system to that of another, especially when one of these is the status quo.

Our current conceptualization of the decision processes that are involved in opting to bring about structural change is much more complex than our earliest version. I will summarize it in this section and conclude by pointing to some parallels between the research that has been reviewed here and some current ideas in the study of social justice.

Although we now recognize that dissatisfaction or perceived unfairness is not a sufficient preconditions to cause people to institute structural changes, we do not believe that dissatisfaction plays no role whatsoever in this process. We rather believe that the dissatisfaction created by the group's failure to maintain the pool or to achieve a relatively equal distribution of the resource triggers an attributional or diagnostic process. This assumption is very much consistent with the findings reviewed by Weiner (1985). After reviewing a number of articles dealing with so-called spontaneous attributional activity, Weiner concludes that there are two types of events that appear to instigate attributional work—failures and unexpected events. The group failures that we have created experimentally are undoubtedly as unexpected as they are failures.

The nature of this attributional or diagnostic process is to determine what is wrong, or what can be done to improve things. We have little data bearing on the nature of this process, but Samuelson (1986) has reported a study that demonstrates its importance. In our standard experimental paradigm, subjects were led to believe that the task they were going to perform was either very easy or very difficult. All the subjects were then exposed to a rapidly declining pool, suggesting that the group was overusing the resource. The subjects were given the choice of proceeding in the second session as they had in the first or by electing a leader to make a collective decision for the entire group. Samuelson predicted that when the subjects believed that the task was an easy one, the explanation for the group failure would tend to be that the group members were either greedy or stupid. Electing them to the position of leader would not be wise. On the other hand, when subjects believed that the task was difficult, the failure could be due to the inability of the group members to coordinate their responses. In this case, a leader could be very helpful. Thus Samuelson predicted that there would be a stronger preference for a leader when the task was perceived as difficult than when it was seen as easy.

The results supported this prediction nicely. Of the subjects in the easy condition, only 30% voted for a leader. In the difficult condition, nearly twice that frequency—57%—did so.

These results attest to the importance of the diagnosed cause of the group's failure to maintain the pool. However, we propose that the subjects try through their own harvesting to keep the pool from depleting. In those conditions in which the pool is dropping relentlessly, subjects tend to decrease their harvest size (although, as I mentioned earlier, cooperators do this more dramatically then noncooperators). If the problem with the group performance can be solved through individual adaptations, then the dissatisfaction can be eliminated or avoided completely. Solving the problem through collective self-restraint may be simpler, less costly, and less uncertain than instituting a change in the allocation system. However, if individual efforts fail to solve the problem, then, we propose, people will consider alternative institutions.

This brings us back to the issue that Thibaut and Kelley (1959) raised by proposing that people compare their current situations to a CLalt and choose one that promises better outcomes. How does the current situation get evaluated? What are the dimensions of this evaluation, or is the only dimension that of strict self-interest? If there is more than a single dimension, how do these dimensions get collapsed into a single judgment that represents the overall goodness or attractiveness of the institution?

The most direct attack that has been made on these problems to date has been conducted by Samuelson (1986). He began by proposing that subjects will evaluate a possible allocation system on at least four criteria. The criteria he assumed to be important were (1) the *efficiency* of the system, by means of which he meant the capacity of the system to allocate the resource effectively and cheaply; (2) the *fairness* of the system: (3) the degree to which the system allowed people the *freedom* to make their own choices; and (4) the extent to which the system promised to benefit one's *self-interest*. Samuelson assumed that people would evaluate a system on these four attributes and then combine these attribute evaluations into an overall rating of the system. The combination rule that he proposed was a weighted average rule in which the weights reflected the importance of each dimension to the individual decision maker.

Dimensional importance could vary both as a function of the situation and of the characteristics of the decision maker.

Samuelson (1986) estimated these importance weights in two independent ways. First, he had each subject simply rank-order the four criteria. In the second method, he estimated the weights indirectly from subjects' evaluations. Each subject was asked to rate the attractiveness of four different allocation systems. They were (1) the free access system used in the first session of the experiment; (2) electing a leader to perform a group harvest; (3) dividing the resource into six equal private pools so that subjects no longer shared resources but controlled their own individual pools; and (4) imposing a harvest cap, lowering the maximum amount that a person could take from the pool. The subjects also rated each of these four allocation schemes on the four criteria discussed. He then regressed the attractiveness ratings for the decision schemes against their ratings on the four attributes and calculated the regression weights implicitly associated with each criteria for each subject.

To illustrate the utility of this type of analysis, Samuelson (1986) had classified his subjects as either cooperators or noncooperators in the same way as did Kramer et al. (1986), Kuhlman and Marshello (1975), and Liebrand (1986). From their rankings of the importance of the four criteria, Samuelson found that cooperators ranked fairness significantly higher and self-interest significantly lower in importance than noncooperators. An analysis of the weights that were inferred from the ratings, moreover, suggests that these weights depend on the environmental circumstances. Roughly half of the subjects of each type witnessed a rapidly declining pool. The other half saw a pool that dropped but that did so more slowly. Furthermore, as in a number of our previous studies, half of the subjects in each of these groups saw relatively homogeneous harvests made by their fellow group members, whereas the other half saw very heterogeneous harvests, some very high and some very low. Samuelson's hypothesis was that the importance of a dimension should reflect not only the values of the decision maker but also the state of the environment. Therefore, one would expect the estimated weights to vary as a function of the experimental conditions.

Support for this hypothesis was found in the form of two significant interactions. For each subject, Samuelson computed a normalized regression weight for each of the four evaluative dimensions. These weights were then analyzed as a function of the experimental variables and the subjects social values. The first significant interaction indicated that cooperators placed a higher average weight on efficiency in the low than in the high variance conditions, whereas the reverse was the case for noncooperators. Presumably, in the high variance condition, where the others were seen to be harvesting extremely different amounts, cooperators were less concerned about efficiency than about the large outcome differences. Noncooperators, on the other hand, placed greater weight on efficiency in the high than in the low variance circumstances.

The second result that Samuelson found was that cooperators placed less weight on self-interest in the extreme than in the moderate overuse condition, whereas noncooperators put somewhat more weight on self-interest when they saw the pool dropping rapidly than when the decline was moderate. This finding adds support to the interpretation offered by Kramer et al. (1986) that noncooperators, when faced with a rapidly declining pool, think of themselves and of getting what they can from the pool, think of themselves and of getting what they can from the pool before it disappears completely. Cooperators, in contrast, tend not to think of themselves but to think instead of the common good.

In summary, our experiments forced us to discard the idea that dissatisfaction with the status quo is a sufficient cause for wanting to change it. Like Martin, Brickman, and Murray (1984), we believe that understanding what causes dissatisfaction may be of limited value in understanding what dissatisfaction causes. We currently think of dissatisfaction as triggering a diagnostic process, the goal of which is to comprehend or eliminate the source of the dissatisfaction. Failing that, we think that people seek out and evaluate alternative institutions that might represent improvements over the status quo. Only little is yet known about the evaluation process.

Social Justice

I will conclude this chapter by commenting on some relationships that I detect between research on social dilemmas, in particular the work that I have reviewed in this chapter, and research that has been done by social psychologists in the area of social justice. To do this, I need to draw two distinctions within the social justice area.

The first of these distinctions is between the concepts of procedural justice and distributive justice. Procedural justice, as discussed by Thibaut and Walker (1975), involves the analysis of procedures that are used to resolve disputes, to mediate disagreements, to judge the guilt or innocence of criminal dependents, to process citizens complaints, to reach collective decisions, or to allocate resources. The focus of attention is on the characteristics and consequences of the procedures or rules that are used to resolve conflicting interests.

Distributive justice (see Deutsch, 1984) is concerned with the outcomes of allocative systems. Is a particular distribution of privileges, rights, opportunities, rewards, or penalties just, and by what criteria can a judgment of that sort be made? By what principles can one justify arrangements that favor one person or group over another? although not meaning to oversimplify the difference between procedural and distributive justice (Walker, Lind, & Thibaut, 1979), the former focuses on the rules and procedures by means of which conflicts of interest become resolved, whereas the latter focuses on the properties of the resolutions themselves, either in two-party disputes or on a more macroscopic level.

In our work on resource dilemmas, the distinction that we make between individual and structural solutions (Messick Brewer, 1983) corresponds closely to the distributional versus procedural distinction of the justice theorists. Peoples' response to the overuse or underuse of a shared resource or their reaction to the equality or inequality of others' harvests may be viewed as responses to or efforts to influence the distribution of outcomes that the group members have or will have in the future. The study of preferences for structural change, on the other hand, is clearly related to procedural justice. The "structures" that we have investigated—free access to a resource, having a leader allocate the resource, dividing it up into private pools, and so on—are really procedures that can be used to allocate the resource.

One important difference between our approach and that of some procedural justice researchers is that our research assumes that there is a default procedure, a status quo, that will be used unless it is replaced with an alternative. Thus it is an implicit assumption in our research that possible new procedures will always be compared to those that are currently in use and that this method of evaluating procedures may be different from a more abstract approach that ignores this fact.

To amplify this point, Rawls (1971) argues that in selecting a rule to serve as the foundation for just social decisions regarding the allocation of goods, rights, and privileges, the deliberations should be made under a "veil of ignorance." This means that no one should know what position one will occupy in society. This implies that the people involved in the decision must disregard, if possible, their personal and collective history. Although this may be an appropriate way to consider principles of distributive justice in the abstract, this does not, and perhaps cannot happen in more realistic contexts. In considering institutions for the allocation of water, whales, or nuclear waste, it would be preposterous to ignore either the institutions that currently exist (having no formal institutions is itself an institution) or the power of the participants to impose or veto an institution.

The procedure, institution, or system that occupies the role of the status quo or default option will be specially favored. First, there will be transition costs. A replacement will have to be enough better to be able to compensate for the costs of the transition. Second, both the advantages and the drawbacks of the current system will be familiar, whereas one can only guess about these features of a system that is not in use. Thus fear of the unknown or risk aversion will tend to favor the status quo. A third factor that supports whatever is the current institution is that we may exaggerate the loss of what we give up relative to the gain of what we obtain (Kahneman Tversky, 1984; Thaler, 1980). Finally, a minority of the group members may be empowered to preserve the status quo. It takes a two-thirds majority of both states and citizens in the United States to amend the constitution. It comes as no surprise, therefore, that it is easier to discover superior procedures for resolving conflicts of interest than it is to get them adopted (see Brams Fishburn, 1983).

Considering distributional justice, there is a further distinction that is often made, especially in economic treatments (Okum, 1975), between efficiency and equality. Efficiency refers to Pareto optimality or whether a distribution of outcomes is as good as it can be in the sense that there is no way to make one party better off without, at the same time, making another worse off. Equality, of course, refers to the extent to which all parties receive equal or equivalent outcomes. The group as a unit will be performing as well as possible if the distribution of outcomes is efficient, but this fact may not swing much weight if one individual is receiving payoffs that are much smaller than another's.

In our experiments, we have also systematically varied efficiency and equality as independent variables. Efficiency, as we have manipulated it, is somewhat different from the strict economic meaning. What we have manipulated is the extent to which the group is using a resource efficiently or, specifically, the extent to which the resource level is seen to be falling or remaining near its maximum level. If subjects believe that the experiment is going to last for a fairly long series of trials, then overuse of the resource is inefficient in precisely the economic sense, because self-restraint on the part of the group members could provide more of the resource to all. However, seeing that the resource is not falling is no guarantee that it is being efficiently used because it is possible that the resource is being underused, that all group members could get more by increasing their harvests. It is perhaps to discover the most efficient level of consumption that subjects who do not see the pool being depleted gradually increase their harvests over time.

Efficiency and equality are two desiderata of distributions of resources. The research that I have described in this chapter may be seen as an investigation of the social psychological consequences of achieving or failing to achieve these qualities. Our work on structural change, from this perspective, involves the study of preferences for procedural change as a function of the success or failure of the group in meeting these two distributional goals. In most of our studies, the status quo procedure permitted subjects free access to a shared resource. I will conclude with the suggestion that similar considerations apply when it is a leader or leaders who allocate the resources.

In the context of social dilemmas, Rutte and Wilke (1984) propose that when leaders are elected to act on the group's behalf, meeting the efficiency requirement defines the leader's external task, whereas satisfying the equality constraint is their internal task. This implies that the dimensions of evaluation of our leaders include (1) how well they do in providing positive outcomes and (2) how fairly the outcomes get distributed. Tyler, Rasinski, and McGraw (1985) present data from public opinion pools that support the idea that political leaders are evaluated both on the extent to which they (1) provide a high level of outcomes for the people whom they represent and (2) are perceived as just or fair. Their data further indicate that judgments of unfairness or injustice are more important determinants of dissatisfaction with political leaders and the political system than are judgments related to outcome levels. The two approaches, therefore, converge on the identification of efficiency and equality as (the?) two important goals for our leaders to meet. If they should fail to meet them, however, the research that I have described in this chapter may shed some light on how their followers might be expected to respond.

ACKNOWLEDGMENT. Much of the research reported in this chapter was supported by Grant BNS 83–02674 from the National Science Foundation, and I am grateful for this support.

References

Allison, S. T., & Messick, D. M. (1985). Effects of experience on performance in a replenishable resource trap. *Journal of Personality and Social Psychology, 49*, 943–948.

Brams, S. J., & Fishburn, P. C. (1983). Approval voting. Boston: Birkhauser.
Brewer, M. B., & Kramer, R. M. (1986). Choice behavior in social dilemmas: Effects of social identity, group size, and decision framing. Journal of Personality and Social Psychology, 50, 543–549.
Cass, R. C., & Edney, J. J. (1978). The commons dilemma: A simulation testing resource visibility and territorial division. Human Ecology, 6, 371–386.
Dawes, R. M., McTavish, J., & Shaklee, H. (1977). Behavior, communication, and assumptions about other peoples behavior in a commons dilemma situation. Journal of Personality and Social Psychology, 35, 1–11.
Deutsch, M. (1985). Distributive justice. New Haven, CT: Yale University Press.
Hardin, G. (1968). The tragedy of the commons. Science, 162, 1243–1248.
Kahneman, D., & Tversky, A. (1984). Choices, values, and frames. American Psychologist, 39, 341–350.
Kelley, H. H., & Grzelak, J. (1972). Conflict between individual and common interest in an N-person relationship. Journal of Personality and Social Psychology, 21, 190–197.
Kerr, N. L. (1986). Motivational choices in task groups: A paradigm for social dilemma research. In H. A. M. Wilke, D. M. Messick, & C. G. Rutte (Eds.), Experimental social dilemmas (pp. 1–27). Frankfurt: Peter Lang.
Komorita, S. S., & Lapworth, C. W. (1982). Alternative choices in social dilemmas. Journal of Conflict Resolution, 26, 692–708.
Komorita, S. S., Sweeney, J., & Kravitz, D. A. (1980). Cooperative choice in the n-person dilemma situation. Journal of Personality and Social Psychology, 38, 504–516.
Kramer, R. M., & Brewer, M. B. (1984). Effects of group identity on resource use in a simulated commons dilemma. Journal of Personality and Social Psychology, 46, 1044–1057.
Kramer, R. M., & Brewer, M. B. (1986). Social group identity and the emergence of cooperation in resource conservation dilemmas. In H. A. M. Wilke, D. M. Messick, & C. G. Rutte (Eds.), Experimental social dilemmas (pp. 205–234). Frankfurt: Peter Lang.
Kramer, R. M., McClintock, C. G., & Messick, D. M. (1986). Social values and cooperative response to a simulated resource conservation crisis. Journal of Personality, 54, 596–677.
Kuhlman, D. M., & Marshello, A. (1975). Individual differences in game motivation as moderators of preprogrammed strategic effects in prisoner's dilemma. Journal of Personality and Social Psychology, 32, 922–931.
Latane, B., Williams, K., & Harkins, S. (1979). Many hands make light the work: The causes and consequences of social loafing. Journal of Personality and Social Psychology, 37, 822–832.
Liebrand, W. B. G. (1986). The ubiquity of social values in social dilemmas. In H. A. M. Wilke, D. M. Messick, & C. G. Rutte (Eds.), Experimental social dilemmas. Frankfurt: Peter Lang.
Marshall, E. (1986). Nuclear waste program faces political burial. Science, 233, 835–836.
Martin, J., Brickman, P., & Murray, A. (1984). Moral outrage and pragmatism: Explanations for collective action. Journal of Experimental Social Psychology, 20, 484–496.
Messick, D. M. (1973). To join or not to join: An approach to the unionization decision. Organizational Behavior and Human Performance, 10, 145–156.
Messick, D. M. (1974). When a little "group interest" goes a long way. Organizational Behavior and Human Performance, 12, 331–334.
Messick, D. M. & Brewer, M. B. (1983). Solving social dilemmas: A review. In L. Wheeler & P. Shaver (Eds.), Review of personality and social psychology Vol. 4, pp. 11–44). Beverley Hills: Sage.

Messick, D. M., & McClelland, C. L. (1983). Social traps and temporal traps. *Personality and Social Psychology Bulletin, 9,* 105–110.

Messick, D. M., Wilke, H., Brewer, M. B., Kramer, R. M., Zemke, P. E., & Lui, L. (1983). Individual adaptations and structural change as solutions to social dilemmas. *Journal of Personality and Social Psychology, 44,* 294–309.

Okum, A. M. (1975). *Equality and efficiency: The big tradeoff.* Washington, DC: The Brookings Institution.

Orbell, J. M., van de Kragt, A. J. C., & Dawes, R. M. (1988). Explaining discussion-induced cooperation in social dilemmas. *Journal of Personality and Social Psychology, 54,* 811–819.

Parker, R., Lui, L., Messick, C., Messick, D. M., Brewer, M. B., Kramer, R., Samuelson, C., & Wilke, H. (1983). A computer laboratory for studying resource dilemmas. *Behavioral Science, 28,* 298–304.

Rawls, J. A. (1971). *A theory of justice.* Cambridge MA: Harvard University Press.

Rutte, C. G., & Wilke, H. A. M. (1984). Social dilemmas and leadership. *European Journal of Social Psychology, 14,* 105–121.

Rutte, C. G., Wilke, H. A. M., & Messick, D. M. (1987). Scarcity or abundance caused by people or the environment as determinants of behavior in a resource dilemma. *Journal of Experimental Social Psychology, 23,* 208–216.

Samuelson, C. D. (1986). *Determinants of preference for structural change in social dilemmas.* Unpublished PhD dissertation, University of California, Santa Barbara.

Samuelson, C. D., & Messick, D. M. (1986a). Alternative structural solutions to resource dilemmas. *Organizational Behavior and Human Decision Processes, 37,* 139–155.

Samuelson, C. D., & Messick, D. M. (1986b). Inequities in access to and use of shared resources in social dilemmas. *Journal of Personality and Social Psychology, 22,* 590–604.

Samuelson, C. D., Messick, D. M., Rutte, C. G., & Wilke, H. (1984). Individual and structural solutions to resource dilemmas in two cultures. *Journal of Personality and Social Psychology, 47,* 94–104.

Schroeder, D. A., Jensen, T., Reed, A., Sullivan, D., & Schwab, M. (1983). The actions of others as determinants of behavior in social trap situations. *Journal of Experimental Social Psychology, 19,* 522–539.

Thaler, R. H. (1980). Toward a positive theory of consumer choice. *Journal of Economic Behavior and Organization, 1,* 39–60.

Thibaut, J., & Kelley, H. H. (1959). *The social psychology of groups.* New York: Wiley.

Thibaut, J. & Walker, L. (1975). *Procedural justice: A psychological analysis.* Hillsdale, NJ: Erlbaum.

Tyler, T. R., Rasinski, K. A., & McGraw, K. M. (1985). The influence of perceived injustice on the endorsement of political leaders. *Journal of Applied Social Psychology, 15,* 700–725.

Van de Kragt, A. J. C., Dawes, R. M., Orbell, J. M., Braver, S. R., & Wilson, L. A. (1986). Doing well and doing good as ways of resolving social dilemmas. In H. A. M. Wilke, D. M. Messick, & C. G. Rutte (Eds.), *Experimental social dilemmas* (pp. 117–203). Frankfurt: Peter Lang.

Walker, L., Lind, A. E., & Thibaut, J. (1979). The relation between procedural and distributive justice. *Virginia Law Review, 65,* 1401–1422.

Weiner, B. (1985). "Spontaneous" causal thinking. *Psychological Bulletin, 97,* 74–84.

Yamagishi, T. (1986). The provision of a sanctioning system as a public good. *Journal of Personality and Social Psychology, 51,* 110–116.

4

Procedural Processes and Legal Institutions

Tom R. Tyler and E. Allan Lind

This chapter has two goals. First, it examines the past decade of research on procedural justice. Our goal in that examination is to discuss the major issues which have been of concern to procedural justice researchers. Second, it explores recent developments in the procedural justice field which suggest the issues that will dominate procedural justice research in the future. In considering both of these questions, we focus most heavily on issues of procedural justice within legal institutions.

The social psychology of procedural justice was first formally defined in legal settings by Thibaut and Walker in their important book *Procedural Justice* (1975). That book both defined the concept of procedural justice and described a series of studies designed to demonstrate its importance.

Thibaut and Walker's basic hypothesis was that the process by which dispute-resolution decisions are made influences litigant satisfaction with those decisions. In their research program, they showed that procedural effects occur and that they are independent of the outcome of the litigant's case. In addition, Thibaut and Walker demonstrated that this procedural effect is based on litigant judgments about the relative fairness of differing methods of dispute resolution

Tom R. Tyler • Departments of Psychology and Political Science, Northwestern University, Evanston, Illinois 60208, and the American Bar Foundation, 750 N. Lake Shore Drive, Chicago, Illinois 60611.   **E. Allan Lind** • The American Bar Foundation, 750 N. Lake Shore Drive, Chicago, Illinois 60611.

and does not simply reflect litigant judgments about the likelihood that each method of dispute resolution will help them to win their case.

Conceptual Contribution

Thibaut and Walker's work has had an important impact on subsequent thinking about the psychology of legal processes. Their contribution was to unite two important social psychological literatures through the articulation of the concept of procedural justice. The first literature underlying Thibaut and Walker's work is the literature on process. Social psychologists have recognized for many years that decision-making procedures influence both the quality and nature of decisions and the reactions of those affected by them. The classic study of Lewin, Lippitt, and White (1959), for example, explored the effect of differing leadership styles on the behavior of group members. In that study, democratically led groups were compared to groups with autocratic and laissez-faire leadership styles. Similarly, Hollander and Julian (1970) have examined the effects of elected versus appointed leadership on the behavior of group members. More recently, Davis has conducted an extensive series of studies on the effects of variation in jury procedures (1980). While all of this research indicated that variations in procedure were important, none of these lines of inquiry produced a theory of the psychology of procedures *per se*.

Thibaut and Walker's work combined a recognition of the importance of procedure with a second important literature in social psychology—the literature on fairness. Social psychologists have also recognized the importance of judgments about distributive (i.e., outcome-based) fairness in both the literature on relative deprivation (Crosby, 1976, 1982) and equity/inequity (Walster, Walster & Berscheid, 1978). Both of these distributive justice literatures suggested strongly that those affected by decisions focus on fairness in reacting to decisions, rather than reacting simply in terms of decision favorability. Thibaut and Walker's theory suggests that the same type of ethical judgments might be important in reactions to *the way that* decisions are made. This combination of process and justice led them to articulate a theory of *procedural* justice (Thibaut & Walker, 1975, 1978).

Empirical Contribution

Having identified the concept of procedural justice, Thibaut, Walker, and their students conducted a series of laboratory experiments designed to demonstrate the importance of that concept. Those studies focused on comparisons of the adversary and the inquisitorial dispute resolution procedures. Adversary procedures place control over definition of the dispute and presentation of the arguments and evidence in the hands of the disputants. In contrast, inquisitorial trial procedures place control over these aspects of the trial in the hands of the judge. Thibaut, and Walker demonstrated that American and European subjects typically view the adversary system as a fairer procedure for dispute resolution. Using college students, law students, lawyers, and judges as subjects and using simulated disputes, Thibaut and Walker demonstrated that resolving disputes through adversary trial procedures heightens satisfaction with the outcome and the process of dispute resolution, irrespective of whether disputants win or lose their case.

A particularly compelling demonstration of the value of subjectively fair dispute resolution procedures is provided by a business simulation study conducted by Thibaut and Walker (Thibaut & Walker, 1975; Chapter 8; Walker, LaTour, Lind, and Thibaut, 1974). In that study, students participated in a complex industrial simulation which allowed the opportunity for gain by cheating. In the course of the simulation, a member of the student's team was accused of cheating, and an adjudication was conducted to decide their guilt. The experimental situation was arranged so that those accused of cheating appeared to be guilty in some conditions and innocent in other conditions. In addition, the outcome of the trial was rigged so that the student's team was judged innocent or guilty independently of their actual guilt or innocence. Finally, the trials were conducted using either adversary or inquisitorial procedures. This complex design allowed the influence of procedures to be assessed independently of apparent innocence/guilt and of verdict. As anticipated, students reacted more favorably to the adversary procedure, irrespective of the trial's outcome. In an especially striking comparison, for example, those apparently innocent and wrongfully judged guilty under the adversary procedure rated that procedure to be fairer (mean = 5.4) than did those apparently innocent students vindicated (judged innocent) under the inquisitorial system (mean 5.0). The students were also more satisfied with the verdicts of adversary trials.

Acceptance of the Procedural Justice Findings

Although the research program conducted by Thibaut and Walker (1975) involved a number of studies, all of which led to similar conclusions, their work was initially greeted with skepticism by the legal community and by other social scientists in the area of sociolegal studies (Anderson & Hayden, 1980–1981; Damaska, 1975; Hayden & Anderson, 1979). One reason for this skepticism was that the conclusions of Thibaut and Walker ran counter to the preconceptions of many lawyers and judges, preconceptions influenced by the law and economics model that has dominated the study of law. That model places a heavy emphasis on issues of outcome favorability, assuming that litigants are primarily concerned with whether or not they win or lose their case. In addition, although Thibaut, Walker, and their students conducted a number of studies, those studies were all quite similar in their approach. Virtually all of the studies used student subjects, and all involved simulated disputes. As a result, their conclusions were open to methodological criticism.

One important task of procedural justice research subsequent to Thibaut and Walker has been to test the degree to which the procedural justice hypothesis generalizes beyond the laboratory arena, that is, to test its robustness across methods of study. These tests were designed in part as a direct response to the criticisms of social scientists outside of social psychology about the laboratory based approach used by Thibaut and Walker, and in part to convey to the legal community the importance of procedural justice issues to litigants.

Methodological Robustness

One type of effort to study procedural justice effects outside of the laboratory has been to look at the results of interviews conducted in natural settings. Studies of this correlational type do not manipulate procedural justice. Instead, they measure naturally occurring judgments about whether fair process is occurring and look at the relationship of procedural fairness judgments to variations in satisfaction.

Typical of this approach is a study of litigants in misdemeanor court conducted by Tyler (1984). In that study, citizens who had recently been to court were interviewed about their courtroom experience. Those interviews asked citizens about several aspects of their case, including the outcome of the case, their assessment of the fairness of the verdict, and their judgment of the fairness of the trial process. In addition, citizens were asked to indicate their overall satisfaction with their courtroom experience and their evaluations of the judge and the court system.

Taking advantage of the ability of correlational research to assess the naturally occurring relationship between variables, Tyler (1984) first examined whether judgments of distributive and procedural justice were distinct from assessments of outcome favorability. He found that the two judgments were distinct, suggesting that fairness judgments were more than simply reflections of the favorability of outcomes.

To determine the role of procedural fairness, judgments in evaluations of the courtroom experience and the legal system, Tyler (1984) used regression analysis. That analysis looked at the ability of one type of judgments to explain variance not explainable using other types of judgments. Tyler found that assessments of fairness (distributive and procedural) consistently had a greater impact on the dependent variables than did issues of outcome favorability. In the case of outcome satisfaction, for example, fairness judgments explained 23% of the variance beyond that explained by outcome favorability, whereas outcome favorability only explained 4% of the variance beyond that explained by fairness. Both distributive fairness (Beta = .48, $p < .001$) and procedural fairness (Beta = .18, $p < .001$) contributed to this influence.

Another example of correlational research testing the importance of procedural justice is provided by Alexander and Ruderman (1987). Their study examined the job satisfaction and turnover intentions of 2,800 federal employees. The approach used was similar to that in the Tyler (1984) study. Employees were interviewed about various aspects of the job environment, including the fairness of the decision making procedures. Their judgments about the job environment were then used to predict job satisfaction and their turnover intentions (i.e., their judgments of their likelihood of quitting their job).

Alexander and Ruderman found that both job satisfaction and turnover intention were influenced by employee assessments of the fairness of decision making within their work setting. Similar findings have been reported by Bies (1985). Unlike Alexander and Ruderman, Bies studied job satisfaction within a private manufacturing company. His results were similar to those of Alexander and Ruderman: judgments that decision-making procedures were unfair negatively influenced job satisfaction, evaluations of supervisors, and loyalty to the company.

Other correlational studies of citizens' reactions to government institutions also provide support for the procedural justice hypothesis within the legal and political arenas (Tyler, Rasinski, & Griffin, 1986). Studies of litigants in court (Casper, Tyler, Fisher, 1988; Landis & Goodstein, 1986; Tyler, 1984, 1990), as well as studies of citizens who have had contact with the police (Tyler & Folger, 1980; Tyler, 1990), all support the argument that procedural justice influences the satisfaction of those involved in real disputes. Similarly, studies of citizen satisfaction with government policies and with the government benefits they receive and the taxes they pay suggest that procedural justice influences satisfaction in the political arena (Rasinski, 1987; Tyler Caine, 1981; Tyler, Rasinski, & McGraw, 1985).

Although the correlational research we have outlined suggests that procedural justice is important in nonlaboratory settings, the use of a correlation approach is itself subject to methodological criticisms. In this case, concerns are typically expressed over issues of internal validity, not external validity. Such concerns are important, however, and suggest that the case for procedural justice would be considerably strengthened through evidence from field experiments. Such studies are higher on external validity than are laboratory studies of the Thibaut and Walker variety but also retain the strong internal validity associated with laboratory experiments.

Further support for the procedural justice hypothesis is provided by several field experiments involving people in realworld settings. One example of such a field study is Earley (1984). That study involved random assignment of workers in an animal care facility to one of three goal-setting procedures. The procedures varied in the extent to which workers were afforded an opportunity to express their views of prospective goals—a procedural feature quite similar in concept to the distinction between adversary and inquisitorial trial procedures. Earley found that those given an opportunity for expression judged the procedures to be more fair and performed better in their jobs.

Also of interest are findings from a nonexperimental field study by Lind, MacCoun, Ebener, Felstiner, Hensler, Resnik, & Tyler (1989). Lind et al. interviewed litigants who were involved in lawsuits in three courts that differed in the procedures used prior to trial: court-annexed arbitration, settlement confererences, and no pretrial procedure. Lind et al. found that procedures judged by litigants to be fairer were more satisfying to litigants. A similar result was obtained in another field study exploring court-annexed arbitration (Adler, Hensler, & Nelson, 1983).

In other words, experimental and quasi-experimental studies that involve real people in the midst of real decisions disputes support the results of correlational studies in suggesting that fair process is an important issue in the evaluation of decisions. Unfortunately, the random assignment needed to produce an experimental design is easier to achieve within the context of a laboratory setting than it is in the field. As a result, there have only been a few field experiments on procedural justice.

As the results outlined above suggest, the initial skepticism concerning the generalizability of the Thibaut and Walker findings has proved to be unjustified. Subsequent studies utilizing nonstudent samples and disputes decisions involving real and important outcomes have supported the suggestion that those affected by decisions care a great deal about the procedures used to make them.

Generalization of Procedural Justice Effects

Research on procedural justice has not simply been directed at testing the robustness of the findings of Thibaut and Walker. Subsequent studies have been concerned with exploring the scope of the study of procedural justice in a variety of ways.

The Evaluation of Authorities and Institutions

One avenue of expansion of the study of procedural justice has been the study of procedural justice effects on evaluations of the authorities and institutions responsible for decision making. Although Thibaut and Walker recognized that an important function of fair procedures was to allow authorities to make unpopular decisions in a way that does not undermine their legitimacy as authorities, they focused their own research on litigant satisfaction with decisions, not satisfaction with authorities.

Studies conducted since the initial work of Thibaut and Walker have explored reactions to decision making authorities, as well as reactions to outcomes. In work settings, several studies have found procedural justice effects on evaluations of supervisors and/or employers (Alexander & Ruderman, 1987; Bies, 1986). In legal settings, procedural justice influences have been found on the evaluations of judges, police officers, and the court system itself (Tyler, 1984, 1990; Tyler & Folger, 1980). Finally, in the political arena procedural justice influences have been found on evaluations of political leaders and institutions (Tyler & Caine, 1981; Tyler, Rasinski, & McGraw, 1985). In other words, studies have universally found that procedural justice matters in the evaluation of authorities and institutions, as well as in personal satisfaction. In fact, direct comparisons of these two dependent variables typically suggest that procedural justice matters more when authorities or institutions are being evaluated (Lind and Tyler, 1988; Tyler, 1986).

Behavior

A second extension of the study of procedural justice has been to the study of behavior. In the legal arena, the behaviors of most interest has been the acceptance of legal decisions and general law abidingness. The influence of fair process on the acceptance of legal decisions is suggested in the work of McEwen and Maiman (1984). McEwen and Maiman studied litigants in small claims courts. In small claims court, many defendants ordered by judges to pay money to the other party to a dispute do not comply with judicial orders. McEwen and Maiman examined the trial factors that led to compliance with judicial orders. They found that mediation, as opposed to adjudication, inhanced compliance. This difference appeared to be linked to issues of procedural justice.

Tyler (1986c) studied not compliance with specific judicial decisions but rather the effects of experiencing fair or unfair procedures in an encounter with the police/courts on later general compliance with the law. Using a sample of 1,574 citizens in Chicago, Tyler explored the effect of encounters with legal authorities on subsequent citizen behavior. He found that procedural fairness in such encounters influenced citizen views about the legitimacy of legal authority and, through that influence, affected citizen compliance with the law.

Research on behavioral influences has also extended beyond the legal arena to work organizations. Alexander and his colleagues have studied the relationship between procedural justice and turnover intention using both correlational (Alexander & Ruderman, 1987) and experimental designs (Alexander, Ruderman, & Russ, 1984; Alexander & Russ, 1985). These studies consistently find that workers who feel that evaluation procedures are unfair are more likely to intend to leave their jobs. Although not overt behavior, such turnover intentions are typically closely related to actual turnover behavior.

An experimental demonstration of the behavioral effects of unfair process is found in Greenberg (1987b). In this study student subjects in a work experiment were subjected to fair or unfair procedures of work evaluation. Following that experience subjects were placed in a room that had a poster with telephone numbers for reporting unfair treatment to the "ethical responsibility board." Greenberg found that unfair process led subjects to take slips of paper with the telephone number attached, suggesting an intention to report unfair procedure to the appropriate authorities.

Procedural justice judgments have also been found to influence political behaviors. Rasinski and Tyler (1987) conducted three studies exploring the influence of procedural justice judgments on political behavior. Two of the studies examined vote choice in the 1986 presidential election. In each study, it was found that citizens' vote choices were influenced by their judgments about the relative fairness of the two presidential candidates (Reagan–Mondale). In the third study, citizen behavioral reactions to public policies (writing a congressman, attending political rallies, etc.) were examined. It was found that participation in political activities was stimulated by feelings of procedural justice.

Other Arenas

Finally, as suggested by some of the studies already described, procedural justice research has been extended beyond the legal arena. Particularly noteworthy has been the tremendous growth of research on the fairness of procedures within work organizations. One example of such research is the study of procedures for evaluating the performance of workers for the purposes of pay increases and promotions. A large number of studies have been conducted in this area, and they have consistently found that employees react more favorably to evaluation procedures that they judge to be fair, irrespective of the outcome of their evaluations (Greenberg, 1987a; Kanfer, Earley, Sawyer, Lind, 1987; Landy, Barnes, & Murphy, 1978; Landy, Barnes-Farrell, & Cleveland, 1980; Lissak, 1983; for a review see Lind & Tyler, 1988, Chapter 8). Typical of such work is Greenberg's demonstration that workers perceive evaluations based on supervisor's diaries of their work as fairer than evaluations without detailed information about work habits, and that they react more favorably to evaluations that use that procedure (Greenberg, 1987a).

Allocation Decisions

The growth in procedural justice research within work organizations illustrates another way in which procedural justice research has expanded since the work of Thibaut and Walker—in its increasing attention to fair ways of making allocations as opposed to resolving disputes. In their work, Thibaut and Walker focused specifically on procedures used to resolve conflicts. That focus was contrary to the focus of the then dominant distributive justice research tradition on issues of allocation. A focus on allocation would lead to a theory of procedural justice more like that of Leventhal (1980). Following Thibaut and Walker's lead, early procedural justice research focused on issues of dispute resolution. Recent research has, however, broadened considerably and studied procedural concerns in allocation. It is now apparent that procedural issues are important in allocation, as well as in dispute resolution. Barrett-Howard and Tyler (1986), for example, found that procedural concerns were as important in the allocation arena as were issues of distributive justice, and both types of justice were more important in allocations than were nonfairness concerns.

New Directions

In the decade since the publication of Thibaut and Walker's book *Procedural Justice*, the dominant concern of procedural justice research has been with demonstrating that procedural justice effects are real and extend beyond the range of the original concerns of Thibaut and Walker. The research to date has not only shown that such effects are real, it has suggested that concerns about procedure are broadly robust, occupying citizen attention in a variety of contexts.

More recent work in the Thibaut and Walker tradition has also focused on integrating procedural justice findings more tightly into the legal literature on dispute resolution. Recently, that literature has been dominated by concerns with court overload, leading to a focus on alternatives to formal courtroom trials as mechanisms for resolving disputes. An important aspect of the evaluation of such alternatives has been establishing the extent to which litigants regard them as procedurally just alternatives to trials. Studies on this topic have provided a new opportunity to examine whether procedural justice judgments mediate litigant reactions to the resolution of their case. Several studies have been conducted by the Institute for Civil Justice of the RAND Corporation which suggest that litigant's satisfaction with nontrial dispute resolution procedures is indeed based on assessments of their procedural fairness (Adler, Hensler, & Nelson, 1983; Lind et al., 1989; MacCoun, Lind, Hensler, Bryant, & Ebener, 1988). These studies also suggest that citizen views about the elements of fair process in such settings may differ greatly from the procedural concerns that dominate the formal structure of courtroom trials.

As noted above, another area in which procedural justice research has recently been developing is that of work organizations. This arena seems an ideal one within which to develop the study of procedure because it touches the lives of most people, who are affected by the decisions made in their own work settings. It is also an arena within which there exist an enormous variety of types of procedures for allocation and decision making. Although the American legal system has been highly standardized toward the adversary approach to dispute resolution, no such standardization exists in the organizational arena. Instead, many procedures have evolved to make decisions within work settings. While the legal arena was an ideal one for testing the hypothesis that procedural justice matters, the arena of work organizations is ideal for exploring the questions about the range of procedural justice phenomena.

What both the recent legal literature on procedural justice and the emerging study of work organizations share is a commitment to working within the context of the procedural concerns that dominate the areas being studied. In both literatures, researchers have made extensive efforts to understand the concerns of actors within the arena and to design research that speaks to those concerns, as well as furthering the study of procedural justice.

In addition to efforts to extend the study of procedure, recent procedural justice research has developed in several other important ways. One development is an effort to move beyond addressing the question of *whether* procedural justice matters, a question to which the answer is now unequivocally yes, to ask *when* procedural justice is more or less important (Tyler, 1986a). Addressing this question requires an effort to develop a theory of procedural justice that allows us to predict when procedural justice will be viewed by people as more or less relevant to decision making and dispute resolution.

Recent efforts to further develop the theory of procedural justice highlight one of the limits of the past decade of procedural justice research. While extensive research has been conducted to explore the range and strength of procedural justice effects, there has been little theoretical advance beyond the initial theoretical efforts of Thibaut and Walker (1975) and Leventhal (1980). Recent efforts to develop procedural justice theory (e.g., Lind & Tyler, 1988, Chapter 10) suggest a growing recognition that a theory of procedural justice is needed that will suggest why people care about procedural justice and, hence, lead to predictions concerning when procedural justice will be more or less important.

An example of a recent effort to understand when procedural justice will be important is the work of Tyler (1986a). That study explores the relationship between the goals a decision-maker is pursuing in making an allocation decision and his or her attention to issues of procedural justice. Tyler found that concerns about the justice of decision-making procedures are especially strongly related to an interest in the interpersonal quality of the relationship.

Another, related, effort to broaden the scope of procedural justice research is found in the work of Sheppard (1983, 1984, 1985). Sheppard's work focuses not on procedural justice per se, but on the choices that third parties make between various procedures that might be used to make a decision. Within that larger question, Sheppard has explored when fairness is considered to be an important characteristic of a procedure by third parties. This work moves beyond the attention given to procedural justice by Thibaut and Walker and explores how people make choices between different ways of making decisions or resolving conflicts. An example of this research is a study by Lissak and Sheppard (1983), which explores the criteria used by managers to choose procedures for dispute resolution. The study found that fairness is an important, although not necessarily the most important, criterion of procedural choice for managers.

Sheppard's work suggests that procedural fairness is one of several criteria against which the value of a process might be assessed. Procedural fairness itself may involve inherent trade-offs between objective and subjective criteria. Sheppard notes that the adversary system has been found to be widely preferred by litigants, but that it suffers from many biases that lead it to produce objectively inferior decisions under many circumstances. Hence, those choosing procedures for dispute resolution often cannot chose the objectively preferable procedure without risking some public dissatisfaction with their procedural choice.

The work of Sheppard suggests an important new direction in procedural justice research—the recognition of trade-offs. Increasingly researchers are recognizing that no process can simultaneously maximize the attainment of the many objectives that might exist for a procedure. As a result, choice of a procedure for dispute resolution inherently involves assessing the value that is placed on various objectives within a given context. Explicating the nature of such trade-offs is an important task for future research on procedural justice.

Examining the Meaning of Procedural Justice

The material presented here shows that procedural fairness judgments are important factors in determining a variety of attitudinal and behavioral reactions to encounters with decision-making and dispute-resolution procedures and that they are one of the most important considerations affecting disputant preferences for different procedures. All of these attitudes and behaviors have long been recognized to be worthy of study, and we now know that we must understand the psychology of procedural justice if we are to understand the causes of these variables.

As the importance of procedural justice has been recognized, attention has been directed toward the question of why procedural justice effects occur. In other words, interest in the psychology of procedure has increased. These efforts have been largely built on the efforts of Thibaut and Walker to address this same question. Thibaut and Walker suggest that the key to understanding procedural preferences is the psychology of perceived control.

Building from a social exchange framework, Thibaut and Walker suggest that disputants are interested in retaining maximum personal control over decisions that influence their lives. For this reason they resist third-party intervention in disputes and often attempt to resolve disputes through bargaining. If, however, disputants come to feel that third-party control is necessary in order to resolve a dispute, then they give up control over decisions about their case to a judge or arbitrator. Under such conditions, disputants attempt to indirectly control case outcomes by controlling the evidence presented at the trial. This type of indirect control is referred to as *process control* or *voice*. Thibaut and Walker assume that litigants believe that they can sway the decision-maker through a persuasive presentation of their case.

According to Thibaut and Walker, the adversary procedure is preferred because it allows disputants to maintain more control over the process of evidence presentation than does the inquisitorial procedure. Both procedures remove "decision control" from the hands of disputants because in both procedures the judge has complete control over the verdict itself. In fact, one of the central themes of the research and theory of the Thibaut and Walker group is that legal and dispute resolution procedures that provide high process control for disputants tend to enhance subjective procedural fairness.

More recent research has confirmed the suggestion of Thibaut and Walker that high process control is associated with procedural fairness. Lind, Kurtz, Musante, Walker, and Thibaut (1980) replicated the original Walker et al. (1974) study with a larger set of measures designed to assess more precisely the effects of the procedure manipulation on disputants' perceptions of the procedure and outcome of the adjudication. Lind et al. measured procedural fairness judgments, distributive fairness judgments, and a variety of other perceptions about the procedures. The independent variables manipulated in the study were the procedure used in the adjudication (either adversary or inquisitorial), the outcome of the adjudication (either win or lose) and the timing of measures of perceptions of various features of the adjudication procedure (either before or after the verdict was announced). Table 1 shows some of the results of the study, indicating that the procedure manipulation had substantial effects on both types of fairness judgments. The experiment also permitted a comparison to be made between the view of procedural features held by subjects who did not know how their case would be decided and the views of subjects who knew whether they had won or lost their case. Lind et al. found that knowledge of the outcome did not change the relative perceptions engendered by the two procedures. Even when subjects received an unfavorable verdict, they showed no inclination to believe that the adversary procedure was corrupt.

The influence of process control on fairness suggests that disputants will perceive greater procedural fairness if the decision-maker allows both parties to a dispute to control the evidence and arguments presented. If the decision-maker restricts process control by requiring that presentation of grievances be limited to legally relevant issues, for example, litigants would feel that the procedure was less fair. Note that the effects of process control restrictions on procedural fairness judgments might run contrary to rules of objective fairness. Some issues might, for example, be irrelevant to the legal questions judges must decide, and it might be unfair in some objective sense to have such issues raised at the hearing. Nevertheless, rules that disallow the presentation of evidence that seems to a disputant to be of importance will restrict process control and the application of such rules to a case is likely to lead to feelings of procedural unfairness, with all of the attendant lowering of satisfaction, support, and compliance documented earlier in this chapter.

In the work on process control effects subsequent to that of Thibaut and Walker, a controversy has developed about the nature of the processes underlying the process control effect on procedural fairness judgments. The debate concerns the extent to which there is something

Table 1. Procedural and Distributive Fairness Judgments of Disputants in Adversary and Inquisitorial Hearings[a]

Fairness measure and outcome of hearing	Hearing procedure	
	Adversary	Inquisitorial
Procedural Fairness Index		
Disputant's team found innocent	.10	−.32
Disputant's team found guilty	.36	−.21
Distributive Fairness Index		
Disputant's team found innocent	2.53	1.93
Disputant's team found guilty	−2.11	−2.61

[a]Values are marginal means for standardized factor scores. Higher values indicate greater perceived fairness. From Lind, Kurtz, Musante, Gilbert, Walker, & Thibaut, 1980, p. 649.

about *process control*, as distinct from other forms of control that might characterize a procedure that is critical to creating the experience of having received procedural justice. Brett and Goldberg (1983) have suggested that the enhancement of procedural fairness judgments by process control is simply one example of a general desire for control over the dispute and that other, more potent, forms of control might result in even greater enhancement of procedural fairness. One could explain the frequent finding of greater procedural justice under high process control by arguing that people react more favorably to procedures that allow them to act to secure favorable outcomes, and that process control is preferred because of its instrumental value in obtaining a favorable outcome in adjudication and other dispute resolution settings. Brett and Goldberg report some field study data showing greater perceived fairness for disputants in a mediation procedure than for disputants in an arbitration procedure (presumably because the former procedure allows disputants more decision control than does the latter). Counterpoised to the instrumental position is the position advanced by Thibaut and Walker (1978), who contend that disputant process control promotes procedural fairness, not because it is seen as promoting *favorable* outcomes, but because it is seen as promoting *equitable* outcomes. A position even more divergent from the instrumental position has been advanced by those who argue that at least part of the process control enhancement of procedural justice is due to factors unrelated to the outcome of the dispute (Lind & Tyler, 1988; Tyler, Rasinski, & Spodick, 1985). This last position is discussed in greater detail in the next section. It is based on research on the procedural justice implications of assuring disputants an adequate opportunity to (1) express their positions and (2) receive consideration of their views. For convenience of discussion, let us label the strong instrumental position *reward-oriented*, the Thibaut and Walker (1978) position *equity-oriented*, and the Tyler, Rasinski, and Spodick (1985) position *expression-oriented*.

Research to date has not provided a definitive resolution of the issues raised by the debate, but it does provide some support for positions, such as the expression oriented perspective, that argue that process control is valued for reasons other than instrumentality in the achievement of favorable outcomes. First, several studies (e.g., La-Tour, 1978; Lind et al., 1980) have shown poor correspondence between ratings of the perceived favorableness of procedures to the disputant (i.e., the disputant's judgment about the likelihood that using a particular procedure will help to win his or her case) and procedural fairness ratings of the same procedures. Second, virtually all of the studies of procedural fairness in dispute resolution have shown process control enhancement of procedural fairness judgments even after litigants have already lost their case's. In the face of a negative outcome it should be obvious to a disputant that process control has been ineffective in securing favorable outcomes. The Lind et al. (1980) study, for example, found little reevaluation of procedures in response to information on the verdict of an adjudication.

All of the studies just mentioned show some results that are inconsistent with reward-oriented explanations of the process control effect. Many of them show results that are also inconsistent with equity-oriented explanations. For example, in the Lind et al. (1980) study, all subjects were given private information that showed conclusively that they were entitled to favorable verdicts. When some of these subjects subsequently received unfavorable verdicts, the outcome was not only unfavorable, it was also clearly inequitable. Nonetheless, these subjects showed higher procedural fairness judgments when they had process control than when they did not.

Several studies show even more clearly that the process control effect involves something other than the ability of process control to influence case outcomes. Lind, Lissak, and Conlon (1983) tested the relative effects of process and decision control on reactions to conflict resolution procedures. Decision control was operationalized in this study as the opportunity to reject the third-party decision offered to resolve the conflict. This type of decision control is a more direct form of control over outcomes than is process control, and if the reward-oriented or equity-oriented views of the process control effect are correct, decision control should have greater effects on perceptions of procedural fairness than does process control. Indeed, one might expect from outcome instrumentality positions that process control would be of little importance, and therefore have little effect, when disputants have decision control.

Lind, Lissak, and Conlon used the same experimental paradigm employed by Walker et al. (1974), LaTour (1978), and Lind et al. (1980) studies, but they independently manipulated the process control and decision control that the hearing procedures afforded disputants. The process control manipulation involved the use of adversary or nonadversary procedures similar to those used in the Walker et al. (1974) study. High disputant decision control was created by including in the procedure either the provision that the judge's decision could be rejected by either disputant (in favor of the option of attempting to negotiate a settlement); low decision control was created by specifying that that judge's decision was final and binding on both parties. In addition, the study included a manipulation of the outcome of the hearing—subjects were told either that they had been awarded two-thirds of the outcomes in controversy or that they had been awarded only one-third of the outcomes in controversy. The results of the Lind, Lissak, and Conlon study indicate that the decision control manipulation had little effect on procedural fairness judgments (see Table 2). Whether decision control was available or not, process control enhanced disputants' perceptions of the fairness of the procedure. These findings are contrary to those one would expect if outcome instrumentality were the major force in the process control effect.

Tyler, Rasinski, and Spodick (1985) used both survey and laboratory data to test whether there was some unique process control effect on procedural justice judgments. Two sets of survey data, one consisting of defendant reactions to trial experiences and the other consisting of student reactions to college courses, were analyzed to determine whether perceptions of process control had any effect on procedural fairness judgments over and above the effect of perceived decision control. In both surveys an independent effect of both process and decision control was found. In their third study, Tyler et al. manipulated the level of process control, the level of decision control, and the allocation setting described in scenarios. Both process control and decision control were found to have independent effects on ratings of procedural fairness. In another round of survey studies, Tyler (1987) had replicated these findings.

There have also been some findings that are favorable to the reward-oriented and equity-oriented explanations of the process control effect. As noted above, Brett and Goldberg (1983) found that mediation procedures received more higher procedural fairness ratings than did arbitration procedures. The difference in procedural justice may have been due to the higher level of decision control given disputants under mediation, or it may have been due to covarying differences in process control or some other feature of the procedures. Other research lends credence to the decision control explanation of

Table 2. Procedural Fairness Reactions to Process and Decision Control[a]

	Disputant Decision Control			
	High		Low	
	Disputant process control		Disputant process control	
Outcome	High	Low	High	Low
Favorable	13.08	11.94	14.23	12.07
Unfavorable	12.21	8.42	10.43	9.33

[a]Values are means of an index constructed by summing two nine-point scales. Higher numbers indicate greater perceived fairness. From Lind, Lissak, & Conlon (1983).

the Brett and Goldberg results. At least one laboratory study of dispute resolution procedures (Houlden et al. 1978) has shown higher procedural fairness under high than low decision control, as has the study of allocation procedures mentioned in the preceding paragraph. Further, the more favorable reactions to mediation than adjudication observed in studies of real-world dispute resolution (McEwen & Maiman, 1984) lead us to suspect that decision control engenders greater procedural fairness.

What can be concluded about the validity of these various explanations of the process control effect? The research conducted to date seems to suggest that process control effects on procedural fairness judgments are due to both outcome-related and expressive features of process control, and that we need to be more complex in our thinking about the relations between various types of control and procedural justice. We need to move to a more sophisticated view of the causes of procedural fairness judgments. There are at least two strategies for generating this more sophisticated view—we can refine and elaborate our conceptions of the various types of control that exist in dispute resolution procedures or we can search for the basic psychological mechanisms that underlie the process and decision control effects. We present next an example of work using the former strategy, and we describe in a later section some studies that have used the latter strategy.

Sheppard (1983, 1984) has presented a conceptualization of control in dispute resolution that analyzes and elaborates control relations between disputants and the third party. Sheppard identifies four different stages of third-party dispute intervention at which control might be exercised, and he distinguishes four different types of control. The four stages of third-party intervention are (1) definition of procedures and issues (2) discussion of information and arguments (3) alternative selection (i.e., choice of a resolution for the dispute) and (4) reconciliation of the parties. Sheppard's four types of control are (1) "process control," control over the choice of processes and procedures; (2) content control, control over the information and arguments considered by the parties; (3) "control by request," taking control of one of the other three types of control at the request of one of the parties; and (4) motivational control, the use of social power to force an action or enforce a decision.

The Sheppard taxonomy permits a more detailed description of the control relations in a procedure, and it emphasizes that procedures can be designed that allocate various types of control in novel ways. This last point is especially important, because it allows us to design procedures that give disputants enough of the types of control that promote procedural fairness, while at the same time avoiding some of the shortcomings, documented later in this chapter, of unlimited adversariness. Sheppard (1985) found that a procedure that called for sharing process control between the disputants and the third party was seen as more fair than a procedure that vested all process control in the disputants. It is noteworthy, we believe, that this "hybrid" procedure allowed the disputants to retain sufficient control to be sure that they would have an adequate opportunity to tell their story.

A growing body of research has addressed the psychological processes that are involved in the traditional process control effect on procedural justice judgments. As we noted in the previous section, there is considerable evidence that the effect involves something beyond instrumental control to assure the favorableness or equity of outcomes. It appears that the opportunity to express one's opinions and arguments, the chance to tell one's own side of the story, is a potent factor in enhancing the experience of procedural justice. A corollary of this finding is that, in order for procedural justice to be experienced in a dispute resolution, one must feel that the third party is giving due consideration to one's views and information (Tyler, 1987).

The Tyler, Rasinski, and Spodick (1985) studies were undertaken to test competing predictions from instrumental and value-expressive views of the function of speech in political contexts. The value-expressive view is based on the notion that there are situations in which the opportunity to speak has value in and of itself, regardless of the capacity of the speech to secure other outcomes. The distinction between instrumental and value-expressive functions of speech was proposed by Katz (1960). Tyler et al. tested these two functions of process control by studying the effects of perceived process control over and above the effects of perceived control over outcomes and vice versa. They found, as mentioned earlier, that the relations between process control and procedural fairness could not be explained by perceived influence over outcomes.

The Tyler et al. (1985) studies showed that the etiology of procedural fairness includes factors other than control over outcomes, and it produced the results predicted by a value-expressive explanation of the process control effect. But additional evidence is needed to assure us that it is expression per se, and not some other nonoutcome function of process control that is the key to the effect. Several studies have shown results that point even more strongly to expression as a key factor in procedural justice.

Among these studies is a field study of procedural fairness judgments of court-annexed arbitration procedures, conducted by

Adler, Hensler, and Nelson (1983). Adler *et al.* asked open-ended questions about what disputants saw as fair or unfair in their arbitration hearings. They found that a majority of the disputants who viewed the hearings as unfair complained that they had too little opportunity to tell their story.

A study by Musante, Gilbert, and Thibaut (1983) provides additional evidence favorable to the proposition that procedural justice judgments are enhanced by an opportunity for the expression of views and opinions, whether or not the expression is instrumental in obtaining favorable outcomes. Musante *et al.* examined the effects of various types of participation in the design of procedures on judgments of the fairness of the procedures and outcomes experienced in a subsequent dispute adjudication. Subjects were assembled into six-person groups. Some groups were asked to discuss and decide on the rules to be used in a later adjudication that would affect the subjects' outcomes. Other groups were told to discuss their preference for the various rules, but these groups were led to believe that their preferences would have no effect on the rules actually used—subjects in these groups were told that the rules to be used had already been selected. In half of these discussion-only groups the rules actually used matched the preferences expressed in the group discussion, in the other groups in the discussion-only condition the rules actually used did not match the group's preferences. Finally, some groups were not allowed to either discuss or decide the rules to be used. Table 3 shows the results of the study. Musante *et al.* found that participation in the form of group discussion and decision making led to the greatest enhancement of procedural and distributive fairness of the subsequent adjudication but that group discussion alone led to some enhancement

Table 3. Procedural and Distributive Fairness Reactions to Group Discussion and Control[a]

| | No control | | Control | |
	No discussion	Preference mismatched discussion	Preference matched discussion	Discussion and choice
Fairness dimension				
Procedural fairness	− 0.995	− 0.559	0.282	1.275
Distributive fairness	− 0.998	− 0.207	0.431	0.779
Influence over decision	1.099	1.338	1.471	2.986

[a]Higher values indicate greater perceived fairness. From Musante, Gilbert, & Thibaut (1983).

of both types of fairness relative to the condition that involved neither discussion nor decision making.

The Musante et al. findings are noteworthy on two grounds. First, they suggest that participation in the design of a procedure can enhance the perceived fairness of the procedure and its outcome. Thus results of the study show that procedural variation in one social decision-making procedure can affect reactions to a subsequent, related procedure. The Musante et al. findings are also of considerable theoretical importance to the issue under discussion in this section: It is remarkable that the study showed some enhancement of fairness in the conditions that encouraged discussion but that explicitly ruled out any influence of this discussion on the decision. It appears that discussion and the expression of preference, even without any action in response to the preference, is one source of favorable procedural and distributive fairness judgments.

These findings support the hypothesis advanced by Tyler et al. (1985) that some process control effects may be due to value expression rather than any instrumentality in achieving outcomes. In the case of the Musante et al. discussion-only condition, an enhancement of fairness was observed in conditions that are purely expressive, conditions in which there was no suggestion whatsoever of control or influence over a decision-making process. Further research has suggested that this process control effect does not occur under all conditions. It is important that the decision-maker be seen as giving due consideration to the views expressed, even if he or she is not influenced by those views.

Tyler (1987) used cross-sectional survey data to test four possible limitations on the process control enhancement of procedural justice judgments. He tested whether the process control effect disappears when (1) the decision-maker is seen as biased; (2) the decision-maker is seen as not acting in "good faith"; (3) the decision-maker is seen as not giving the disputant's views due consideration; and (4) the outcomes involved were substantial. Each limitation was tested by selecting individuals who did not believe they had any control over the decision and who believed that the limitation in question was operative in their case. Within each set of individuals thus selected, the procedural fairness judgments of those who had experienced varying levels of process control were compared. Tyler's results showed that only the third limitation, the lack of due consideration, removed the process control effect. Process control enhanced procedural justice even when the decision-maker was seen as biased, when he or she was seen as acting in bad faith, and when the outcomes were important, but not when the decision-maker was seen as not giving consideration to the respondent's views and arguments. A recent laboratory study showed results that are congruent with those of Tyler's survey, suggesting that consideration of arguments is an important factor in procedural justice. Conlon, Lind, and Lissak (1989) studied the effects of various levels of outcomes in the context of an adjudication. They tested whether compromise outcomes induce feelings of injustice. Conlon et al. hypothesized that compromise outcomes might be interpreted as showing inadequate consideration of a disputant's views, because a compromise can be suggested without considering the difficult issues of right and wrong that underlie many disputes. Conlon et al. suggest this in turn might lead to judgments that the procedure and outcome are less fair when a judge issues a compromise decision than when an all-or-nothing outcome is issued.

The experimental paradigm used was an adaptation of that used in the Walker et al. (1974) study, using only the adversary procedure. As in the Walker et al. study, a dispute arose in an experimental competition and a trial was held to decide whether cheating had occurred and who should receive the prize that was to be awarded to the winner of the competition. Some subjects were told that their team had been found innocent of all counts charged and would receive the full prize, some were told that their team had been found innocent on most of the counts and would receive two-thirds of the prize, some were told that their team had been found guilty of most of the counts and would receive only one-third of the prize, and some were told that their team had been found guilty on all counts and would receive none of the prize. The major dependent variables were indices of perceived procedural and distributive fairness and ratings of the extent to which the judge considered the arguments favoring the subject's side of the case. Outcome effects on consideration ratings were clearly nonmonotonic. As the outcomes moved from a total loss to a total win, fairness judgments first decreased and then increased. Ratings of the extent to which the judge considered all aspects of the case showed a nonlinear outcome effect quite similar to that seen on the procedural fairness index.

As this review suggests, the research on the relationship between control and procedural preference stimulated by Thibaut and Walker has not simply confirmed their initial suggestions. The research has suggested that the relationship between control and procedural preference is more complex than Thibaut and Walker realized. Subsequent studies have suggested that one reason process control is valued is that it allows litigants to indirectly influence outcomes by influencing the decisions of third parties. In addition, though, it is now clear that the opportunity to state one's case has value in itself. Recent studies suggest that this expressive value of speech may be more important than its instrumental influence on decisions. It is certainly more intriguing! At the same time, recent studies have suggested that process control effects do not occur under all circumstances. Disputants only value voice if they feel that the decision-maker is giving consideration to what they say.

It is also important to note that research into the meaning of procedural justice has almost exclusively examined the issues of control raised by Thibaut and Walker. A broader procedural justice framework proposed by Leventhal (1980), in which control is only one procedural justice criterion, has received less attention. Several studies that do consider a larger framework of procedural justice have suggested that issues of decision and process control are only one of several factors considered by those judging the fairness of procedures (Sheppard & Lewicki, 1987; Tyler, 1988).

Outcome Effects on Procedural Fairness

Many of the studies described above included manipulations of the outcome of the procedure: Subjects were led to believe they had received either a positive or a negative outcome from the dispute resolution process. Although there have been instances of studies showing no outcome effect on procedural fairness (e.g., Lind et al., 1980), most of the studies have shown that procedural fairness judgments are higher following a favorable outcome than following an unfavorable outcome. With the exceptions noted next, outcome effects appear to operate independently of other determinants of procedural fairness, raising or lowering the patterns of perceived fairness caused by other factors.

There are a few instances in which outcome effects are complicated by interactions with other factors. Lind and Lissak (1985) used the Walker et al. (1974) paradigm to examine the effects of flaws in the enactment of an otherwise fair procedure. They exposed subjects to an enactment of an adversary procedure that either did or did not include evidence of what might be viewed as an improper interpersonal relationship. In conditions with an unflawed procedure, the hearing was conducted without any information about the personal relationships of the judge and lawyers conducting the hearing. In conditions with a flawed procedure, the subjects saw an apparently friendly social interaction between the judge and the lawyer representing the subject's opponent. The "flaw" or impropriety manipulation was crossed with a manipulation of the outcome of the hearing—the subject was told that he or she had either won or lost the case. Table 4 shows the results of the study. When the procedure was enacted without any suggestion of improper personal relationships, no outcome effect was observed. However, when the ostensible impropriety was present, procedural fairness judgments were decreased by an unfavorable verdict and enhanced by a favorable verdict and enhanced by a favorable judgment. Lind and Lissak speculated that the presence of a flaw in the procedure instigated a more complete attributional analysis (cf. Wong & Weiner, 1981) of the procedure. This more extensive cognitive analysis led to the procedure being evaluated more in terms of its outcome than would otherwise be the case.

Conclusion

Our goal in this chapter has been to review past research on procedural justice. While it has not been possible for us to discuss all of the research that has occurred in this rapidly expanding area, we have discussed representative examples of what we regard as the major areas of procedural justice research. Our review suggests that the initial findings of Thibaut and Walker about the importance of procedural justice have been strongly confirmed. In fact, procedures matter far more than was suggested in their early work. In addition, the experience of procedural justice has been found to have predictable antecedents and important consequences. We now know that the consequences of procedural justice judgments include effects on a wide variety of social attitudes and behaviors. Similarly, we now know much more about the antecedents of procedural justice than we did a decade ago. Our understanding of the meaning of procedural justice has also advanced beyond the control-based theory of Thibaut and Walker. In contrast to research on the importance of procedural justice, which has nearly universally supported Thibaut and Walker's work,

Table 4. Procedural Fairness Reactions to Impropriety in the Enactment of Procedures[a]

| | Impropriety | |
Outcome	Absent	Present
Disputant's team found innocent	6.28	6.85
Disputant's team found guilty	5.89	5.26

[a]Values are means of an index constructed by averaging five rating scales. Higher values indicate greater perceived fairness. From Lind & Lissak (1985, Table 1, p. 24).

research on control judgments has suggested that the relationship between control and judgments of procedural justice is more complex, and may be fundamentally different, than that suggested by Thibaut and Walker. In particular, expressive aspects of process control have emerged as more central to fairness than was envisioned by Thibaut and Walker.

The work we have described has set the stage, we believe, for further advances in both the theory and application of procedural justice concepts. It has been thirteen years since Thibaut and Walker (1978) advanced their theory of procedure and eleven years since Leventhal's (1980) theory of procedural justice was published. As research findings have accumulated it has become increasingly clear that some procedural justice phenomena cannot be explained by these early theories. One example we have outlined in some detail is the fairness-enhancing propensity of noninstrumental expression. We hope that the next few years will see more theory building in the procedural justice arena.

Equally exciting is the prospect of new applications of procedural justice findings to the legal and work settings. As we have noted, research in both of these areas has shown that strong procedural justice effects occur. Increasingly, procedural justice concerns have figured in efforts to develop and evaluate innovations in these areas. For example, in the legal arena, alternative dispute resolution procedures have been evaluated, in part, in terms of their perceived procedural justice. As recognition of the central role of procedural fairness to the reactions of affected parties in allocation and dispute resolution we would expect this focus on procedural justice to grow.

References

Adler, J. W., Hensler, D. R., and Nelson, C. E. (1983). Simple justice. Santa Monica, CA: RAND.

Alexander, S., & Ruderman, M. (1987). The role of procedural and distributive justice in organizational behavior. Social Justice Research, 1, 177–198.

Alexander, S., Ruderman, M., & Russ, T. L. (1984, August). The nature of procedural justice and its influence on organizational behavior. Paper presented at the American Psychological Association Meetings. Toronto.

Alexander, S., & Russ, T. L. (1985, August) Procedural and distributive justice effects: The role of social context. Paper presented at the American Psychological Association Meetings. Los Angeles, California.

Anderson, J. K., and Hayden, R. M. (1980–1981). Questions of validity and drawing conclusions from simulation studies in procedural justice. Law and Society Review, 15, 293–304.

Barrett-Howard, E., & Tyler, T. R. (1986). Procedural justice as a criterion in allocation decisions. *Journal of Personality and Social Psychology, 50,* 296–304.

Bies, R. J. (1985). The influence of leader's concerns for task, teamwork, and fairness on subordinates satisfaction and organizational evaluations. Unpublished manuscript, Northwestern University.

Brett, J. M., & Goldberg, S. B. (1983). Grievance mediation in the coal industry: A field experiment. *Industrial and Labor Relations Review, 37,* 49–69.

Casper, J. D., Tyler, T. R., & Fisher, B. (1988). Procedural justice in felony cases. *Law and Society Review, 22,* 483–507.

Conlon, D. E., Lind, E. A., & Lissak, R. I. (1989). Nonlinear and nonmonotonic effects of outcome on procedural and distributive fairness judgments. *Journal of Applied Social Psychology, 19,* 1085–1099.

Crosby, F. (1976). A model of egoistical relative deprivation. *Psychological Bulletin, 76,* 85–113.

Crosby, F. (1982). *Relative deprivation and working women.* New York: Oxford University Press.

Damaska, M. (1975). Presentation of evidence and factfinding precision. *University of Pennsylvania Law Review, 123,* 1083–1106.

Davis, J. H. (1980). Group decision and procedural justice. In M. Fishbein (Ed.), *Advances in Social Psychology* (pp. 157–229). Hillsdale, NJ.: Erlbaum.

Earley, P. C. (1984). Informational mechanisms of participation influencing goal acceptance, satisfaction, and performance. Unpublished manuscript, University of Illinois.

Greenberg, J. (1987a). Using diaries to promote procedural justice in performance appraisals. *Social Justice Research, 1,* 219–234.

Greenberg, J. (1987b). Reactions to injustice in payment distributions: Do the means justify the ends? *Journal of Applied Psychology, 72,* 55–61.

Hayden, R. M., & Anderson, J. K. (1979). On the evaluation of procedural issues in laboratory experiments. *Law and Human Behavior, 3,* 21–33.

Hollander, E. P., & Julian, J. W. (1970). Studies in leader legitimacy, influence, and innovation. In L. Berkowitz (Ed.), *Advances in Experimental Social Psychology* (Volume 5, pp. 33–69) . New York: Academic Press.

Houlden, P., LaTour, S., Walker, L., and Thibaut, J. (1978). Preference for modes of dispute resolution as a function of process and decision control. *Journal of Experimental Social Psychology, 14,* 13–30.

Kanfer, R., Sawyer, J., Earley, P. C., and Lind, E. A. (1987). Fairness and participation in evaluation procedures: Effects on task attitudes and performance. *Social Justice Research, 1,* 235–249.

Katz, D. (1960). The functional approach to the study of attitudes. *Public Opinion Quarterly, 24,* 163–204.

Landis, J. M., & Goodstein, L. I. (1986). When is justice fair? *American Bar Foundation Research Journal, 1986,* 675–708.

Landy, F. J., Barnes-Farrell, J. L., & Murphy, K. R. (1978). Correlates of perceived fairness and accuracy of performance evaluation. *Journal of Applied Psychology, 63,* 751–754.

Landy, F. J., Barnes-Farrell, J. L., & Cleveland, J. N. (1980). Perceived fairness and accuracy of performance evaluation. *Journal of Applied Psychology, 65,* 355–356.

LaTour, S. (1978). Determinants of participant and observer satisfaction with adversary and inquisitorial modes of adjudication. *Journal of Personality and Social Psychology, 36,* 1531–1545.

Leventhal, G. S. (1980). What should be done with equity theory? In K. J. Gergen, M. S. Greenberg, & R. H. Weiss (Eds.), *Social exchange: Advances in theory and research* (pp. 27–55). New York : Plenum Press

Lewin K., Lippitt, R., & White, R. K. (1959). Patterns of aggressive behavior in experimentally created "social climates." *Journal of Social Issues, 10,* 271–299.

Lind, E. A., Kurtz, S., Musante, L., Walker, L., & Thibaut, J. (1980). Procedure and outcome effects on reactions to adjudicated resolution of conflicts of interest. *Journal of Personality and Social Psychology, 39,* 643–653.

Lind, E. A., & Lissak, R. I. (1985). Apparent impropriety and procedural fairness judgments. *Journal of Experimental Social Psychology, 21,* 19–29.

Lind, E. A., & Lissak, R. I., & Conlon, D. E. (1983). Decision control and process control effects on procedural fairness judgments. *Journal of Applied Social Psychology, 4,* 338–350.

Lind, E. A., MacCoun, R. J., Ebener, P. A., Felstiner, W. L. F., Hensler, D. R., Resnik, J., & Tyler, T. R. (1989). *The Perception of Justice: Tort Litigants' Views of Trial, Court-Annexed Arbitration, and Judicial Settlement Conferences.* Santa Monica, CA: RAND.

Lind, E. A., & Tyler, T. R. (1988). *The social psychology of procedural justice.* New York: Plenum Press..

Lissak, R. I. (1983). Procedural fairness: How employees evaluate procedures. Unpublished dissertation. University of Illinois.

Lissak, R. I., & Sheppard, B. H. (1983). Beyond fairness: The criterion problem in research on dispute intervention. *Journal of Applied Social Psychology, 13,* 45–65.

MacCoun, R. J., Lind, E. A., Hensler, D. R., Bryant, D. L., & Ebener, P. A. (1988). *Alternative adjudication: An evaluation of the New Jersey Automobile Arbitration program.* Santa Monica, CA: RAND.

McEwen, C. A., & Maiman, R. J. (1984). Mediation in small claims court: Achieving compliance through consent. *Law and Society Review, 18,* 11–50.

Musante, L., Gilbert, M. A., & Thibaut, J. (1983). The effects of control on the perceived fairness of procedures and outcomes. *Journal of Experimental Social Psychology, 19,* 223–238.

O'Barr, W. M., & Conley, J. M. (1985). Litigant satisfaction versus adequacy in small claims court narratives. *Law and Society Review, 19,* 661–702.

Rasinski, K. (1987). What's fair is fair . . . or is it? Value differences underlying public views about social justice. *Journal of Personality and Social Psychology, 53,* 201–211.

Rasinski, K., & Tyler, T. R. (1987). Fairness and vote choice in the 1984 Presidential election. *American Politics Quarterly, 16,* 5–24.

Sheppard, B. H. (1983). Managers as inquisitors: Some lessons from the law. In M. Bazerman & R. Lewicki (Eds.), *Negotiating in organizations* (pp. 193–213). Beverly Hills CA: Sage.

Sheppard, B. H. (1984). Third party conflict intervention: A procedural framework. In B. Staw and L. Cummings (Eds.), *Research in organizational behavior* (Volume 6, pp. 141–190). Greenwich, CT: JAI Press.

Sheppard, B. H. (1985). Justice is no simple matter: Case for elaborating our model of procedural fairness. *Journal of Personality and Social Psychology, 49,* 953–962.

Sheppard, B. H., & Lewicki, R. J. (1987). Toward general principles of managerial fairness. *Social Justice Research, 1,* 161–176.

Thibaut, J., & Walker, L. (1975). *Procedural justice.* Hillsdale, NJ: Erlbaum.

Thibaut, J., & Walker,L. (1978). A theory of procedure. *California Law Review, 66,* 541–566.

Tyler, T. R. (1984). The role of perceived injustice in defendants' evaluations of their courtroom experience. *Law and Society Review, 18,* 51–67.

Tyler, T. R. (1986a). Procedural justice in organizations. In R. Lewicki, M. Bazerman, & B. H. Sheppard (Eds.), *Research on negotiation in organizations* (Volume 1, pp. 7–73). Greenwich, CT: JAI Press.

Tyler, T. R. (1986b). Justice and leadership endorsement. In R. R. Lau and D. O. Sears (Eds.), *Political cognition*. Hillsdale, NJ: Erlbaum.

Tyler, T. R. (1987). Conditions leading to value expressive effects in judgments of procedural justice: A test of four models. *Journal of Personality and Social Psychology, 52*, 333–344.

Tyler, T. R. (1988). What is procedural justice? Criteria used by citizens to assess the fairness of legal procedures. *Law and Society Review, 22*, 301–355.

Tyler, T. R. (1990). *Why people obey the law*. New Haven: Yale University Press.

Tyler, T. R., & Caine, A. (1981). The influence of outcomes amd procedures on satisfaction with formal leaders. *Journal of Personality and Social Psychology, 41*, 642–655.

Tyler, T. R., & Folger, R. (1980). Distributional and procedural aspects of satisfaction with citizen-police encounters. *Basic and Applied Psychology, 1*, 281–292.

Tyler, T. R., Rasinski, K., & Griffin, E. (1986). Alternative images of the citizen: Implications for public policy. *American Psychologist, 41*, 970–978.

Tyler, T. R., Rasinski, K., & McGraw, K. (1985). The influence of perceived injustice on the endorsement of political leaders. *Journal of Applied Social Psychology, 15*, 700–725.

Tyler, T. R. Rasinski, K., & Spodick, N. (1985). The influence of voice on satisfaction with leaders: Exploring the meaning of process control. *Journal of Personality and Social Psychology, 48*, 72–81.

Walker, L. LaTour, S., Lind, E. A., & Thibaut, J. (1974). Reactions of participants and observers to modes of adjudication. *Journal of Applied Social Psychology, 4*, 295–310.

Walster, E., Walster, G. W., & Berscheid, E. (1978). *Equity: Theory and research*. Boston: Allyn and Bacon.

Wong, P. T. B., & Weiner, B. (1981). When people ask "why" questions and the heuristics of attributional search. *Journal of Personality and Social Psychology, 40*, 650–663.

5

Aspects of Distributive and Procedural Justice in Quality of Working Life

Jacques Allegro, Henk Kruidenier, and
Herman Steensma

Introduction

This chapter offers an indicative review of the uneven distribution of
the quality of working life. After presenting a conceptual model
concerning humanization and the quality of working life, it gives
objective indicators of the quality of working life, followed by data on
blue- versus white-collar workers indicating social injustice. Next, it
provides some ideas on strategies of improvement, that is, humanization strategies in relation to automation, giving an example and
including, in the final paragraph, a theoretical reflection.

A Model of Humanization and Quality of Working Life

Humanization of working life can be defined as a *process* directed at
obtaining more safety, health, and well-being in the work situation. In
this respect, humanization of working life should be distinguished
from quality of working life, which means the *assessment* of the level

Jacques Allegro • Department of Psychology, University of Leiden, P.O. Box 9555,
2312 KM Leiden, The Netherlands   Henk Kruidenier • Dutch Institute for the Working Environment, Amsterdam, The Netherlands   Herman Steensma • Department of
Social and Organizational Psychology, University of Leiden, P.O. Box 9555, 2312 KM,
Leiden, The Netherlands.

of working life in terms of safety, health, and well-being. Before the issue of humanization of working life can be settled, the starting point—*quality of working life*—must be made clear. Inspection of several definitions in the publications of the International Labour Organisation (ILO), the Organization for Economic Cooperation and Development (OECD), the Dutch National Institute for Preventive Health Care (TNO/NIPG), and the Dutch Scientific Council for Governmental Policy (WRR) produces four common categories of quality of working life:

1. Job content—job qualifications, work load, autonomy
2. Material working conditions—dirt, noise, toxic material
3. Industrial relations—works council, job consultation, social relations with colleagues, supervisors and coworkers, the relationship with union and management
4. Working conditions—reward allocation, form of reward allocation, working hours (and other aspects of personnel management)

Next we go into the process of *humanization of working life*, asking which elements/dimensions can be distinguished in the policy to obtain better safety, health, and well-being and how are these different from former policies concerning the improvement of working life? Gradually, new approaches are being introduced in the development of humanization of working life, in which four elements can be distinguished:

1. The goal of humanization of working life (a pure social goal)
2. Control of people (give workers more say)
3. A multidimensional approach
4. Focus on processes of the introduction of planned change.

A Pure Social Goal

In a publication of TNO-NIPG (1979), the following statement is interesting in this respect: "the essential part [of a social goal settlement] is that the requirements are directly based on assumptions concerning the well being of working people." In this formulation a pure social aim is the central element. In our view and that of others (e.g., De Galan et al., 1980; Social and Cultural Planning Office (SCP), 1984), the actual influence of such humanization of working life—directed at purely by social goals—is still very slight.

More Say

A sparkling new element in the humanization approach is more say and participation for the workers involved. More say is effected through formal channels such as the works council, the ARBO Council and the VWG committees,[1] as well as through informal channels such as job consultation.

In this respect, we assume that both formal and informal strategies should be integrated, preferably with an emphasis on informal say, as in our view the new working situation must be linked as closely as possible to those who are directly involved. The required approach should be contrary to for instance, the Committee for the Developmental Policy of Organizations (COB) experiments in co-management (1981), where formal, structural co-management is prominent.

A Multidimensional Approach

A third new element is that, in some projects of humanization, several elements as described will be applied simultaneously. This approach concerns not only work redesign but also changes in other areas.

Focus on Issues Concerning Introduction of Planned Change

A fourth element deals with the growing attention to the process of introduction of planned change. There is an increasing awareness that production of blue prints is insufficient and that it is essential to pay more attention to the manner in which the goals should be reached. From earlier studies, it is evident that these processes of change will take years rather than months.

The aforementioned issues of humanization of working life are summarized in Table 1. Thus, humanization is a process that should lead to work situations characterized by better safety, health, and well-being of all workers involved. The objects of the planned change concern job content, material working conditions, job relations, as well as working conditions and other aspects of personnel management. Job

---

[1]Work council and VGW committees (safety, health, and well-being committees) are formalized systems that allow representatives of workers to participate in decision making within organizations. There is an extensive amount of legislation concerning these systems. The ARBO Council is a council consisting of representatives of employers, labor unions, and government. Its task is to advise the Dutch government on QWL legislation.

Table 1. Model of Humanization of Working Life

Humanization of working life

Objects	Goals
Job content	Safety
Work environment	Health
Policy on working relations	Well-being: involvement and
Working conditions	critical satisfaction
Personnel management	

Participation

Formal	Informal
Work's council	Job consultation
ARBO-committee	Quality circles
VWG-committee	

control of the participants must be at the core of the process of humanization of working life.

From a societal perspective, decreasing attention is being given to the improvement of the quality of working life. However, more emphasis is being placed on which conditions of the humanization of working life and efficiency of production can be combined (Allegro, 1985).

Facts on Quality of Working Life in The Netherlands

According to the WRR (1981), although some improvements in the *objects* of the model can be observed, in several other areas, the problems concerning quality of working life have increased. The four objects in the model illustrate this state of affairs.

1. *Job content.* Problems arise from the discrepancy between the on-average higher educational level of the workers and the level of the jobs offered; an increasing number of workers have a higher educational level than their job requires. From research findings of Conen and Huijen (1983), based on labor counts in 1971 and 1977 in The Netherlands, it can be concluded that for all educational levels, the quality of working life has decreased, specified for the level of job content. From Central Office of Statistics (CBS) findings (1985), it can be observed that there is a growing tendency for people to experience a negative connection between work content and educational level and/or work experience. Moreover, for the various professional areas, there are several developments taking place.

2. *Material working conditions.* According to WRR (1981) and SCP (1984), physical working conditions tend to improve in the course of time. Although this improvement is generally accepted, it is also recognized that large groups of the Dutch industrial population still work in damaging circumstances (see also Fortuin & Wijnen, 1980; Terra & Tappèl, 1986).

3. *Labor Relations.* Labor relations, in terms of institutional structures, have slowly but steadily developed. Since the new act on the works council, there is, for instance, the right of consent of the council concerning certain parts of social policy. However, job consultation often still shows evidence of a deficient development. The Work Environment Act could mean a stimulant, despite the delay in its planned enforcement. Altogether, one could wonder whether the aforementioned developments are keeping pace with the changing norms of authority and of work and leisure time, even though, in the present economic situation, other values, such as keeping one's job, have clearly become more and more evident.

4. *Labor conditions.* Since the 1970s the development of primary labor conditions has, at best, been stabilized. For a great many workers, job insecurity increases, sometimes resulting in health problems (Bastiaansen et al., 1983–1985).

Summarizing, one may conclude that these developments do not contribute to optimism. In some places, therefore, the developments require a certain policy concerning humanization of work, aimed at better safety, health, and well-being.

Inequality in the Distribution of Quality of Working Life

Next we will present—as an illustration of social inequality in working life—some data on the unequal distribution of quality of working life as shown in the goal section of the model (Table 2). In the presentation, we will distinguish between different professional groups (blue and white-collar workers). We will also provide some indexes of health and

Table 2. Percentage of Working People with a Negative Attitude toward Working Conditions

	Noise	Dirt	Stench	Danger	Physical hard work	High speed	monotony
White collar	-13^b	-5	-4	-3	-3	42	16
Blue collar	$+44^a$	$+57$	$+20$	$+23$	$+42$	40	19

[a] +significantly higher than population mean.
[b] −significantly lower than population mean.

Table 3. Percentage of Working People with a Positive Attitude toward Working Conditions

	Growth	Connection work/education	Security of job	Good chances of promotion	Good reward system
White collar	+60[a]	+60	+73	+30	+71
Blue collar	+56	+61	−50[b]	−18	−56

[a] +significantly higher than population mean.
[b] − significantly lower than population mean.

illness for these professional groups. The data are derived from a CBS survey (1985) of the social climate of the Dutch population over 18 years of age, based on a sample (1983) of 4,000 respondents, half of whom had a paid job.

From these findings, we can infer that blue-collar workers work under considerably worse conditions than do white-collar workers, with the exception of high speed and monotony.

Table 3 shows that blue-collar workers judge their working conditions more negatively than the population mean. Concluding, we may state that blue-collar workers are worse off with regard to several material labor conditions and circumstances than the average Dutch professional population. These findings are in agreement with results found elsewhere (Katz & Kahn, 1978).

If health and illness findings are presented for the same professional groups, the following picture can be shown (Table 4) Also, according to health indexes, blue-collar workers are worse off than white-collar workers. Our concluding remark is that there is an unequal distribution of quality of working life for professional groups. This unequal distribution calls for changes. The global tendencies in task content and working conditions are especially negative.

Humanization of Working Life and Automation

The question is how improvement can be achieved. We will try to answer this question in relation to the radical changes in the develop-

Table 4. Percentage of Absenteeism and Disability for Blue and White Collar Workers

	Absenteeism[a]	Disability[b]
White collar	5.4	0.7
Blue collar	12.5	2.2

[a] Percentage of absenteeism in 1983 according to CCOZ data.
[b] Kruidenier (1982). These percentages are related to male workers.

ment of new technologies, especially automation, a development that has launched a new assault on the quality of working life and on its equal distribution. Therefore, we will first describe the cause and consequences of automation and next ask the question whether or not automation can be introduced in such a way that both efficiency and a better quality of working life are possible. Then we will describe one of the most important movements of humanization of working life, that is, the open sociotechnical systems approach, including planned change and research methodology. In the following paragraph, a case study will be presented: However, it is not one directed at the situation of blue-collar versus white-collar workers but one proving that the quality of working life can be influenced.

Cause

The introduction of new technologies based on microelectronics primarily stems from economic and technical causes (SER, 1982). From these points of view, the rapidly developing automation seems a success, although there are also complaints about (too) high introduction costs and less efficiency than expected.

At the same time, the social costs seem high as a result of loss of labor and the frequently observed low quality of working life, expressed in the low utilization of the expertise of users, in stress and in resistance against changes (Algera & Koopman, 1983; Butera & Thurman, 1984; Mumford, 1985; Weggelaar & De Boer, 1984). From a societal point of view, there is, in The Netherlands, growing attention to this problem from the authorities, both employers and employees (Ekkers, 1984), although from different perspectives.

Problem Definition

Is it possible to introduce automation that leads both to the desired efficiency and to a higher quality of working life? And if so, under what conditions can this goal be reached? In this respect, we assume that the relations between efficiency and quality of working life may be positive, neutral, or negative, depending on the circumstances. Earlier we showed more generally that, under certain conditions, efficiency and quality of working life coincide (Allegro, 1985).

In order to answer this specific question, we must first explain the position on the introduction of automation in terms of organization theory and planned change. From literature on the introduction of

automation (see especially the summarizing studies of Butera & Thurman, 1984; Van der Vlist, 1985), we learn that automation is defined as
a technical (economical) problem, where the social–organizational
consequences come last. In fact, this viewpoint represents the scientific management approach of organizations, where people are viewed
as extensions of machines. Related to this scientific management
approach is the idea of technological determinism (Davis & Taylor,
1976) that says that (1.) technical development has its own internal
dynamics; (2.) only engineers and technicians determine the application of technology; and (3.) technology determines the structure of the
organization. In the aforementioned section, the negative effects of
scientific management have already been shown.

However, when the introduction of automation is considered as a
process of planned change in the organization—where techniques,
organization, people, and tasks change—new perspectives arise. From
literature on organization development (Bruining & Allegro, 1981), it is
stated that the manager/advisor/researcher has to reconsider his basic
assumptions on the desired future organization (theories of organizations) and the methods by which this organization will hopefully be
reached (theories on change). In this respect, we should be aware that
the analytical difference between goal and method earlier referred to is
not based on completely independent factors but must be seen as a
consequence of the fact that most organization theories are static.
Moreover, for researchers, it is important to indicate the most efficient
evaluation method.

Theoretical, "Planned Change," and Methodological
Backgrounds

The Open Sociotechnical System Approach. In this theoretical
viewpoint, organizations have two subsystems (a social and a technical
one) in an open connection with the environment. This implies that the
behavior of individuals and groups in the organization can only be
understood and changed by the interaction between the technical
system (machines and the production process needed for production)
and the social system (individuals, with their capacities and needs and
the formal and the informal task, and organization structure). From an
analytical point of view (Emery, 1959), there is no question of an
economic subsystem, but from an economic point of view, there is an
evaluation of the relationship between both subsystems.

An essential concept in this respect is joint optimization, in short,
the idea that an organization only operates optimally, according to

standards of efficiency and social policy, when one of the subsystems does not dominate. It is also stated that, contrary to technological determinism, organizational choice should be made in designing tasks, when new techniques are introduced. These theoretical ideas are successfully applied in planned change projects in which new forms of task designs and work organization were introduced (Emery and Thorsrud, 1969, Trist, 1981, Mumford, 1985, Davis and Cherns, 1975, Allegro 1973, and Masselink and Zandvliet, 1986).

In such projects, it is essential from the very start to apply technical as well as social criteria in the design of systems. Initially, the effect of this conception was concentrated on new forms of task design and work organization at the lower levels. In more recent projects, new departments and new plants were designed, in which attention was also given to working circumstances and labor conditions. The results of these projects were higher involvement of the workers, lower absenteeism and turnover, and higher productivity (see Pasmore, 1982).

In The Netherlands, De Sitter (1980) has defended the same, afore-mentioned ideas. Katz and Kahn (1978), however, have pointed out that, with the exception of the projects of Volvo Kalmar and Saab Scania in Sweden, there were only minor changes in the technical system. Several other researchers have presented critical opinions on, for instance, the limitations of the joint optimization concept and the lack of attention to planned change projects, especially in the earlier projects. They have also pointed out a number of theoretical and methodological objections. And they have stated that the choice for or against technological determinism in respect to organizational freedom of choice in automation is far too absolute to explain the influence of automation on task and organization design.

Planned Change Strategies. The next question concerns the way in which planned change should be realized. According to Chin and Benne (1971), we call this aspect *strategies of planned change*. Chin and Benne distinguish the following types of strategies: empirical rational strategies, requiring an expert role of the change agent; normative–reeducative strategies, requiring a counseling role; and power coercion strategies, requiring a political role.

Several authors (Bruining & Allegro, 1981) assume that, depending on the circumstances, a mixture of different roles should be applied or, in other words, the so-called contingency approach of organization development. This means that, apart from the role of the expert, especially important in the scientific management approach, the coun-seling role also plays an important part. For the participants, we apply the more general concept of users' participation; users' participation has been defended by scientists with different viewpoints (Blokdijk, 1981; Butera & Thurman, 1984; Den Hertog & Van der Wee, 1982; Mumford, 1985). Some of these writers emphasize a democratic value perspective, whereas others emphasize the knowledge and skill of the directly involved users, as well as the acceptation motive. At the same time, some of the authors state that users' participation is a difficult matter, for which several different guidelines for solutions are presented. Furthermore, attention must also be paid to (inter)group processes, not only to processes of task structuring.

Methodological Approach. Roughly speaking two types of evaluation research (necessary to assess the effects of planned change projects) can be distinguished. The first type, the more applied of the two, is based on stringent causal models and is primarily directed at transversal data gatherings and data-analytical techniques. The second is a process type of evaluation. A process evaluation methodology, apart from attention for effects, is directed at the self-development of processes during planned change in a group or a department. Many data-gathering techniques will usually be applied to account for the error variation of each technique. Emphasis is especially put on the interpretation of the total pattern of data of the several data-gathering techniques. In our own research, we make use of both types of evaluation research.

Application at Automation

Although the aforementioned conceptions are not developed in the application of new techniques, in this area some new approaches can be distinguished with positive effects on efficiency and quality of working life (Butera & Thurman 1984; Den Hertog and Van der Wee (1982). For example, the open sociotechnical systems approach that is presented in different variations by Mumford (the Ethics method), Allegro and De Vries (1979) and others; and the STAA approach from Kranendonk and others. Moreover, there are a number of more "traditional system development methods" where the social–organizational component is a central part (the prisma method, the isac method, and others).

An Example

A successful example of the open systems approach has been described by Allegro and de Vries (1979) and is presented here.

Introduction

As a predecessor of several participation projects, funded by COB, a 3 year planned project was carried out in cooperation with insurance company Centraal Beheer, Apeldoorn, and the Foundation Bedrijfs-kunde, Delft, The Netherlands from November 1974 to September 1977 (evaluation 1983). The most important goals of the project were to increase the level of participation of workers and of the humanization of the working situation. The instrument of planned change consisted mainly of designing and introducing new types of task and work organization and of realizing job consultation. The goals had to be realized at the introduction of an automation project in the life insurance department. In fact, the question was how automation could be carried out so that quality of working life could also be maintained.

The Organization at the End of 1974

The cooperative association Centraal Beheer is an administration office with (in 1974) about 1,073 employees. Its most important activities are life and indemnity insurances, investments, and a computer service office. During the past years, a number of drastic changes have been made, changes that are still taking place. These changes include removal from Amsterdam to Apeldoorn and the introduction of a number of complex automation projects. The economic results are positive.

At the life insurance department where automation was intro-duced, four subdepartments (225 employees) were distinguishable with a strict differentiation in functions and a rather strong hierarchy. The project was supervised by a representative counseling group, whereas during analyses, the design and implementation period, extensive participation of employees—especially the middle manage-ment—was realized.

Planning of the Project

Stage 1: General Orientation. During this stage, the researchers/advisors became acquainted with the organization, where ample atten-tion was given to both the technical administrative system and the social system. The most significant result of this stage was discovering the use of this project because the chosen automation system left room for the needs and wants of the employees. It turned out, however, that the project had to be carried out under considerable time pressure. At the same time, it was observed that, apart from job satisfaction itself, there were a great many problems in the field of personnel and organization policy. There was a strong need for more information on the planned automation.

Stage II: Analysis of the Life Insurance Department (January–July 1975). After a thorough analysis of the life insurance department by representative task groups, the decision was made to introduce contract control groups. This meant that a whole cycle of activities such as proposals, insurance and social security benefits, administration, and control was the responsibility of the group. Next, procedures and working instructions were developed.

Stage III: Design of New Tasks and Realization of the Action Program (January–September 1977). Based on the results of the organization analysis, a new task and organization structure was introduced in close cooperation with employees and management. This took place before the actual introduction of the automation that, due to technical problems, was not carried out until the autumn of 1977. At the same time, a system of job consultation was introduced and, together with a number of representative work groups, problems concerning automation and humanization were tackled. Parallel to these activities, issues in the personnel policy area were dealt with. These issues concerned the training of personnel, the introduction of a new system of job classification, and the improvement of the evaluation system.

Stage IV: Evaluation of the Project. Several evaluation studies of the project were carried out in 1977, 1978, and 1983 in order to determine whether or not restructuring tasks in a participative way led to the desired goals. It was discovered that the employees had an important say in the restructuring of the new situation. In the job consultation sessions, the degree of decision control on the distribution of work and on social policy was increased. Most groups of employees were more satisfied with their work, although a lot remained to be done. Most negative opinions concerned the lack of sufficient results in the field of personnel and organization policy, for example, job-classification and job evaluation system. Efficiency proved to be at an acceptable level.

In order to find out more about the long-term effects, an evaluation took place 1 year after the end of the project (September 1978). It was seen that a stabilization of participation had been achieved, but a decrease in satisfaction was observed. The employees were negative about the job consultation and moderately positive about contract-directed work. Employees were most negative about the absence of sufficient results in the field of personnel and organization policy. Economic criteria were not measured.

The most important explanation for this development seems to be the actual introduction of automation (November 1977), the reorganization of divisions, and the lack of adaptation to existing norms and values. In September 1983, managers and administrative personnel of the Life and Indemnity Division were interviewed in order to establish whether in daily working life there were any traces left from the intervention. It was perceived that, in the Life Insurance Division, contract control groups functioned sufficiently, in spite of the many problems arising from the automation process. Job consultation on the floor had become solidly rooted. In the field of personnel and organization policy, there was a development toward increasing users' participation. Analog developments occurred elsewhere in the organization, however, with the emphasis on management problems.

Discussion

On this project, too, we have assumed that automation is not a technologically determined development but a social–organizational problem. Although attention was given to automation at a relatively late stage, it proved possible to arrive at an appreciable degree of user participation. This fact has resulted in the ultimate package of tasks for the "contract management groups" that must clearly be regarded as favourable. Summarizing, we can say that the project has shown a number of both inhibiting and encouraging factors in the field of humanization of work, especially with regard to the problems of office automation. We also have to remark that quality of working life is unequally divided (between professional groups), that there are a number of technological developments that influence this distribution negatively, but that there are organizational approaches to counteract these developments. These societal/organizational phenomena can be placed in the theoretical framework of social justice, as will be shown in the next paragraph.

Quality of Working Life and Theories of Justice

A distinction can be made between two general classes of theories on justice: theories on distributive justice and theories on procedural justice. Equity theory, perhaps the best-known theory of distributive justice, (Adams, 1965, Walster, Walster, & Berscheid, 1978) may be summarized as follows: In social relationships, a person struggles to balance his or her inputs (factors like, e.g. effort, experience, ability, performance) and their outcomes (monetary and nonmaterial rewards, status, etc.). From the point of view of *interpersonal* (social) comparison, an equitable relationship exists if the ratio of outcomes to inputs for a person (P) equals the ratio of outcomes to inputs for a comparison other (O).

From the point of view of *intrapersonal* comparison, inequity is experienced if the outcomes to inputs ratio deviates from an "internal standard" that is considered fair (Pritchard, 1969). Inequity is distressing and motivates persons to restore equity. The greater the inequity, the more distress individuals will feel, and the harder they will try to restore equity. Restoration of equity may be accomplished by an actual or psychological altering of inputs and/or outcomes. In a situation of underreward, for instance, equity may be restored by reducing effort (i.e., reducing inputs).

Equity theory is, like most theories of distributive justice, individualistic; it embodies principles of microjustice (i.e., it focuses on the fairness of rewards to individual persons). Recently, *macrojustice* has been distinguished from microjustice. Principles of macrojustice concern the aggregate fairness of "outcomes" in a society (Brickman, Folger, Goode, Schul, 1981; Cook Hegtvedt, 1983). People seem to have preferences for the overall shape of an outcome distribution *per se*, not simply for the microlevel principles by which such outcome distributions may be produced.

Micro- and macrojustice may conflict. Strict application of principles of microjustice may result in an aggregation considered highly unfair by most persons (Brickman *et al.*, 1981). We should note that people have preferences for the shape of an overall outcome distribution, and that in general, these preferences appear to be rather egalitarian. Applied to the distribution of QWL characteristics, this means that at least part of these differences in QWL will be considered unfair by most people. Most people endorse both principles of microjustice and principles of macrojustice, but the relative weight of the principles seems to differ according to the characteristics of outcomes to be divided (Brickman *et al.*, 1981). Therefore, we may speculate that group differences in sickness rates and the number of job disabilities, as well as group differences in labor conditions, are considered unfair. These differences cannot be justified in a meaningful way by principles of microjustice. For most other QWL differences, it is possible to specify input characteristics that justify part of the differences, for example, academic schooling is an investment and may therefore result in higher monetary rewards. It should be noted, however, that even in these instances application of principles of macrojustice tends to level differences that are considered fair when only principles of microjustice are applied.

In the first parts of this chapter, we mentioned that QWL of blue-collar workers in general is lower than QWL of white-collar workers. According to the principles of macrojustice and to the principles of microjustice (e.g. equity), this could lead to feelings of injustice. This perceived injustice, in its turn, can be the cause of lower work motivation and lower levels of job satisfaction. These are effects of injustice at the microlevel of the individual person. But, of course, these effects are detrimental at the mesolevel of organizational output, effectiveness, and efficiency, too.

Thus, improving QWL seems to be a wise policy. These improvements in QWL should lead to a fairer distribution of outcomes. But what must be done to reach such a distribution? Or, stated differently, what is the best procedure?

Theories of procedural justice focus on the methods, the procedures by which outcomes are distributed. Perceptions of fair procedure may be influenced by several aspects: clarity, absence of bias, apprehensiveness (understandable rules), correctability. Most authors seem to recognize that the *control of procedures* is of central importance in procedural justice (see, e.g., the review by Lerner Whitehead, 1980). People want to have a say in the procedures. Here we have a remarkable resemblance to our model of humanization of work. This model stresses the importance of participation of workers in improving the quality of working life.

We have been involved in several action-research projects to improve QWL (Allegro, 1973; Allegro & De Vries, 1979; Masselink & Zandvliet, 1986; Steensma & Knip, 1982, Steensma & Vrooland, 1986). In these projects, several dimensions of QWL were improved. Workers participated in planning and implementing the improvements. All projects demonstrate the usefulness of the participative approach. In conclusion, it should be noted that data on QWL and the strategies to improve QWL may be reinterpreted within the framework of theories of justice. Such reinterpretation has at least two positive effects:

- Theories of justice are illustrated by vivid, exciting examples. In other words, societal relevance is very clear.
- Up to the present, data on QWL generally have been collected in

an ad hoc way. Using theories of justice offers a way to select data in a meaningful way and to accumulate a body of knowledge by systematically testing hypotheses.

References

Adams, J. S. (1965). Inequity in social exchange. In L. Berkowitz (Ed.), Advances in experimental social psychology (Vol. 2). New York: Academic Press.

Algera, J., & Koopman, P. (1983). Automatisering: ontwerpproces en implementatie [Automation: Design and Implementation] In P. J. Drenth, e.a. (red.), Handboek Arbeids en Organisatiepsychologie. [Handbook of Industrial and organization psychology]. Deventer: Van Loghum Slaterus.

Allegro, J. T. (1973). Sociotechnische organisatie-ontwikkeling. [Sociotechnical organizational development] Leiden: Stenfert Kroese.

Allegro, J. T. (1985). Humanisering van de arbeid: een plaatsbepaling. [Humanization of work: The state of the art] In H. Steensma, R. van der Vlist, & J. T. Allegro (Eds.), Modern organiseren en menselijker werken (pp. 1–17) [Modern forms of organizing and humanizing work]. The Hague: VUGA.

Allegro, J. T., & de Vries, E. 1979). Project Humanisering en Medezeg-genschap Centraal Beheer [Project Humanization and Codetermination]. The Hague: COB-SER.

Bastiaansen, J., Verkley, H., Spruit, I., & Van Nieuwenhuizen (1983–1985). Werk, Werkloosheid en Gezondheid [Work, unemployment, and health]. Leiden: Instituut voor Sociale Geneeskunde.

Blokdijk, A. (1981). Systeemontwikkelingsmethodiek SASO [The SASO System Development Methodology]. Informatie, 23, 222–237.

Brickmann, Ph., Folger, R., Goode, E., Schul, Y. (1981). Microjustice and macrojustice. In M. Lerner & S. Lerner (eds.), The justice motive in social behavior (pp. 173–202). New York: Plenum Press.

Bruining, G. R. P. & Allegro, J. T. (1981). Organisatie-ontwikkeling. [Organizational development] In P. J. Drenth e.a. (Eds.), Handboek arbeids- en organisatiepsychologie [Handbook of industrial and organizational psychology] Deventer: Van Loghum Slaterus.

Butera, F., & Thurman, J. (1984). Automation and workdesign. Amsterdam: North-Holland.

CBS (1985). Supplement bij de Sociaal-Economische Maandstatistiek, no. 4 [Supplement to Monthly Socio-Economic Statistics]. The Hague: Staatsuitseverij.

Chin, R., & Benne, K. D. (1971). General strategies for effecting changes in human systems. In W. G. Bennis, W. W. Banne, & R. Chin (Eds.), The planning of change (pp. 32–60). New York: Holt, Rinehart & Winston.

COB (1981). Voortgang van het programma experimenten medezeggenschap [Continuation of the Program "Experiments in Codetermination"]. The Hague: COB/SER.

Conen, G., & Huijgen, F. (1983). De kwalitatieve structuur van de werkgelegenheid in 1960, 1971 en 1977 [The qualitative structure of employment in 1960, 1971, and 1977]. In Economisch-Statistische Berichten [Economic–Statistical Bulletin] 27–4.

Cook, K., & Hegtvedt, K. (1983). Distributive justice, equity and equality. Annual Review of Sociology, 9, 217–241.

Davis, L. & Cherns, A. (1975). The quality of working life. New York: Free Press (Volumes 1 and 2).

Davis, L. E. & Taylor, J. C. (1976). Technology, organization and job structure. In R. Dubin (Ed.), Handbook of work, organization and society. Chicago: Rand McNally.

Ekkers, C. L. (1984). De invloed van technologische en wetenschappelijke ontwikkelingen op de Arbowet [The influence of technological and scientific developments on the Dutch Work Environment Law]. Amsterdam: Paper Arbo-congres.

Emery, F. (1950). Characteristics of sociotechnical systems. London: Tavistock.

Emery, F., & Thorsrud, E. (1969). Form and content in industrial democracy. London: Tavistock.

Fortuin, R. J., & Wijnen, D. (1980). Evaluatie subsidieregeling arbeidsplaatsverbetering 1977 [Evaluation of the Dutch Work Improvement Act]. The Hague: Ministerie van Sociale Zaken en Werkgelegenheid.

Galan, L. de, Van Gils, M. R., & Van Strien, P. J. (1980). Humanisering van de arbeid [Humanization of Work]. Assen: Van Gorcum.

Hertog, J. F. den, & Wee, E. van der (1982). Gebruikersparticipatie: uitgangspunt bij het inschakelen van gebruikers in automatiseringsprojecten [User's participation as the starting point in involving users in automation projects]. Informatie, 24, 141–151.

ILO (International Labour Organisation). (1981). The effects of technological changes on the employment and working conditions of non-manual workers. Geneva: ILO.

Katz, D., & Kahn, R. L. (1978). The social psychology of organizations. New York: Wiley.

Kruidenier, H. (1982). Arbeidsbelasting en de kans op langdurige arbeidsongeschiktheid [Job stress and the risk of long-term disability] In V. Vrooland (Ed.), Werk en Gezondheid [Work and Health]. Alphen a/d Rijn: Samson.

Lerner, M. J., and Whitehead, L. A. (1980). Procedural justice viewed in the context of justice motive theory. In G. Minula (Ed.), Justice and social interaction (pp. 219–256). Bern: Hans Huber.

Masselink, W., & Zandvliet, C. (1986). Vernieuwing van werk en organisatie [Renewing work and organization]. Amsterdam: CCOZ.

Mumford, E. (1985). De ETHICS-methode. In P. A. Cornelis & J. Van Oorschot (Eds.), Automatisering in sociaal perspectief (The social perspective in automation). Deventer: Kluwer.

Pasmore, W. (1982). Overcoming road blocks in work restructuring. Organizational Dynamics, 10, 54–67.

Pritchard, R. D. (1969). Equity theory: A review and critique. Organizational Behavior and Human Performance, 4, 176–211.

SCP [Sociaal Cultureel Planbureau]. (1984). Sociaal en Cultureel rapport 1984 [Report on social and cultural conditions]. The Hague: Staatsuitgeverij.

SER (1982). Rapport werkgelegenheidseffecten en micro-electronica. [Report on new technology and its effects on employment]. The Hague: Sociaal Economische Raad.

Sitter, L. K. de. (1981). Op weg naar nieuwe fabrieken en kantoren [On designing New Factories and Offices]. Deventer: Kluwer.

Steensma, H. & Knip, J. (1982). Werkvoldoening en organisatie-ontwikkeling [Job satisfaction and organizational development]. Utrecht: Gemeentelijke Drukkerij.

Steensma, H., & Vrooland, V. (Eds.). (1986). Winst voor werk en organisatie [Profits for work and organization]. Amsterdam: CCOZ.

Terra, N. G. M., & Tappel, B. J. (1986). Het werkt anders, een overzicht van maatregelen tegen veel voorkomende problemen met de kwaliteit van de arbeid van arbeidsplaatsen in de industrie [It's working differently: A review of actions to improve problems of Quality of Working Life in Dutch industry]. The Hague: Ministerie van Sociale Zaken en Werkgelegenheid (Dutch Ministry of Labor and Employment).

Thorsrud, E. (1977). Democracy at work, Norwegian experiments with nonbureaucratic forms of organization. Journal of Applied Behavioral Sciences, 13, 410–421.

TNO–IPG. (1979). *Humanisering van de Arbeid: mogelijkheden en voorwaarden voor TNO-onderzoek* [Humanization of work: Conditions and possibilities for applied research]. Leiden: NIPG.

Trist, E. (1981). *The evolution of sociotechnical systems.* Toronto: Ontario Quality of Working Life Centre.

Vlist, R., van der. (1985). Effecten van automatisering op de kwaliteit van de arbeid in een supermarktketen[effects of automation on the quality of working life in department stores]. In H. Steensma, R. van der Vlist, & J. T. Allegro (Eds.), *Modern organiseren en menselijker werken* (pp. 73–103) [Modern forms of organizing and humanizing work]. The Hague: VUGA.

Walster, E., Walster, G. W., & Berscheid, E. (1978). *Equity: Theory and research.* Boston: Allyn & Bacon.

Weggelaar, M., & De Boer, K. (1984). *Micro-electronica en vrouwenarbeid, II Verslag van vier case-studies* (Micro-Electronics and women's work: Four case studies]. The Hague: Ministerie van Sociale Zaken en Werkgelegenheid.

WRR (Wetenschappelijke Raad voor het regeringsbeleid) [Scientific Council for Governmental Policy]. (1981). *Vernieuwingen in het arbeidsbestel* [The renewal of work]. The Hague: Staatsuitgeverij.

II

Macrojustice

6

Social Justice, Income Distribution, and Social Stratification in The Netherlands: A Review[1]

Piet Hermkens and David van Kreveld

Introduction

A major aspect of social justice in human relations concerns the income level of individuals, in particular the way the incomes in a society are distributed. Income is desirable because it enables a person to obtain attractive goods and services as a result. The inequalities in income become visible and therefore important for the evaluation of social inequalities. Moreover, they are often congruent with differences in power, prestige, and the like. In that sense, the distribution of incomes is part of a social stratification: a system of layers in the society, in which people are categorized according to several criteria and ordered according to a hierarchy. Examples of such criteria are possession of means of production (capitalists, laborers), sources of income (working, nonworking), status and characteristics of occupations (e.g., physicians, managers, office workers, industrial laborers). The income distribution is to an important extent, if not fully, the result of the balances of power in the society (e.g., Homans, 1974; Walster & Walster, 1975). Nevertheless, it is an object not only of analysis but also of pleadings to change it.

[1]The authors wish to thank Bernard J. M. Verlaan for tracing part of the references.

Piet Hermkens • Department of Planning Organization and Policy Studies, Faculty of Social Sciences, University of Utrecht, P.O.Box 80.140, 3508 TC Utrecht, The Netherlands   **David van Kreveld** • Institute of Social Psychology, University of Utrecht, P.O. Box 80.140, 3508 TC Utrecht, the Netherlands

For the social stratification to remain stable, the members of the society must perceive it as legitimate. Legitimacy refers to the total of values and norms justifying the distribution of attractive and scarce goods and services. This leads to two questions: how the distribution process ought to be achieved ("procedural justice") and what the acceptable results of this process ("distributive justice") are. We will deal here mainly with the latter question.

The norms used in attributing advantages and disadvantages to the members of a society can well be analyzed on the basis of research on the justice of the distribution of incomes. Individuals claim a specific income based on individual characteristics (merit, need, etc.), without taking the resulting distribution of all incomes into account. Brickman, Folger, Goode, and Schul (1981, p. 173) call this "microjustice," contrasting it with "macrojustice," which refers to the distribution of incomes in the society more specifically. Macrojustice deals with matters like the desired distance between lowest and highest incomes, the differences in incomes between social categories, and the line, or in general, the shape of the distribution of incomes.

Many of the publications dealing with income distribution refer to the specifics of a particular society whereas others are not easily accessible. Therefore, we review publications dealing especially with the income distribution in The Netherlands.

This subject cannot fully be understood without taking the historical background into account. In our opinion, the development of income distribution, at least during this century, had been governed by two principles: microjustice and macrojustice. These two principles lead in this case to opposite results. The first is the principle of free enterprise in a country in which the struggle for independence was crucial for its origin and survival. Although a considerable proportion of the population is of Roman Catholic origin, Protestant values, if not Calvinistic values in particular, have played a crucial role in this process. This influence led to a preference for equity, to each according to his or her investments. The other governing principle is an emphasis on social concern or responsibility. This led to a preference for equality or at least an aversion to what were considered as too large differences in income. The compromise between these principles can be typified as something like the following: in freedom to each according to what comes out, as long as the differences do not become too large (see also Arts 1984, 1985).

This review deals with four general topics, each of which will be treated in a separate section. First, it discusses the nature of income distribution and changes unit over time. Second, it pays attention to possible causes of income distribution and the changes in it. Then, it considers some studies on judgments of income distributions. Finally, it offers some concluding remarks on the Dutch situation.

The Distribution of Incomes

We begin this section with a matter of macrojustice—general income distribution in The Netherlands. The income distribution of several groups in the Dutch society is represented in Figure 1. It turns out that the position of some typical income groups largely depends on whether the source of income is a paid job or social security (unemployment benefits, disability benefits, old age pension plan, etc.). The distribution of incomes as depicted in Figure 1 is fairly stable. The rank order of the several positions has remained exactly the same over the years: demographical characteristics, as well as the source of income (paid job or social security), determine the position in the income distribution (Social and Cultural Planning Office, 1985). A household with the legal minimum wage is located in the fourth of fifth decile,

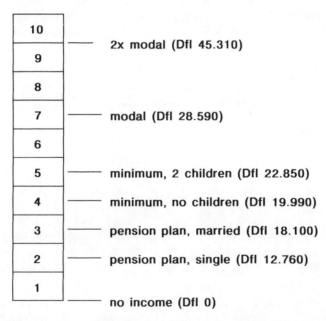

Figure 1. Position of some typical income groups in the secondary income distribution 1981 in The Netherlands (in Dutch guilders; in July 1986, a Dutch guilder had a value of about .40 U.S. dollars, but it has varied through the years between .28 and .50). Redrawn from Figure 4.3 from: SCP (Social and Cultural Planning Office), Berekend Beleid,'s Gravenhage, Staatsuitgeverij, 1985, p. 99.

depending on whether children's allowance is received. In this distribution, income after tax is used as income concepts because we are
interested in a comparison of all incomes, of workers and nonworkers,
in The Netherlands. The figure shows also that the lower income
deciles are fairly close together. An occasional, small, extra bit of
income moves the family easily into the next decile. These small
differences between the low-income groups have received much attention in the discussion of a just income distribution in The Netherlands,
for they constitute a matter of macrojustice.

When The Netherlands was building the welfare state after World
War II, the guiding principle was the position of the low-income
groups (the old, the unemployed, etc.), who would also obtain a just
income. The present system was constructed in the 1950s and 1960s
(Van Wijngaarden, 1982, pp. 15–68). For a comparison with the
obvious situation, we refer to an early and quite respectable investigation on low incomes in the year 1939 reported by Verwey-Jonker in
1943.[2] Although it deals with only one city, Eindhoven, the study is
quite representative of the situation in The Netherlands in general
(p. 17). Following the eighteenth-century mathematician Bernouilli,
Verwey-Jonker claims that the appreciation of income is proportional
to the log of income; she concludes from her data that the distribution
of incomes is a symmetrical Gauss curve and that there are as many
people who consider themselves wealthy as those who consider
themselves poor (pp. 159–161). The year 1939 was neither one of
depression nor of prosperity (p. 169), so her generalization over at least
that period seems legitimate.

Verwey-Jonker compared her results to a much earlier similar
study performed by Rowntree (1901) in the English city of York around
the turn of the century. Rowntree had concluded that 28% of the
population lived in poverty, of which 10% were in primary poverty,
which means that their income was insufficient for primary living
needs. Four decades later, Verwey-Jonker came to a similar conclusion
in Eindhoven. Many of the poor people were aged (pp. 176–180) and
quite often children had to start earning money early. They were thus
cut off from a good education and the resulting good income, a
situation that is an injustice toward them and a waste of talent for the
society (pp. 180–181).

Recently, Verwey-Jonker (1985) compared the results of her study
from 1939 with those of two other studies on poverty in The Nether-

---

[2]The book by Mrs. Verwey-Jonker is a doctoral thesis. Because of war circumstances, the
public defense planned in 1943 was canceled. The defense took place after the liberation
in 1945.

lands (Van Praag, Hagenaars et al., 1984 Wieberens 1981). She concludes that for the late 1970s and the early 1980s, not much has
changed: A difference is that poverty became less painful and got a
new face. The question concerning macrojustice remains the same, in
spite of the construction of the welfare state: How can the low-income
groups participate as much as possible in the prosperity?

When we look only at the incomes of employed workers, income-
distribution affects a much smaller number of people. According to the
personal income distribution in 1981 (CBS, 1984b), there were
2,843,000 families in The Netherlands in which the head participated
in the labor process and 1,711,000 in which the head did not perform
labor. So, the "actives" comprise 62% of the total.

When comparing socioeconomic categories, we will limit ourselves here to private enterprise on the one hand and to government on
the other.[3] The statistical information concerns wages before tax of
male laborers and employees from 23 to 65 years of age (CBS, 1984a).
In private enterprise, the relative inequality has increased in the period
from October 1977 until October 1983: the minimum before tax
increased 30%, the increase reached 41% for the ninth decile, and was
39% for the tenth decile. After tax, the picture is different: the relative
inequality has become slightly smaller. The income of the lowest paid
employee with three children rose 29% during the mentioned period of
time, whereas the income of an employee with three children in the
highest decile rose 21%.

For government employees, the developments from 1977 to 1983
were different; also, before tax the inequalities became smaller. For the
lowest paid employees the increase was 22%, and the increase became
smaller until 11% in the tenth decile. After tax, the extremes for
government employees ranged from an increase of 21.5% for a married
man with three children having the lowest income, to 10% for an
otherwise similar person in the highest decile (Van der Werf &
Fierloos, 1984).

Results of the so-called "package comparison" also appeared (Van
Schaaijk, 1986). It was found that the total package of income parts for
lower government employees and those whose incomes are coupled to
these is slightly better than for employees having similar jobs in the
private sector. For middle groups, the reverse turned out to apply and
stronger so for higher groups.

It has been a topic of political debate in The Netherlands whether
the inequalities have become smaller and whether they should become

---

[3]Salaries paid by lower government (city, province, etc.) and subsidized foundations
follow pretty much those paid by the central government.

smaller. Over somewhat longer periods, the inequalities have definitely become considerably smaller. Pen and Tinbergen (1977) estimate that, in the period from 1938 to 1972, the relative differences
decreased by 50%, that is, by about 2% per year. De Kleijn and Van de
Stadt (1985) estimate a decrease of 5% from 1970 to 1975. This process
has been considerably weaker from 1975 to 1982: the Theil coefficient[4]
became 0.7% smaller. In an analysis of the Central Bureau of Statistics
(De Kleijn & Van de Stadt, 1985, p. 1006), it was concluded that the
average income after tax increased by 11% over the years 1970 to 1982,
or by 0.9% per year. For the independent, this increase is 0.5% per
year for the employees 1.4% per year, and for the nonworkers 1.7% per
year. The average incomes of the several socioeconomic categories
have grown closer. Inequality among the independent is largest and
quite variable. Inequality among the employed and unemployed is
much smaller and decreased from 1970 to 1982.

De Kleijn and Van de Stadt have some reservations about these
data, because of the level of aggregation and the slight modification of
the definitions of income after tax. Nevertheless, it can be concluded
that inequalities have decreased for the employed and for the nonworkers. For the independent, the fluctuations in income are so large that no
conclusions can be drawn.

Possible Causes of the Income Distribution

Several theories have formulated to explain the shape of the income
distribution (see Van der Hoek, 1985; Hartog 1980). The assumption of
stochastic theories is that many factors simultaneously and independent of each other determine the level of incomes. The probability of
increases and decreases in income per category can be described by
means of Markow chain models. Dependent on the specific assumptions made, a lognormal or a Pareto distribution arises. The disadvantage of stochastic theories is that they do not specify the influences of
the independent factors. They can merely lead to a description of a
resulting distribution, seem more promising, that is, at best in terms of
macrojustice.

The *human capital theories* they start off from the decisions taken
by (future) employees to improve their chances in the labor market.
Higher investments should lead to higher incomes. Investments in
schooling cost time and lead to a shorter period of employment.

---

[4]The Theil coefficient is a measure of inequality. It ranges from 0 = full equality to 1 =
maximal inequality. It is discussed by Odink and Van Imhoff (1982).

Therefore, these theories proceed from the total income earned during one's lifetime. In another version of these theories, Grootings and Hövels (1981), grounding themselves on Becker (1964), define human capital in terms of the investments made by the employer. Of course, human capital is a matter of mutual investments of employee and employer.

We mention further the scarcity, matching, or allocation theories that consider labor and income as matters of supply and demand. According to these theories, the income structure is balanced if there exists a balance between qualities offered by employees and demanded by employers (Hartog 1980, 1981; Tinbergen 1953, 1956, 1975). Matching processes take place via changes of income. Based on this mechanism Tinbergen (1953) specified a principle of justice: justice exists between two persons if neither of them wishes to exchange positions. If a person accepts a job higher or lower than his or her level of capacities, supposedly a tension arises for which a financial compensation will be requested. If only a small number of persons can fulfill the requirements of the job, this will lead to high financial compensations. If the distributions of requested and offered characteristics coincide to a large extent, the income differences will become smaller. Tinbergen (1975) describes a race between technological development and education. He estimates the marginal productivity of individuals with a specific educational level in several jobs, and he indicates which long-term developments in the relative payment of different individuals can be expected.

So far, the development of education had been faster than the demand for it, a situation that has resulted in decreased rewards for the educated (Huijgen, Riesewijk, & Conen, 1983) and brings up the question of whether exists "overeducation" exists in Dutch society, that is, if too much schooling is provided for the jobs available. Hartog (1985) does not come to this general conclusion, although in his opinion it may hold for some fields. Hartog doubts whether education is merely a costly sorting machine of differences in expected productivity without adding much to it, as is sometimes asserted, and considers the effect of education on production as unknown.

Finally, we mention the dual labor market theories or segmentation theories which suggest that wages depend on exogeneous factors, in particular, institutional and power factors. Jobs differ in the relative costs the employer has to sustain to train a person for an adequate job fulfillment. These costs supposedly are not so much sustained before the person enters the job market, but during employment, "on the job." Employers estimate the costs to be made and select those persons for whom these costs are minimal. Determining factors are supposed to be education, sex, age, personality, and the like. In this connection, Thurow (1975, p. 177) mentions the phenomenon of "statistical discrimination." That is, an individual is judged in terms of the average characteristics of the category the person belongs to; if a person has characteristics that on average are favorable in terms of training costs, this person is more likely to be hired. This reasoning can explain why women have lower wages. Supposedly, when employed, they are available to a lesser extent (because of their task in raising children); therefore, they are not so easily employed and have to accept a lower income.

Based on these theories, several analyses of income distribution have been made (e.g. Hartog et al., 1985). Income level turns out to be mainly determined by educational level, age, and sex of the persons seeking a job as well as by level of the job to be fulfilled. Other factors, such as whether there is a collective labor agreement or not, regularity of working times, size of enterprise, and the line turn out to play a small role (Mourits-Ruiter & Van Driel, 1984). The influence of the several factors seems hardly to have changed. In particular, getting a good education is a good strategy to obtain a higher income, although importance of this factor is decreasing. As the number of well-trained persons rises, their relative incomes become lower, mostly because of the resulting relative increased importance of age and the time when enter the job market. When these factors are held constant, education still pays off, though to a decreased extent (Hartog et al., 1985).

In addition, research based on the segmentation theories stresses the importance of factors influencing the chance of obtaining a higher income. For instance, traditionally, women are concentrated in specific, lower-paid jobs. Also, institutional factors, like legal status, the power of labor unions, and internal recruitment for higher positions play a role. This is true particularly for persons who already have a job and who can use the job as a stepping stone to obtain a better-paid job.

This leads to the already mentioned differences between persons with paid jobs on one hand and those who are dependent on social security on the other hand. When both categories are included in the income distribution (Figure 1), it turns out that then 39% of the variance of the distribution in 1981 is explained by the following factors: family stage, age, education, and sources of income of the head of the family and a possible partner (SCP, 1985, p. 93–96). Family heads under 26 or over 65 years of age less often have a partner and have a lower net income. In the second place, income is determined by performing a paid job and having a high education.

Also, unemployment itself is determined by social stratum. Van Schaaijk (1985) shows that unemployment in a poor economy is unequally distributed as well. The increase in unemployment is highest in categories in which unemployment is already high, that is, in categories with a low educational level and in geographical areas having a low-income level, among young workers and those having a high unemployment rate already.

The human capital theories deal only with microjustices; that is, justice is defined in terms of individual capacities collected during a person's lifetime. The scarcity, matching, and allocation theories focus mainly on matters of macrojustice; that is, the scarcity of individual characteristics determines the shape of the income distribution. A more equal income distribution requires a decrease on individually different capacities. In that sense, an increase in macrojustice depends on an increase in microjustice.

Segmentation theories also deal with questions of macrojustice. They stress the persistence of the mutual difference resulting from individual characteristics. These theories are more pessimistic than the matching theories with regard to the possibility of changes in the income distribution; in short, individual capacities (microjustice) are less decisive than institutional factors (macrojustice) for obtaining a certain income.

Judgmental Studies on Income Distribution

Questions on the justice of income differences do not deal only with objective differences of income, but at least as much with the *perception* of differences of income. In this section, we discuss investigations of this topic. After that we will review some investigations dealing with macro- and microjustice.

Several studies have dealt with the way incomes are perceived. Bunjes, Van Geffen, Keuzenkamp, Lijftocht, and Wijga (1977) interviewed 180 employees working in several organizations. The respondents were divided into six salary levels. The data were collected briefly after considerable public discussion on the salary of the prime minister. Nevertheless, persons belonging to level 1 (the lowest level) underestimated this income to a considerable extent and those of the levels 2 and 3 overestimated by just as much. Although the frequent changes in the legal minimum wage are published in the press, knowledge of it turned out to be poor on all levels, even among those who themselves belong to the lowest income level, of which the legal minimum wage is a subset. The salary of their own company director was underestimated by one-third on the average.

Research dealing with curiosity about salary information and the tendency to compare one's own salary to that of others was investigated by Von Grumbkow (1980). One reason for this curiosity is that the need to determine one's own position and improvements in it can be fulfilled on a scale type with a high measurement level. Sums of money can more easily be compared than social values. Von Grumbkow found, in accordance with Festinger's social comparison theory (1954) (compare also the analysis by Syroit, 1984), that people first want "individual" information (information on their own salary, its components, reasons for it, etc.) and only after that "social" salary information (dealing with others' salaries). This result holds similarly for information on the range of the salaries for their own type of function compared to other functions in the company. However, the stronger the perceived competition, the more curiosity for others' salaries there was. The desire to know their own relative position among those of colleagues turns out to be somewhat stronger the higher their own position is. Von Grumbkow found a tendency to underestimate most of the salaries in the company; exceptions were the range of one's own salary category as well as the next lower function. The respondents also reported a tendency in accordance with equity theory; that is, the more favorable the ratio of outcome to input, the stronger the tendency to be satisfied with their own salary and the weaker the desire to reduce their own inputs; no effect was found, however, on the desire to raise their own outcomes.

An important conclusion by Von Grumbkow (pp. 130–131) is that the tendency toward equality sometimes found in experimental research (e.g., Leventhal, 1976; Van Kreveld & Van Beemen, 1978; Van Kreveld, Morgan, Staats, & Verplanken 1981; Kemp & Van Kreveld 1986) is not shown by the opinions he collected in the field.

Some of his findings are applied by Von Grumbkow (1983) on his discussion on the planned but repealed law on the publicity of incomes. This law would have required only a limited amount of information per company to be made public: the number of employees per income category, age, sex, and level of function, as well as the system of determining factors of incomes. One criticism Von Grumbkow expresses on publicity of incomes is that many people will realize that the relationship between effort and results is only weak. This recognition will create a sense of powerlessness and alienation. Therefore, information on the personnel judgment and career system should also be publicized. The proposed law would have hardly provided for publicity on *individual* incomes. Von Grumbkow is in favor of such publicity, to avoid the impression that the differences are unjust, and if they are considered unjust, to begin societal process leading to justness. Social relationships would profit from couplings between behavior and rewards, acceptance of the factors determining these couplings, as well as the confidence that differences in incomes arise according to procedural justice (pp. 137–142).

An interesting and productive line of research is represented by a series of studies on how people evaluate different levels of income (Van Praag & Kapteyn, 1973; Kapteyn, 1977; Van Praag, Kapteyn, & Van Herwaarden, 1979). These investigations demonstrate that an increase of income does not lead to a proportional increase in the satisfaction with that income. Van Praag et. al. distinguish two effects. First there is a preference drift that reflects how individual preferences adapt to individual circumstances. In other words, when an individual's income increases, the need also increase and thus a part of the satisfaction with the income dissipates. After a while, more income is needed for the person to be as satisfied as previously was the case. The second effect is a reference drift: If the average income of the reference group increases, the individual needs more income to remain on the same level of satisfaction.

Kapteyn, et al., (1985; see also Goedhart et al., 1977) mention that in a country with a small income inequality, the subjective minimum (poverty) is located higher than in a country with a large income inequality. Not so much the absolute level of prosperity but rather the income distribution determines the social security; that is, the possibility of paying expenses is considered necessary. In a country with a high prosperity, relatively equal incomes and a high subjective minimum, the social security can be experienced as acutely as in a country in which the income distribution is less favorable. Adaptation or comparison levels change easily, at least upward, a well-known phenomenon of experimental psychological research that holds for social justice as well.

Bunjes et al. asked also which salaries and which differences in salary were considered just, predominantly in terms of macrojustice. Primarily, but not only, in the lower income groups, the respondents were advocates of smaller differences, to be achieved by decreasing high incomes and increasing low incomes. These opinions are a function not only of one's own income but also of the accuracy of the estimations as well: The respondents were in favor of raises the more they underestimated salaries and then were in favor of reductions the more they overestimated salaries. In other words, opinions about the injustice of incomes could in part be explained by misinformation. But in using estimates as a starting point, the respondents on all levels advocated smaller differences, though they did so to a lesser extent the higher the respondents's own income. The obtained opinions are hardly those of revolutionaries: There were practically no advocates of changes in the rankings.

Szirmai came to the same conclusion (1982, p. 60; see also, Szirmai, 1984). He asked his respondents to estimate the incomes of a number of well-known jobs and functions, on a scale from 0 to 300,000 Dutch guilders before tax. After that, he asked them to rate the level of incomes considered just. The implied desired changes are depicted in Table 1. The results reveal a strong expressed desire to level the differences; two thirds of the respondents prefer a redistribution à la Robin Hood: take from the wealthy, give to the poor. Hardly anybody advocates deleveling; in fact only 4.1% want to give more to the wealthy and less to the poor. In a similarly designed Flemish pilot study, Lagrou, Overlaet, and Schokkaert (1981) came to a similar conclusion: a preference for a sizable reduction of the four highest incomes and a small increase of the lowest incomes. Szirmai refers to an ethic of equalization: In all strata of the Dutch population, people are in favor of leveling—however, without always being aware of the consequences to their own income.

Studies by Van Wijngaarden (1982) and Hermkens (1983), preceded by Hermkens and Van Wijngaarden (1977), are a larger extent focused on the *microjustice* of income distributions. In the 1977 study, respondents had to rate 15 criteria justifying differences in wages for labor. On a scale (from 1 to 10), all criteria except one, age, were considered of at least average importance (scale value 6). Also, the results were very similar for all subgroups, whatever their own salary. The only exception was length of working week, which was quite important for respondents having a low income. The authors distinguished between compensating and noncompensating differences in income. Compensating differences result from the working situation,

Table 1. Desired (De)leveling Patterns for Five Highest and Five Lowest Incomes.[a]

High incomes lower, low incomes higher	580	(67.8%)
High incomes the same, low incomes higher	22	(2.6%)
High incomes lower, low incomes the same	68	(7.9%)
High incomes lower, low incomes relatively lower	100	(11.9%)
High incomes higher, low incomes relatively higher	30	(3.5%)
High incomes the same, low incomes the same	20	(2.3%)
Distance between high and low incomes larger	34	(4.1%)
Total	854	(100.0%)

[a]Highest estimated incomes: prime minister, manager of a large enterprise, family doctor, high school teacher, head of a personnel department. Lowest estimated incomes: car mechanic, typist, unskilled laborer, pension plan, and poverty plan. From Szirmai, 1982, p. 75, table 6.8.

like unfavorable working circumstances. Noncompensating differences refer to optimal use of labor, aimed at finding a balance between supply and demand; examples are personal characteristics, performance, custom. Generally as expected, most of the compensating differences were considered relatively more important than noncompensating differences to justify differences in income. Van Kreveld performed some related studies on judgments based on comparison criteria, that is, in terms of microjustice as well. Vermunt and Van Kreveld (1981) used 19 criteria of job evaluation and made respondents judge the desirability of higher or lower payment. Numbers of hours turns out to be considered of prime importance for equity and received supervision least. For the deviation from equality of payments, the following criteria are most important: danger and the number of hours. The least important are status, need, and monotony. The 19 criteria could well be grouped into three factors: personal investment, such as effort, dirty work, responsibility, experience, danger, and supervision; working circumstances, such as draught, humidity, and noise; and production, such as quality and the number of hours. Also found was an age effect: Older people are directed more toward prosperity in the sense that they think people have to devote themselves and perform; younger people are in favor of an optimal working situation, and if that cannot be created, they think workers have to be compensated in pay.

Van Kreveld, Vermunt, and De Vries (1985) investigated to what extent respondents judged that differences in the three factors obtained in the previous study should lead to differences in reward. Rewards were distinguished in two general classes: goods and benefits, represented by pay and recognition (Van Kreveld & Van Beemen, 1978). The respondents judged that devotion must be compensated with recognition, not with pay. Poorer working circumstances have to be compensated with more pay. Better working circumstances, or higher or lower production, do not have to lead to differences in rewards. Also an effect of political preference of the respondents was found. Low inputs have to lead to lower rewards, according to respondents with a right-wing political preference, but not so or to a lesser extent, according to respondents with a left-wing political preference. Wong and Van Kreveld (1983) obtained similar findings: Left-wing respondents were more in favor of equality than right-wing respondents. Also, left-wing respondents took need to a larger extent into account, whereas right-wing respondents were to a larger extent led by equity considerations.

In part based on the previously mentioned research performed with Hermkens, Van Wijngaarden (1982) holds a plea for a national job classification system. In such a system, a balance can be sought between justice and efficiency of the economic system. Of the several advantages described by Van Wijngaarden, we want to mention the possibility of including the independent as well and of using job classification in the national income policy (pp. 185–186). Introduction of such a system depends on whether the national government is willing to promote it as well as whether it is possible for the government to effectively exert so much control.

Most of the aforementioned studies deal specifically with the inequality of income from labor. In several studies, the incomes of households have been judged without restricting the source of income as obtained from a paid job. A vignette survey on judgments of incomes as being too high or too low was performed by Hermkens (1983; see also Hermkens, 1986). A vignette is a short description of a person or a situation containing information that is considered relevant and is to be judged by respondents. (See also Alves & Rossi, 1978; Jasso & Rossi, 1977; Rossi & Nock, 1982.) In this study, hypothetical households were described in terms of specific combinations of the following attributes: occupation, educational level, source of income, sex, number of persons, age, and net family income. Like other authors, Hermkens reports a desire for a decrease in income differences but not to zero. In vignettes with low incomes combined with a high prestige and a long education, the respondents are clearly in favor of increasing incomes. For the lower incomes, the number of family members contributing to the income has no influence on the justice ratings; for higher incomes, the desirable income is higher if more family members contribute to it. Mainly for higher incomes, quality of performance is considered relevant. Amount of working experience does not turn out to have much influence on the judgments.

Hermkens investigated the effects of the respondent's characteristics as well. In general, the effect of these characteristics on the justice ratings is quite small. The assumption that ratings of justice and injustice are self-serving is not confirmed. One's own income does serve as a reference: Respondents who consider their own income as too high do so for other income as well.

An average of 60% of the respondents consider the existing distribution of incomes as unjust (Hermkens, 1983). The low-income groups consider their own income as too low; the others consider their income as adequate. If there exists no possibility of a general raise, the general opinion is that raises should go to the lowest incomes. A large majority of members of higher incomes are, however, against a decrease of their own income.

Comparable to Hermkens' vignette procedure is the procedure applied by Wong and Van Kreveld (1983), who also made respondents judge examples of imaginary payment situations. They compared nonconstant sum situations with opposed interests to constant sum situations (in which interests are necessarily opposed). Many claims for societal changes imply nonconstant sum changes, for instance, more for the poor, but not, or not fully, at the cost of the wealthy (e.g., Table 1). In nonconstant sum situations, there turned out to exists less tendency to favor an equal distribution and more to take account of differences in contribution than in constant sum situations. Primarily equity, but also need and contribution, play an important role as distribution criteria.

Concluding Remarks

Finally, we want to comment on the problem of the income distribution in The Netherlands in general. The findings reviewed indicate a fairly continuous preference to reduce the differences between incomes. The justice criteria born out by these investigations coincide to a considerable extent with the criteria that are actually applied to bring about these income differences. Phillips (1983, p. 318) notices that:

> "although these various investigations differ in their theoretical and methodological approaches to studying the normative standing of economic inequalities, all appear to reach a similar conclusion: what most people find fair, just, equitable, or legitimate in regard to distribution is generally consistent with the actual distribution of rewards or outcomes. This finding is very much in line with Homans' observation that "what is, is always turning into what is right."

We referred already to a similar observation by Walster and Walster (1975).

The question remains which income distribution is meant. Functionalists consider the society as "open": That is, persons can obtain knowledge and abilities and thus reach an attractive position. Conflict theorists refer to conflicting interests and to structural handicaps in reaching an attractive position. It becomes obvious that presently, large numbers of people do not obtain a paid job they are seeking and that the prospect of obtaining that job is unfavorable. This makes it desirable to use not only a job stratification but also another stratification as well to judge justice of income differences, which will probably make the shape of the income distribution more important, in particular in increasing the range of the income distribution. These arguments are in terms of the principles of macrojustice rather than of microjustice, not only hold for the employment situation, but also for the tax situation.

Unemployed persons have not only a financial problem but also other problems as well. Many unemployed want to keep involved in some kind of a working network, in order to improve their chances of a return into the work force, to meet other people, to avoid status loss, to maintain a favorable self image, and the line. If they receive financial gains from these activities, these are partly deducted from unemployment benefits. In connection with this situation, two issues are being discussed on a large scale: how unfair competition with regularly paid jobs can be avoided and to what extent the unemployed should be entitled to keep these gains without the unemployments benefits being reduced. This discussion is complicated by the fact that at the bottom of the scale the differences are so small that sometimes unemployment benefits together with small additional gains result in higher earnings than those of persons regularly employed (see Figure 1).

The macrojustice desire to avoid extremes is one of the causes of high and progressive taxes. For instance, the marginal rate for the income tax is 67% for incomes of approximately f 100,000, and even 77% for incomes of approximately f 240,000. The high rate of the purchase tax is 19% at present. The need for microjustice and—according to the opinions of at least some people—the desire to make possible unobtrusive cuts in social security led to a complicated system of sizable tax deductions. Together with a tradition of relatively weak punishments, these have been conditions for considerable semilegal as well as illegal practices. Recently, indications of both an increase of negative consequences of illegal practices as well as arguments in favor of a simplified taxation system and lower taxes can be noticed.

One consequence of the Dutch tax system is that net incomes are hard to compare. The many and high taxes and deductions confuse any comparison. One could hypothesize that there exists a tendency to be strongly aware of, if not to overestimate and exaggerate, others' advantages and their own disadvantages, as compared to their own advantages and others' disadvantages. Also the result would be not only confusing but biased as well, burdening a morally loaded discussion.

The greater attention for principles of macrojustice leads to comparison of several social groups. The resulting discussion on the application of justice principles is interesting. Should, for instance, the higher government employees be treated as equal to their counterparts in private enterprises, who are better off? Or should they display solidarity with government employees with lower appointments and incomes—and with the still lower incomes of the unemployed who obtain government benefits? The unemployed themselves are supposed to sacrifice in order to contribute to a later decrease of unemployment, which they are supposed to believe will come, at least later and for other members of their social stratum. They are likely to consider this application of macrojustice as unjust. In our opinion, the debate on the justice of income distribution in The Netherlands is dominated by preference for moderately leveling the income distribution in the society (a principle of macrojustice) and not so much paying attention to the determinants underlying such differences (which would be a principle of microjustice). This situation leads to a dilemma in applying principles of justice. The preferences for limiting the differences in income interferes with its application, for instance, the merit principle. Most people are not aware of the dilemma this may create and favor both principles. The resulting tension seems a promising topic of investigation.

References

Alves, W. M., Rossi P. H. (1978). Who should get what? Fairness judgements of the distribution of earnings. *American Journal of Sociology,* 84 541–564.

Arts, W. A., (1984). *Eerlijk delen. Over verdelende rechtvaardigheid en inkomens-beleid* [To each his due. On distributive justice and incomes policy]. Amsterdam: Kobra.

Arts, W. A. (1985). To each his due: Ideas of social justice and Dutch income. *The Netherlands Journal of Sociology,* 22, 318–350.

Becker, G. S. (1984). *Human capital.*. New York: Colombia University Press.

Brickman, P. Folger, R. Goode E.& Schul Y. (1981). Microjustice and macrojustice. In M. J., Lerner S. C. Lerner (Eds.), *The justice motive in social behavior* (pp. 173–202). New York, Plenum.

Bunjes, A. M., Geffen, L. M. H. J. van, Keuzenkamp, T. M., Lijftocht, S. G., Wijga, W. (1977). *Inkomens op tafel* [Incomes above board]. Alphen aan den Rijn: Samsom.

CBS. (1984a). *Verdiende lonen van werknemers in nijverheid en dienstensector ontleend aan het halfjaarlijks loononderzoek,* [Semiannual survey of earnings]. The Hague: Staatsuitgeverij.

CBS. (1984b). *De personele inkomensverdeling 1981, individuen, huishoudens.* [Personal income distribution 1981. Individuals and households]. 's-Gravenhage: Staatsuitgeverij.

Festinger, L. (1954). A theory of social comparison process. *Human Relations,* 1954, 7, 117–140.

Goedhart, Th., Halberstadt, V., Kapteyn, A., & Van Praag, B. M. S. (1977). The poverty line: Concept and measurement. *The Journal of Human Resources,* 1977, 12, 503–504

Grootings, P., & Hövels, B. (1981). *Sociale ongelijkheid in het arbeidsbestel* [Social inequality on the labor market]. Nijmegen: Instituut voor Toegepaste Sociologie.

Grumbkow, J. von. (1980). *Sociale vergelijking van salarissen* [Social comparison of salaries]. Groningen.

Grumbkow, J. von. (1983). *Openbaarheid van inkomens, Psychologische aspecten van het wetsontwerp* [Publicity of incomes. Psychological aspects of a bill]. 's-Gravenhage: Vuga.

Hartog, J. (1980). *Tussen vraag en aanbod* [Between supply and demand]. Leiden: Stenfert Kroese.

Hartog, J. (1981). *Personal income distribution: A multicapability theory.* Boston: Martinus Nijhoff.

Hartog, J. ,(1985). Overscholling? [Overeducation?]. *Economisch-Statistische Berichten,* 70, 152–156.

Hartog, J., Ophem, H. V., and Pfann. G. (1985). *Allocatie en beloning* [Allocation and remuneration]. 's-Gravenhage: Staatsuitgeverij, 1985.

Hermkens, P. L. J. (1983). *Oordelen over de rechtvaardigheid van inkomens.* Verslag van een vignetonderzoek [Judgements on the fairness of incomes; A report on a vignette survey] Amsterdam: Kobra.

Hermkens, P. L. J. (1986). Fairness judgements of the distribution of incomes. *The Netherlands Journal of Sociology,* 1986, 2, 61–71.

Hermkens, P., & van Wijngaarden, P.(1974). *Inkomensongelijkheid en rechtvaardigheidscriteria* [Income inequality and criteria of justification]. 's-Gravenhage: Staatsuitgeverij.

Hoek, M. P., van der. (1985). *Inkomensverdeling: Theorie en beleid* [Income distribution: Theory and policy]. Leiden: Stenfert Kroese.

Homans, G. C. (1974). *Social behavior, its elementary forms.* New York: Harcourt Brace.

Huijgen, F., Riesewijk, B. J. P., Conen, G. (1983). *De kwalitatieve structuur van de werkgelegenheid,* [The qualitative structure of employment]. NPOA-publicatie no. 17. 's-Gravenhage: Staatsuitgeverij.

Jasso, G., Rossi P. H. (1977). Distributive justice and earned income. *American Sociological Review,* 42, 639–651.

Kapteyn, A. (1977). *A theory of preference formation,* PhD dessertation University of Leiden.

Kapteyn, A., Van de Stadt, H., Van de Geer, A. (1985). *Uitkeringen, armoede en welvaart* [Benefits, poverty, and welfare]. *Economisch-Statistische Berichten* 70, 384–389.

Kemp, W., van Kreveld D., (1986). Het verdelen van goederen en voordelen. In A. van Knippenberg *etal.* (Eds.), *Fundamentele sociale psychologie* (pp. 75–94) [The distribution of goods and benefits]. Tilburg: Tilburg University Press.

Kleijn, J. P. de, Stadt, H. van de (1985). Ontwikkelingen in de inkomensverdeling sinds 1970 [Developments in income distribution since 1970]. *Economisch Statistische Berichten,* 70, 1004–1009.

Kreveld, D. van, Beemen E. K. van. (1978). Distributing goods and benefits: A framework and review of research. *Gedrag,* 6, 361–401.

Kreveld, D. van, Morgan, D. F. Staats, H., Verplanken, B. (1981). Gelijkheid is het hoogste goed: het verdelen van een niet-konstante som [Equality is most important: The distribution of a nonconstant sum]. *Gedrag,* 9, 203–218.

Kreveld, D. van, Vermunt, R., de Vries, H. (1985). *How much of what does a person desire for what?* Paper presented to a group meeting, "Justice and Injustice in Interpersonal Relationships," of the European Association of Experimental Social Psychology, Katowice (Poland) Sept. 26–30.

Lagrou, L., Overlaet, B., Schokkaert, E. (1981). Beoordeling van inkomensverschillen, [Judgements of income differentials]. *Psychologica Belgica,* 123–147.

Leventhal, G. S. (1976). The distribution of rewards and resources in groups and organizations. In L. Berkowitz (Ed.), *Advances in experimental social psychology,* Vol. 9. New York: Academic Press.

Mourits-Ruiter, T., van Driel, J., (1984). Achtergronden van beloningsverschillen, [Income differentials]. *Social-economische Maandstatistiek* (Suppl. 5), 5–19.

Pen, J., & Tinbergen, J. (1977). *Naar een rechtvaardigere inkomensverdeling* [Toward a more just income distribution]. Amsterdam: Elsevier.

Phillips, D. L. (1983). The normative standing of economic inequalities. *Sociologische Gids*, 318–350.

Praag, B. M. S. van, Hagenaars A. J. M. *et al.* (1984). GPD-inkomensenquête [GPD income survey]. Leiden: Centrum voor onderzoek van de publieke sector en Gemeenschappelijke Persdienst.

Praag, B. M. S. van Kapteyn A. (1973). Further evidence on the individual welfare function of income: An empirical investigation in The Netherlands. *European Economic Review*, *42*, 33–62.

Praag, B. M. S. van Kapteyn A., van Herwaarden, F. G. (1979). The definition and measurement of social reference spaces. *The Netherlands Journal of Sociology*, *19*, 13–25.

Rossi P. H., Nock, S. L. (Eds), (1982) *Measuring social judgments: The factorial survey approach*, Beverly Hills: Sage.

Rowntree, B. S. (1901). *Poverty: A study of townlife*. London.

Schaaijk, M. van (1985). Starre beloningsverhoudingen, starre werkloosheidsverhoudingen? [Fixed income differentials, fixed unemployment Differentials?]. *Maandschrift Economie*, *49*, 56–69.

Schaaijk, M. van (1986). Pakketvergelijking [Comparison of wages]. *Economisch Statistische Berichten*, *71*, 438–440.

SCP (Social and Cultural Planning Office). (1985). *Berekend Beleid* [Calculated policy]. 's-Gravenhage: Staatsuitgeverij.

Syroit, J. E. M. M. (1984). *Interpersonal injustice: A psychological analysis illustrated with empirical research*. Ph.D. thesis, University of Brabant.

Szirmai, A. (1982). *Matigingsbereidheid en nivelleringsgeneigdheid* [Acceptance of income restraint and preference for income equalization]. Onderzoeksmemorandum 119. Groningen: Economic Institute. 1982.

Szirmai, A. (1984). How do we really feel about income equalization. *The Netherlands Journal of Sociology*, *20*, 115–133.

Thurow, L. C. (1975). *Generating inequality*. New York: Basic Books.

Tinbergen, J. (1953). Naar een rechtvaardiger inkomensverdeling [Toward a more just income distribution]. *Socialisme en Democratie*, *1953*, 354–361.

Tinbergen, J. (1956). On the theory of income distribution. *Weltwirtschaftiches Archiv*, Bd. 77 (no.2), pp. 155–173.

Tinbergen, J. (1975). *Income distribution. Analysis and policy*. Amsterdam: North-Holland.

Vermunt, R., van Kreveld, D. (1981). Vergelijkbare betalingen? De invloed van diverse vergelijkingscriteria op wenselijk geachte betalingsverhoudingen, Gedrag [Comparable payments? The influence of several criteria of comparison on the desirability of payment relations], *Gedrag*, *9*, 125–143.

Verwey-Jonker, H. (1943). *Lage inkomens. Een statistisch onderzoek naar de verdeling der inkomens beneden de belastinggrens in de gemeente Eindhoven* [Lower incomes. Statistics of income differentials in Eindhoven]. Assen: Van Gorcum.

Verwey-Jonker, H. (1985). Poverty in the past and poverty today. *The Netherlands Journal of Sociology*, *21*, 99–109.

Walster, E., Walster G. W. (1985). Equity and social justice. *Journal of Social Issues*, *31*(3), 21–43.

Werf, R. E. J. van der, R. A., Fierloos. (1984). (Ontwikkelingen van bruto loonverschillen 1977–1983 [Development of gross wage differentials, 1977–1983). *Social Maandstatistiek* (Supplement 4, pp. 11–24)

Wiebrens, C. J. (1981). Inkomen en rondkomen, de financiële [positie van huishoudens

in Nederland [Lower incomes. Financial positions of households in The Nether-
lands]. *Social and Cultural Studies 2*, SCP. 's-Gravenhage: Staatsuitgeverij.
Wijngaarden, P. J. van. (1982). Inkomensverdelingsbeleid in de verzorgingsstaat [In-
come distribution in the welfare state). Rechtvaardigingskriteria voor inkomensverschillen uit arbeid, Utrecht, 1982.
Wong, R. A., & van Kreveld, D. (1983). Voorkeuren voor verdelingen zoals bepaald door
situationele en persoonlijke factoren [Preferences for distributions determined by
situational and personal factors). *Mens en Maatschappij*, *58*, 240–254.

7

What Is "Fair" in Japan?

Louise H. Kidder and Susan Muller

Tales of Samurai Honor

In Japanese poetry and folklore, the honorable samurai is often compared to a cherry blossom, destined to die after a brief but glorious blooming. A samurai was expected to sacrifice his own and his family's life for his lord and other samurai. Honor, or "giri," which characterizes the samurai code can be translated as "duty," "obligation," "justice," or "social courtesy" (Saikaku, 1981). The following excerpt from a seventeenth-century Japanese writer illustrates the samurai's sense of duty, obligation, and justice:

> One day the Lord of Itami Castle ordered one of his samurai, Shikibu, to take the lord's son on a long journey to some distant islands. Shikibu took along his own son as well as the sixteen-year-old son of a fellow samurai. Shikibu was responsible for all three boys as well as the group of retainers who helped with the horses and supplies. Rains had swollen the rivers and Shikibu, fearing the waters might be too dangerous, always made his own son cross first to test the current rather than risk the life of his lord's or friend's child. At one particularly dangerous crossing, Shikibu's son reached the other bank safely, but the horse carrying his friend's son stumbled and the boy was swept down the river and disappeared. Shikibu turned to his own son and said, "If you remain alive, I will not be able to fulfill my duty to Lord Tango and preserve my honor as a samurai. And so you yourself must die at once." With true samurai spirit, his son dove into the dangerous waters and disappeared. (Saikaku, translated by Callahan, 1981, pp. 45–47)

Louise H. Kidder and **Susan Muller** • Department of Psychology, Temple University, Philadelphia, Pennsylvania 19122.

Shikibu and his son were acting according to the samurai code of honor or giri—duty, obligation, social courtesy, and justice. The days of samurai law and practice are long gone, but the code of honor in Japan today still contains elements of duty, obligation, and justice reminiscent of Saikaku's story. The problem we explore in this chapter is how the conceptions of obligation and duty that characterize Japanese culture affect what is considered just or fair. We want to be careful not to reify a stereotype of Japan as a "shame culture." Ruth Benedict used that label to describe Japan in 1946 in contrast to the "guilt culture" of the West. That distinction is still useful in understanding some cultural differences such as the meaning of suicide in the two countries (Iga, 1986), but it should not overshadow cultural similarities. For instance, despite the difference in how Americans and Japanese regard persons who occupy positions of authority, there are important similarities in how they react to wrongdoings by authorities (e.g., Hamilton & Sanders, 1983). Therefore, though we are primarily interested in cultural differences, we do not want to ignore commonalities.

In this chapter we explore some of the bases for both the differences and similarities in perceptions of what is "fair." Our interest in this problem was piqued by the senior author's observations of an apparent paradox: In a society so attuned to obligations and entitlements there is no word for "fair" (Kidder, 1986).

Obligations and Social Courtesy

A special set of obligations and social courtesy are enacted daily in the practice of gift giving in Japan. Office workers and neighbors routinely give gifts when they return to work and home after a journey, even if they have been gone for only a weekend. They return with "omiyage" (something "given from the place seen") that are like souvenirs but more obligatory. One's coworkers and neighbors are pleased to receive the gifts, but they also expect them and would be disappointed if there were none. The vacationer acts out of duty and obligation. Giving and receiving omiyage is predictable and almost routine; train stations and bus depots are surrounded by shops that specialize in gift-wrapped souvenirs suitable for office mates and neighbors. Boxes of sweets with logos depicting the temples, lakes, or mountains in that area are appropriate and favored gifts.

Obligatory gift giving is the positive side of a system of social relations based on duty rather than spontaneity. Obligatory self-sacrifice, as portrayed in the story of Shikibu story, is the negative side.

In either case, the donor is obliged to give, and the receiver is obliged to accept the gift or sacrifice. The donor says humbly, "This is nothing, it's worthless, but please accept it," and the recipient accepts with thanks but without adding "you shouldn't have done this," because both know it had to be done.

These are small scenes from a much larger drama of mutual obligations. Gift giving is one of many arenas where there are clear patterns of entitlement in the Japanese system of relationships bound by social courtesy, duty, and respect. The problem we pursue in this chapter is how the question of what is "fair" is both addressed and ignored in a culture where there are such clear and strong patterns of entitlement (cf. Lerner, 1986, paper and personal communication, Leiden).

No Word for "Fair"

There is no word for "fair" in Japanese, at least none that is used in the same way as in English. In conversations with the first author, several scholars and students made the following observations:

> M: We don't even have a word or expression for "fairness." So if you tried to ask people about it, they wouldn't even be able to answer you.
>
> LK: What would the closest word be?
>
> M: Kohei . . . that means fairness, but if you used that word people might assume you were talking about sports . . . fair play, or playing according to the rules . . .
>
> T: Yes, and I think you wouldn't hear that word much in ordinary common conversation. It's just not used much. And I think it's a rather new word.
>
> LK: Since when?
>
> T: Maybe since the Meiji period [1868–1912] . . . Before that it didn't exist . . . Also, the word for "justice" is not used so commonly, and people might not know why you were using it.
>
> LK: What is it?
>
> M: Byoodo . . . that means "justice" but not fairness.

Byoodo means equality, and it is generally used in the context of talking about courts or legal justice.

A student who had spent a year in an American high school added, "I think Americans say "that's not fair" much more than we do." Another student, when asked what he would say in Japanese if someone did something that Americans would describe as "unfair,"

replied "Sore wa 'fair' zya nai" ("That is not 'fair' "), interjecting the
English word because there is no equivalent in Japanese.

There are other terms in Japanese that pertain to justice issues:
"seiji" is roughly equivalent to "politics" and "kohei" means "im-
partial," but neither captures the meaning of "fairness."

The word for "rights" (kenri) was first used in the nineteenth
century when Japanese legal scholars translated Dutch and French
legal codes (Rosch, 1983, p. 709). Even after this word was introduced,
however, it was not used to describe individuals' rights in the same
manner as in France and Holland. Instead it referred to the government's rights to control individuals. The American military and legal
officers who framed the Japanese constitution after World War II and
introduced new institutions to make Japan more like the United States
believed that they could promote greater individualism as an antidote
to what they perceived as totalitarianism in the "old" Japan (Rosch,
1983). In 1948 members of the American occupation and the Japanese
Ministry of Justice established the Japanese Civil Liberties Bureau to
promote individual rights by enabling persons to bring claims against
the government. Citizens used the civil liberties bureaus to settle
community disputes instead, and the heads of the bureaus served as
mediators, settling family and neighborhood disputes. For instance,
one resident of an apartment building came to the civil liberties bureau
to complain that other members of his building did not greet him but
seemed to shun him. He wanted to be recognized and properly treated,
and he presumably received some satisfaction. Rather than change
Japanese values, the civil liberties bureaus buttressed the traditional
emphasis on social rights—"how group members ought to treat each
other and how people of higher status ought to treat those of lower
status" (Rosch, 1983, p. 710). The citizens and bureau heads transformed this new institution so that it served Japanese tradition rather
than replacing it with American customs.

Japanese language and culture place great emphasis on certain
forms of entitlement—entitlement to respect, to politeness, to honor.
Workers use honorific verbs to describe their boss's acts, humble verbs
to describe their own. A wife speaks respectfully of her own husband
as "master," and even more respectfully of someone else's as "honorable master," particularly if she is speaking to an older person. A man
refers to his own wife as kannai or "the person taking care of the
family, inside the house" and refers to another man's wife as okusan or
"honored woman inside the house."

A person refers to another's house with the honorific prefix o
attached to the polite word for "dwelling" and uses a different and
more humble word to refer to her own. One's elders, supervisors,

teachers, and acquaintances are entitled to honorific prefixes, suffixes, and an entire class of verbs and nouns reserved for speaking "up."

Japanese language and culture are finely tuned for expressing respect, honor, and politeness. Do these entitlements enhance or submerge a concern with "justice"? Is it of significance that there is no equivalent of the English word for "fair"? (cf. Shotter, 1986)

Hamilton et al. (1983) point out that there are some universal reactions to wrongdoing (p. 208). Japanese and Americans share a concern for justice and make similar judgments about actors' responsibility for wrongdoing. Respondents in both cultures hold authorities more responsible than equals for harm they have done. And in both cultures, respondents assigned more responsibility to a wrongdoer who acted out of anger than to one who inflicted harm through carelessness. Japanese respondents, however, assigned more responsibility to authorities than Americans did, and Americans placed more emphasis on the harmdoer's emotional state than Japanese do. Therefore, Hamilton and Sanders found main effects of authority and emotional state in both cultures and also interactions between those variables and the respondents' culture.

This experimental evidence that authorities in Japan are held more responsible for wrongdoing than their counterparts in the United States is consistent with the public apologies that leaders of Japanese industry and government have made in the past. When Japanese residents in the town of Minamata suffered severe deterioration of the nervous system in adults and birth defects in children, they expected the president of the chemical company responsible for their mercury poisoning to make a public apology as well as restitution (Wagamatsu and Rosett, 1986). They regarded him as personally responsible.

If we believe these experimental, anecdotal, and historical examples, we must conclude that far from being unconcerned with justice, the Japanese are intensely concerned. But the conception of what is fair and whether it is so named differ in important ways from American and European conventions.

Japanese language and culture involve elaborate expressions of respect and humility. The person who is older and higher in authority is entitled to honorific terms of address; the younger and lower status person is obliged to use humble self-referents. Do these conditions enhance or obscure a concern with what is "fair"? Is it possible that the linguistic and cultural conditions that place a premium on honor and respect shroud what Americans would call questions of "fairness" despite the otherwise strong concerns with justice and responsibility for wrongdoing.

We will examine the system of entitlements contained in the

language and culture of respect to see how that might determine
"what's fair." And we will describe the context in which Japanese
students and employees work very hard to succeed—with a premium
on collective instead of individual well-being—to see whether "what's
fair" takes on different meanings.

Speaking Humbly and Honorifically

The language and culture make respect, honor, humility, and politeness very salient. Like many European and non-European languages,
Japanese has polite and plain verb forms. Speakers also attach honorific prefixes to nouns, including the otherwise humble words like *toilet*
and the word that describes the dried husks of soy beans left over after
everything edible has been extracted. The prefix is a sign of respect—
even the humble soy husks deserve to be honored for all they have
provided.

If these forms of honor and respect were used by all speakers, the
language would tell us about a universal code of respect. They are used
differentially, however, and the asymmetrical use of polite language
makes it difficult for people of lower status to talk about and perhaps
even to perceive "injustice."

Men and Women Talking

Compared with men's language, women's language is replete with
honorifics. The different words for "I" are just the beginning. Women
should never use the man's term ("'boku"') because it sounds crude and
impolite. Men use the women's word for I ("'watashi"') when they want
to sound respectful and considerate. Speaking to a superior or in polite
company, they say "I" as women do; speaking among friends or
family, they use the cruder "boku."

Parents explicitly teach their daughters not to speak like sons. A
Japanese instructor was disturbed when she heard junior-high-school
girls talking "like boys," and she corrected her daughter if she spoke
that way. They were not curse words that she forbade but the less
polite, less respectful forms. Non-Japanese women who marry Japanese
men and learn the language from their husbands can be a source of
amusement. Their language sounds rude or crude, but they are excused
because they are foreigners. Foreign men who learn the language from
their Japanese wives sound inappropriately polite and humble.

The first author was particularly struck by the irony of a discussion about language with a radical feminist, an organizer of a rape crisis center in Japan:

> LK: I'm interested in the use of language . . . men's and women's . . . and whether there's any movement to change that.
>
> Organizer: Why do you think women should change? Don't you think it's nice that we speak politely . . . I mean, I think that's one of the nice things about Japanese society. . . our politeness.

She added that she uses honorific words when speaking to a superior and uses humble terms in reference to herself because "we have to, you know, or we get into a lot of trouble."

The risk of "getting into a lot of trouble" was echoed by feminist scholars talking about the words they must use when referring to husbands and the words husbands use when referring to wives:

> TS: One of the things Japanese women are talking about now is how to call their husbands . . . whether to call them "master" or not.
>
> LK: What are the alternatives?
>
> TS: Alternatives? "Shujin" [meaning "master"] is what we should say when we talk about our husbands, and "goshujin" [honorable master] if we are talking about someone else's husband. But now some women don't want to. I say "goshujin" if I'm talking to an older person . . . or talking to my boss . . . but inside it doesn't feel right . . . I don't like it.
>
> YM: And when husbands call their wives, you know what they say [they both laughed] "dirty old pig . . ."
>
> LK: Really? What is the word . . . is it "oi"? [I had been told previously that husbands sometimes call out "oi" when they want their wives' attention. No one could give me a translation of the term, other than to say it means what it sounds like.]
>
> YM: They say "kannai" when they're talking about their own wives . . . but that really has no direct translation in English . . . it means literally "person inside the house."
>
> TS: Some women are talking about whether to call their husbands by first names . . . that's what I do with my husband. But many women wouldn't do that. And around older people, you can get into trouble if you don't say "shujin" or "goshujin." So we still do that around them. Because they wouldn't understand. They would think something about us, like that we are impolite. And it's so important in Japanese society to be polite.

These women were able to talk about their language and how it places men and women because they also spoke another language—English—and could compare the two. They all thought it was unlikely, however, that most Japanese women would think about these issues:

YM: . . . especially for Japanese women . . . I don't think they think
much about "fairness." They think mainly about enduring . . . and
accepting . . . and making do

Language as a Social Issue

When the first author asked Japanese students and colleagues about
language as a "social issue" they often answered with another question. Some respondents asked, "Don't you think it's nice that we speak
politely?" Others said simply, "What do you mean?" For some people
the question "What do you think of the issue of men's and women's
language . . . Do you think there should be any changes?" sounded as
bizarre as "What do you think of the issue of men's and women's facial
hair . . . Do you think women should grow beards?"

Other respondents did recognize language as a social issue with a
set of attendant problems. Students who anticipate working in offices
know they will have to change how they speak:

H: I noticed some friends of mine who are working now and talking so
differently . . . they've gone to work for companies and they really
talk differently.
LK: You mean more formally . . . ?
H: Maybe that's it . . . it just sounds strange now when I meet them . . .
they've changed.

Some students attend special language courses before they enter
the work world. They practice the most honorific forms of address
before meeting the boss.

Two other informants, one a sociologist and the other a student of
linguistics, said they have noticed that men and women living in rural
Japan speak more plainly and more like each other than people living
in the cities:

T: I noticed that out in the small villages in the countryside, men and
women talk the same to one another. They don't use this different kind
of language that women and men use here in the city . . . it's like what
you were saying before. I noticed this and it seemed strange. But I
think maybe they're more equal there in the country than here in
Tokyo. We think we're so modern and more liberated, and they are
traditional, but maybe in some ways the women in the villages have
more equality. I remember noticing this in how they talked with men.

Even in the cities, not all women speak politely all the time. They
use plain language when they are among friends. And junior-
high-school girls have become notorious for using crude language—

they refer to themselves with the man's "I" ("boku"), much to their parents' and teachers' dismay. Nonetheless, the obligation to be polite and humble is an almost omnipresent burden carried by most speakers of Japanese. Even those who regard language as a social issue have few visions of changing it. A speaker who violates the rules risks "getting into trouble" and being discredited in the very act of speaking. A speaker who respects the rules and talks humbly and politely about how language constrains relationships and shrouds injustice works under the handicap of humility.

Speech is not the only conveyor of honor and humility or politeness and consideration. Proper speech is accompanied by proper nonverbal behavior. Nonverbal signs of respect are naturally learned and conveyed in all cultures. They stand out in greater relief in Japan, however, because bowing is a pronounced and conscious act.

Ranks—Verbal and Nonverbal Markers

An essential part of an introduction in Japan is the immediate exchange of business cards, handed to one another just before bowing. This permits each to note the other's title and rank. With this quick glance, the speakers know which one should be accorded more respect, expressed in the choice of verbs and nouns and in the nonverbal language of the body. The person of lower status bows first, lower, longer, and more frequently; the body mirrors the words.

People who are bilingual in Japanese and English are bilingual in body as well as words. A Japanese student who had lived in the United States for 6 years returned to Tokyo for research in the summer. When he was introduced to a Japanese office manager and then to an American faculty member, there was a marked change in his bearing. Asked if he noticed any differences in how he felt when he was speaking Japanese and English, he said, "Yes, I guess it's in the muscle tension." He held himself taut, bowed carefully, and directed his gaze down toward his feet while talking with the office manager. When the same student spoke with an American professor, he relaxed his body and looked directly into the other's face.

Foreigners who learn to speak Japanese can "get into trouble" if they learn only the verbal forms of honor. An American visiting professor spoke Japanese well enough to address the woman of the house with the most honorific words ("oksamma" instead of the plainer "oksan"). The woman's son knew something was wrong, however, as he watched his mother's reaction. The professor's words were correct, but his body betrayed him. He was too relaxed, he sat with his legs crossed and his arms folded. If he really meant "ok-samma," he would have sat on the edge of his chair, arms at his side and legs together. The net effect was insulting—his words sounded hypocritical because his body conveyed no respect.

The postural markers of respect in Japan are taught explicitly; parents teach their children how to bow and to whom even before the child can walk. A parent takes the head of a babe in arms and bows it while saying "hello" or "goodbye" to someone else. Office workers also receive lessons in bowing. (The Western tradition of teaching children to bow or curtsy was also explicitly taught in former days. Now children in the West learn more by observation than by direct instruction, and few of them bow or curtsy.)

Another Vertical Society

Military language and culture similarly construct and protect hierarchical relationships. Military manners are finely tuned to recognize status and pay respect. Forms of address are asymmetrical. The verbal and nonverbal markers of respect inhibit discussions about "injustice" in that context.

Terms of address like "sir" are analogous to the honorific forms of address in Japanese, and saluting is similar to bowing—the lower rank person salutes first, longer, and more frequently. In social relations with such clearly prescribed verbal and nonverbal forms of respect and obedience, subordinates do not openly question the "fairness" of the relationship because the hierarchy is taken for granted. Inequality is the ground rather than the figure, and the Gestalt is preserved by the asymmetrical verbal and nonverbal communications. This is the nature of vertical society (cf. Nakane, 1971).

Collective versus Individual Well-Being

The social psychological literature on cultural differences in distributive justice presents a mixed picture. Several scholars have proposed that China, Japan, and Korea have a collective rather than individualistic orientation to justice and persons living in those societies should accordingly prefer less "selfish" solutions to problems of distributive justice (e.g., Bond, Leung, & Wan, 1982; Hofstede, 1984; Hui, 1984; Hsu, 1972). In an experimental paradigm where the "subject" completes more work than a coworker, the subject should choose to divide the rewards equally; and when the subject performs less well than a coworker, the subject should choose a proportional or equitable distribution. By contrast, in individualistically oriented societies like the United States, Canada, or Western Europe, people would be expected to maximize their own gains by choosing equality when they have performed less well and equity when they have performed better than their coworkers.

Some research has borne out these predictions (e.g., Bond, Leung, & Wan, 1982; Leung & Bond, 1982; Leung & Bond, 1984). Chinese subjects sacrificed self-gain to benefit in-group members more than American subjects did. Lerner's theoretical model of the justice motive also includes a consideration of the nature of the relationship between persons and portrays an in-group or "unit" relationship as more conducive to self-sacrifice or equality (Lerner, 1975).

Not all of the cross-cultural data fit the predicted pattern. Not all Chinese, Korean, and Japanese subjects respond more collectively or self-sacrificially than all North American subjects (e.g., Leung & Iwawaki, 1988). Nonetheless, the general principle is still useful and interesting.

Controlling Oneself Rather Than Others

Avoiding conflict and confrontation does not necessitate being passive. On the contrary, it can mean trying actively to fit in, to be part of a group, to maintain good social relations. Some of the social–psychological conceptions of what it means to be instrumental or "in control" are particularly middle class and American. For instance, Michelle Fine has described how one rape survivor maintained control over her fate by *not* reporting the rape to the police and not prosecuting the assailant (Fine, 1985).

Trying to influence the world through personal agency or domination is what Weisz, Rothbaum and Blackburn (1984) call "primary control." An alternative means of control, "secondary control," is trying to fit one's own expectations, interpretations, and goals to existing reality (Weisz, Rothbaum and Blackburn, 1984). Japanese tend to exhibit the latter and Americans the former means of control. Neither is by definition "more controlling," but their different modes create the conditions for cultural misunderstanding. Americans are likely to be seen as "pushy" and "selfish" and Japanese as "devious" or "inscrutable" (Weisz et al; 1984). Americans have an internal and Japanese an external locus of control (Mahler, Greenberg, & Hayashi, 1981; Weisz et al; 1984;). Japanese have lower scores on the Just World

Scale, prefer equality over equity, and believe that individuals have only limited effectiveness when they act alone (Mahler, Greenberg and Hayashi, 1981).

Horizontal Ties That Obviate What Is "Fair"

We have so far portrayed Japan as a vertical society. Honor, respect, and politeness are cultural values that derive from and sustain a hierarchy. Two additional values that promote horizontal rather than vertical relationships also tend to preclude a concern with "fairness" as we know it in the West. One is the value of harmony and, consequently, the avoidance of conflict. The other is an emphasis on group identity and consequent loyalty.

Wa—The Japanese Way, the Way of Harmony

The written character, pronounced WA, that refers to "Japanese," as in "Japanese food" or "Japanese clothing" or a "Japanese-style room," is also the character for "harmony." It represents the picture of many voices speaking together, harmoniously not disputatiously. Harmony is highly prized, and it is part of the "Japanese way."

People who do not act with respect, politeness, and harmony, are regarded as "not Japanese." For instance, in talking about a child who was aggressive and brusque by Japanese standards, a neighbor said "she does not seem like a Japanese girl." And a Japanese-American woman who returned to Tokyo to visit relatives was told that her daughter did not act like a Japanese.

Rudeness is not part of the "Japanese way." A rough quality, even a readiness to fight, is , by contrast, associated with American culture, as illustrated in the following scene from televised English language lessons in Tokyo:

> A husband and wife are talking at the breakfast table. He finishes reading the newspaper and stands up, saying, "I'm going for a walk in the park." She replies, "Now dear, you're not going to get into a fight, are you?"

This sequence was enacted to illustrate the use of a question that has the form "You're not going to do such-and-such, are you?" The scene struck the senior author as peculiar—a middle-class couple with fancy tea cups and silver, his talk of going for a walk in the park followed by her admonition not to get into a fight. Why were those words chosen to illustrate that grammatical point? Perhaps our normal daily interactions (in the United States) appear so impolite by Japanese standards that we appear ready to "get into a fight" at any moment. The Japanese emphasis on harmony constrains considerations of justice at both the interpersonal and intergroup levels. When the first author was teaching social psychology in Tokyo, her students discussed American race relations with great clarity and interest. They talked freely about American racial stereotypes and about discrimination in employment, housing, and social relations. When the professor suggested that the class examine some Japanese examples, such as the position of Koreans living in Japan or another group known as the Burakumin (literally, "village people" whose ancestors were butchers and leather workers and were considered polluted), the class became silent. No one wanted to discuss discrimination in employment, marriage, and other social relations among groups living in Japan. After class, a student asked whether the professor thought social problems would be resolved more effectively by talking about them or by ignoring them. He thought harmony would be best served by not discussing difficult issues.

Someone who says "this is not fair" risks creating disharmony. Naming an injustice breaks the surface of what previously seemed like natural or normal social relations. Naming, blaming, and claiming are stages in the emergence of disputes that are by their nature the antithesis of harmony (cf. Felstiner, Abel & Sarat, 1980–1981.

An American informant who has lived in Tokyo for 7 years made the following observations:

> S: You have to forget your American ways of thinking to understand the women's movement here. It's nothing like in the U.S. Because the whole culture is so different . . . The culture is based on the value of harmony, and you'll never see the kind of confrontational tactics used here that were used in the women's movement in the U.S. . . . There was one confrontational group . . . called the Pink Helmets, and their leader would go around with female body guards . . . That kind of thing gets the media attention but it doesn't attract a following here in Japan.

The value of harmony is consistent with the requirements of respect, honor, and politeness. Even without those vertical markers, however, the desire to maintain harmony by itself prohibits a loud cry for "justice."

Maintaining group harmony is often at odds with making claims for individual rights. If relations within the group become discordant, persons might appeal to some higher authority to restore their rights. Our earlier example of an apartment resident who felt shunned by his neighbors described a claim filed by one individual against others—but it was an effort to restore rather than disrupt group harmony (Rosch, 1983).

Uchi—My Home, My Group

"Uchi" means "my house," as opposed to "your house." It is a humble term because it refers to oneself, and it expresses a sense of belonging. The same word that refers to my house also refers to my workplace, my team. Belonging together implies being loyal, and one's loyalty to the group places further constraints on any claim for individual rights. A loyal member who is asked to make some sacrifice for the group should not turn around and say, "that's not fair." The group's interests should come first. The following incident illustrates the choice between group and individual interests.

Randy Bass is an American baseball player who was hired by the Hanshin Tigers in Japan. He broke batting records, which endeared him to his team members, but he also broke social conventions in ways that risked his career. In the middle of the 1984 baseball season, Randy rushed home to see his father who was suddenly hospitalized for a massive heart attack in Oklahoma. His father died and Bass returned to his team in Japan amidst strong criticism for leaving in midseason. He was unfavorably compared with a Japanese player who had left his own father's wake early to play that evening's game. Bass had placed loyalty to his own family ahead of loyalty to his team and this was a breach of obligation to the "uchi" or "house" that hired him. He was not forgiven until he wept publicly as Japanese reporters questioned him about his unusually long absence (Neff. 1987). When individual entitlements run counter to collective interests, the group's rights prevail in Japan, and the "house" one joins has a greater claim to one's loyalty than the group we ordinarily call "home."

Conclusion

Perhaps "what's fair" is a peculiarly American obsession. Children in the United States learn at an early age to say "that's not fair" not only about sports and games but also about parents' rules and restrictions and about teachers' exams and grades. They question authority, create conflict,and split apart from their group if they think they have been treated unfairly; and they appear to have a low threshold for perceiving unfairness. Japanese language and culture anchor the other end of the spectrum. Elaborate systems of respect and honor create and sustain a vertical society where "what's fair" is less important than "what's respectful or polite." The horizontal bonds of harmony and group identity further deemphasize individual entitlement. So it comes as no surprise that there is no word for "fair."

References

Benedict, R. (1946). The chrysanthemum and the sword: Patterns of Japanese culture. New York: New American Library.

Bond, M. H., Leung, K. & Wan, K. C. (1982). How does cultural collectivism operate? The impact of task maintenance contributions on reward allocation. Journal of Cross-Cultural Psychology 13, 186–200.

Bond, M. H., & Tornatzky, L. G. (1973). Locus of control in students from Japan and the United States: Dimensions and levels of response. Psychologia, 16, 209–213.

Doi, T. (1973). The anatomy of dependence. Tokyo: Kodansha International Ltd.

Felstiner, W., Abel, R., & Sarat, A. (1981). The emergence and transformation of disputes: Naming, blaming, and claiming. Law and Society Review, 15 (3).

Fine, M. (1983–1984). Coping with rape: critical perspectives on consciousness. Imagination, Cognition and Personality, 3 (3), 249–267.

Hamilton, V. L. & Sanders, J. (1983). Universals in judging wrongdoing: Japanese and Americans compared. American Sociological Review, 48, 199–211.

Hofstede, G. (1984). Culture's consequences: International differences in work-related values. Beverly Hills: Sage.

Hsu, F. L. K. (Ed.). (1972). Psychological anthropology. Cambridge, MA: Schenkman.

Hui, H. C. C. (1984). Individualism-collectivism: Theory, measurement, and its relation to reward allocation. Unpublished doctoral dissertation, University of Illinois at Urbana–Champaign.

Iga, M. (1986). The thorn in the chrysanthemum: Suicide and economic success in modern Japan. Berkelev, CA: University of California Press.

Ihara, S. (1981). Tales of samurai honor (Buke giri monogatari; trans. Caryl Ann Callahan). Tokyo: Monumenta Nipponica, Sophia University.

Kidder, L. H. (1986). No Word for "Fair" Notes from Japan. Paper presented at the International Conference on Social Justice in Human Relations, University of Leiden, The Netherlands.

Lerner, M. J. (1991). Integrating societal and psychological rules. The basic task of each social actor and fundamental problem for the social sciences. In Riël Vermunt and Herman Steersma (Eds.) Social Justice in Human Relations, Volume 1: Societal and Psychological Origins of Justice (pp. 00–00). New York: Plenum Press.

Lerner, M. J. (1975). The justice motive in social behaviour: introduction. Journal of Social Issues, 31 (1), 1–20.

Leung, K. (1987). Some determinants of reactions to procedural models of conflict resolution: A cross-national study. Journal of Personality and Social Psychology, 53, 898–908.

Leung, K., & Bond, M. H. (1982). How Chinese and Americans reward task-related contributions: A preliminary study. Psychologia, 25, 32–39.

Leung, K., & Bond, M. H. (1984). The impact of cultural collectivism on reward allocation. Journal of Personality and Social Psychology, 47, 793–804.

Louise H. Kidder and Susan Miller

Leung, K., & Iwawaki, S. (1988). Cultural collectivism and distributive behavior: A cross-national study. *Journal of Cross-Cultural Psychology, 19*, 35–49.

Mahler, I, Greenberg, L., & Hayashi, II. (1901). A comparative study of rules of justice: Japanese versus American. *Psychologia, 24*, 1–8.

Nakane, C. (1970). *Japanese society*. Berkeley: University of California Press.

Neff, C. (1987). The hottest American import in Japan: Hanshin's Randy Bass found fame a long way from home. *Sports Illustrated, 66*, 72–79.

Rosch, J. (1983). Institutionalizing mediation: The evolution of the civil liberties bureau in Japan. *Law and Society Review, 18*(1), 701–724.

Saikaku, I. (1981). Tales of samurai honor (Buke giri monogatari). Trans. Caryl Ann Callahan. Tokyo: Monumenta Nipponica, Sophia University.

Wagatsuma, H., & Rosett, A. (1986). The implications of apology: Law and culture in Japan and the United States. *Law and Society Review, 20* (4), 461–498.

Weisz, J. R., Rothbaum, F. M., & Blackburn, T. C. (1984). Standing out and standing in: The psychology of control in America and Japan. *American Psychologist, 39* (9), 955–969.

8

Distributive Justice and Social Welfare Institutions

Guillermina Jasso

Introduction

This chapter* describes how the basic sense of distributive justice leads to predictions concerning the emergence and maintenance of social welfare institutions. To accomplish this purpose, it is necessary to adopt as working tools, first, a definition of social welfare institutions, and, second, a theory of the distributive-justice force. Distilling from the literature on institutions, we define an *institution* as *a patterned individual and/or social behavior, a prevailing way of doing something, with variation possible across space and time.* Narrowing the focus, we take a *social welfare institution* to be an institution that *promotes the social welfare of the population.* For the working description of the distributive-justice force, from which we will derive implications for the emergence and maintenance of social welfare institutions, we use the theory proposed by Jasso (1980).

The theory of the distributive-justice force provides a mathematical description of the operation of the sense of distributive justice, a process whereby individuals, reflecting on their holdings of goods they value, experience an instantaneous particular magnitude of the justice

*This chapter, written in June 1987, is a revised version of a paper presented at the International Conference on Social Justice in Human Relations, in July 1986. Subsequent work, reported in Jasso (1988b, 1989ab, 1990ab), provides a simpler and more general axiomatization, a more compact notation, and elaboration of the predictions.

Guillermina Jasso • Department of Sociology, University of Iowa, Iowa City, Iowa 52242.

evaluation J, a magnitude that captures their sense of being fairly or unfairly treated in the distributions of the natural and social goods. The justice evaluation J spans the full real-number line, so that zero represents the point of perfect justice, the positive segment represents degrees of unjust overreward, and the negative segment represents degrees of unjust underreward. The theory proposes that J may play a part in the determination of many phenomena at both the individual and social levels. At the individual level, both instantaneous J and intertemporal sequences of J are of interest, whereas at social levels, parameters of instantaneous distributions of J and of temporal sequences of J distributions are thought to govern many diverse phenomena. Particularly pertinent to the present chapter, the theory proposes that individual well-being is an increasing function of instantaneous J and that the arithmetic mean of a collectivity's distribution of instantaneous J measures the collectivity's *social welfare*.

Thus the theory of the distributive-justice force offers a way to systematically explore the connections between particular institutions and the collectivity's distribution of the justice evaluation J, in particular, its mean the social welfare.[1] The theory, grounded at the individual level, enables disciplined inquiry of effects at both micro- and macrolevels.

In this chapter we first derive the basic social welfare institutions that can be predicated from the relations embodied in the social welfare relation. Next we focus on two sets of institutional phenomena, monastic institutions and societal selection of valued goods. Both kinds of institutions have played important parts in the history of the human species. Yet little is known about their causal origins. Why did monasticism arise? Why do some societies value birth, whereas others value wealth? Under what conditions would monasteries and new valued goods arise? Under what conditions would they disappear? We shall formulate models that yield the distributive-justice theory's answers to these questions. And, although we are innocent of the number and kind of forces jointly operating to produce these institutions and, as well, offer no more than a child's approximation to the workings of the distributive-justice force, nonetheless our hope is that the work reported in this chapter may lead others to more faithful descriptions and hence to more precise understandings.

The chapter is organized as follows: Section 2 summarizes the basic elements and formulas of the theory of the distributive-justice

---

[1] As well, the theory provides a way to map the connections between institutions and the magnitudes and magnitude changes of the J of individuals. That task, however, is beyond the scope of the present chapter.

force. In Section 3 we investigate the social welfare postulate, describing the effects on social welfare of economic inequality, population size, and variability in what individuals regard as just for themselves. Section 4 reviews the idea of an institution and reports derivation of the three basic social welfare institutions that can be predicted from the theory. In Section 5, we formulate a collectivistic model of how societies choose the goods they value and, using tools from the study of probability distributions, derive general predictions concerning the choice of valued goods in two-goods contests. Section 6 reports derivation of the theory's predictions concerning the social welfare benefit that monastic institutions confer on the noncloistered world. A brief summary concludes the chapter.

Basic Elements of the Theory of the Distributive-Justice Force

The Individual's Sense of Distributive Justice

Basic Postulates. The distributive-justice theoretical framework begins with a core of four basic postulates, which jointly describe the operation of the sense of distributive justice:

Postulate 1. Self-Assessment. Humans (behave as if they)[2] reflect on their goods—that is, those endowments, attributes, and possessions that rational persons are presumed to want and that are thought to increase happiness. Humans (behave as if they) measure (1) their holdings of nonadditive, nontransferable goods (termed quality goods), such as beauty, intelligence, or athletic skill, by their relative rank within a specially selected comparison group termed the comparison aggregate, and (2) their holdings of additive, transferable goods (termed quantity goods), such as wealth, income, or land, in the good(s)' own units. The generic label for an individual's actual amount or level of a good is actual term.

Postulate 2. Notions of Justice. Humans (behave as if they) form notions of the amount or level of a good they regard as just for themselves. These just holdings are measured in the same way as the actual holdings, namely quantity goods in their own units and quality goods as relative ranks within a comparison aggregate. The generic label for an individual's just amount or level of a good is just term.

---

[2]The "as-if" qualifiers are inserted in the statement of the opening postulates in order to highlight the metaphorical nature of a scientific theory. Later, for convenience, they are omitted but remain implicit.

Postulate 3. Comparison. Humans (behave as if they) compare their actual amount or level of a good to the amount or level they regard as just for themselves.

Postulate 4. The Justice Evaluation. The basic operation of the sense of distributive justice produces an (instantaneous) magnitude termed the *justice evaluation* (J). The measurement scale employed for the justice evaluation assigns the positive segment of the real-number line for the condition of overreward and the negative segment for underreward, with zero denoting the point of perfect justice. The justice evaluation is specified as the logarithm of the ratio of the actual term to the just term, a form that quantifies the common human opinion that deficiency is felt more keenly than comparable excess.[3]

As this statement of the core postulates shows, the theory of the distributive-justice force proposed in Jasso (1980) may be regarded as a self-consistent formalization of basic ideas in several literatures, especially the ideas of Homans (1974) and of Berger, Zelditch, Anderson, and Cohen (1972), animated by the logarithmic specification of the justice-evaluation function, which was found empirically through Jasso's (1978) analyses of factorial survey data generated by Rossi's method (Alves, 1982; Rossi 1978; Jasso & Rossi, 1977; Rossi 1951, 1979; Rossi & Anderson 1982; Rossi & Berk 1985).[4]

The statement of the four basic postulates incorporates into the self-assessment and notions-of-justice postulates the basic measurement principle, which distinguishes between cardinal and ordinal goods and which plays an important part in all subsequent theoretical

---

[3]The words we use to name the basic force we are attempting to describe—the distributive-justice force—and to name the concepts upon which operations are performed—for example, actual term and just term—do not share in the fundamental character of the force, the concepts, and the operations. These labels seem appropriate in one language, English, and may seem less or more appropriate in others. Indeed, it is humbling that the words we use are absent from some languages (see Kidder, 1986). Perhaps what Mendelssohn said about music applies to social science theory: The ideas are too precise for words and require a nonverbal language, such as music or mathematics, for their expression.

[4]Jasso (1980) traces the origins of the propositions in the theory to classical, Patristic, Scholastic, and Renaissance social thinkers and to the contributions and analyses of Merton and Rossi (1950), Kelley (1952), Festinger (1954), Merton (1957), Hyman (1968), and Sherif (1968). The form of the theory owes much to the lessons of Berger, Zelditch, and Anderson (1972). For extensions, refinements, applications, and commentary concerning the theory of the distributive-justice force, see Soltan (1981), Jasso (1981, 1982, 1983a, 1986, 1987a, 1988a,), Wagner and Berger (1985), Gartrell (1985, 1987), Markovsky (1985), Markovsky and Ford (1987), Shepelak and Alwin (1986), Alwin (1987), and Mirowsky (1987). The framework yields testable implications for a wide range of human individual and social phenomena.

analysis. We note that this statement may be unduly restrictive in its characterization of the second postulate. That is, it is possible that the essential feature is that humans form *expectations*, as theorized by Berger and his associates (Berger, Fisek, Norman, & Wagner 1985; Ridgeway & Berger 1986) and that notions of justice constitute merely one subclass of a wider and more basic class of expectations.

Basic Distributive-Justice Formulas. The postulate core yields immediately the basic general formula of the justice evaluation *J*:

Justice evaluation $= ln$ [(actual term)/(just term)]   (1.a)

Justice evaluation $= ln$ (actual term) $- ln$ (just term).   (1.b)

The basic general formula can be restated in a form that notices whether the valued good is a quantity good or a quality good:

$$J = \begin{cases} ln \text{ [(actual amount)/(just amount)], quantity good} \\ \\ ln \text{ [(actual rank)/(just rank)],} \qquad \text{quality good.} \end{cases} \quad (2)$$

At this point a problem arises: Although the theory provides the specification of the justice-evaluation function and although the numerator of the argument of the log is more or less discernible, the denominator of the argument is not. The theory does not include a postulate to describe *determination* of the just term.[5] Thus, it is necessary for us, in order to proceed, to use a *representation* of the just term, one that, albeit not descriptive of its origins, is faithful to its value. Following the reasoning in Jasso (1980), as extended and refined in Jasso (1986), we propose to represent the just term by the product of two factors, (1) the arithmetic mean of the distribution of the valued good in a collectivity, and (2) an idiosyncratic factor, denoted phi (ø), capturing all individual-specific influences on formation of the just term. Formally:

$$J = \begin{cases} ln(\phi N/\phi S), & \phi > 0, & \text{quantity good} \\ \\ ln[2i/\phi(N + 1)], & 0 < \phi < 2, & \text{quality good,} \end{cases} \quad (3)$$

where x denotes the individual's amount of a quantity good, i denotes his/her rank-order statistic (arranged in ascending order of magni-

---

[5]A theory of the distributive-justice force is incomplete without a postulate describing how individuals come to regard certain states or outcomes as just for themselves and how these notions of justice fluctuate even within time periods as short as a day. This is a lively topic of theoretical and empirical research at the present time.

tude, namely with "1" assigned to the lowest-ranked person); S denotes the total amount of the quantity good in the collectivity, N denotes the population size, and ∅ denotes the factor incorporating all individual-specific influences on the just term. The quality good formula is obtained by using the fact that the arithmetic mean of the set of relative ranks (i.e., the mean of the unit rectangular distribution) is equal to one-half.

As can be seen in expression (3),this representation of the just term combines generality with precision. That is, it is accurate for all possible values of the just term.

The theory provides the combinatorial rule for specifying the instantaneous justice evaluation in the case where two or more (K) goods are *simultaneously* valued:

$$J^* = (1/K) \Sigma J \tag{4}$$

The theory further proposes that each person may be regarded as having a distinctive time series of justice evaluations—termed the *distributive-justice profile*. Important parameters of this profile include, for any interval of time, the arithmetic mean, range, variance, jumps between contiguous J, gaps during which no J is experienced , means of the overrewarded and underrewarded truncates, and the like.

Specification of Justice-Dependent Behaviors of the Individual. The theoretical framework described leads in a simple and straightforward manner to the specification of many and diverse justice-dependent behaviors of the individual.[6] Two general classes may be discerned. The first consists of phenomena related to the instantaneous-justice evaluation J and the second of phenomena related to parameters of the distributive-justice profile.

In turn, the class of phenomena related to the instantaneous justice evaluation J contains four subclasses of justice-dependent behavioral phenomena, corresponding to the four possible combinations of two binary considerations. The first consideration, following Coleman (1973), is whether the behavior under investigation is a responsive or purposive behavior. The second consideration is whether the behavior is a function of the *magnitude* of J or instead of the *absolute magnitude* of J, that is, whether or not it notices the distinction between overreward or underreward. These classes are described in Jasso (1986). For our present purpose, it suffices to note that two of these subclasses, those in which the outcome is an increasing function of J, will be pertinent to this analysis. These effects may be formally stated:

---

[6]The phrase *justice-dependent* denotes dependence on the operation of the distributive-justice force.

(a) Responsive/J-sign-attentive behavior

$$Y^R = Y^R(J, \Gamma, \epsilon) \qquad (5.a)$$

where

$$\delta Y^R/\delta J > 0 \qquad (5.b)$$

and where the superscript R denotes the responsive type of behavior, Γ denotes a vector of other factors relevant to the determination of Y, and ϵ denotes a random disturbance. The class of Y^R phenomena thus includes subjective states in which the condition of overreward generates happiness like conditions and underreward generates unhappiness like conditions, as well as responses such as healthiness.

(b) Purposive/J-sign-attentive

$$Y^P = Y^P(G, \Gamma, \epsilon) \qquad (6.a)$$

where

$$\delta Y^P/\delta G > 0, \ \delta Y^P/\delta J_2 > 0, \text{ and } \delta Y^P/\delta J_1 < 0 \qquad (6.b)$$

and where the superscript P denotes the purposive type of behavior, J_1 denotes the current value of J, J_2 denotes the expected future value of J, $G = J_2\text{-}J_1$, and all other terms are as in (5) and (6). The derivatives with respect to J_2 and to J_1 follow from the definition of G. The "purpose" underlying the relation expressed in (6) is to maximize J and, therefore, G.

The second general class of justice-dependent individual-level behavioral phenomena consists of behaviors specified as functions of a *parameter of the individual's distributive-justice profile.* That is, this set of phenomena respond to (one or more of) such parameters as, for any interval of time, the arithmetic mean, the range, and the variance of the person's time series, the jumps between contiguous J, the gaps during which no J is experienced, and the means of the overrewarded and underrewarded truncates. The distributive-justice profile enables investigation of cyclical phenomena and of aging effects.

The general form of the equation for this class of phenomena is:

$$Q = Q(P, \Gamma, \epsilon), \qquad (7)$$

where Q denotes the dependent phenomenon, P denotes the parameter(s) of the distributive-justice profile, and other terms are as previously defined.

Distributive-Justice Effects at the Social Level

The theory of the distributive-justice force suggests that a collectivity, any collectivity of any size, may be represented by the instantaneous *distribution of justice evaluations* among its members. Further, the parameters of the *J* distribution are regarded as exercising a special hegemony over distinctive areas of the social life. These parameters include the distribution's arithmetic mean, lower extreme value, proportion overrewarded, proportion underrewarded, and other quantities. Two of the parameters of the *J* distribution are of special interest; these are the arithmetic mean and the Gini's mean difference. By postulate, the first becomes the theory's measure of social welfare and the second that of social cohesiveness.

The theory proposes the arithmetic mean of the distribution of justice evaluations in a collectivity as a basic measure of the theoretical term *social welfare*, denoted SW. Formally:

Postulate 5. Social Welfare.

$$\text{Social Welfare} = E(J). \qquad (8)$$

Social distance is defined in the theory as a pairwise phenomenon, the absolute difference between the justice evaluations of two individuals. The collectivity's *social cohesiveness* is assumed to depend jointly and equally on the social distance property of all pairs in the group, a quantity exactly captured by the Gini's mean difference (GMD), with the smaller the GMD the greater the cohesiveness, or, equivalently, the greater the GMD the greater the propensity to dissolution.[7] Formally:

Postulate 6. Social Cohesiveness.

$$\text{Cohesiveness} = -\text{GMD}(J). \qquad (9)$$

This chapter shall have no more to say concerning social cohesiveness.

A Sampler of Predictions

The theory of the distributive-justice force yields testable implications for a wide variety of human behavioral and social phenomena. Among these implications are the following[8]

1. Persons who are blind or deaf have fewer dimensions of self-evaluation, per unit of time, than otherwise comparable persons.

---

[7]As in Blau's (1977) pioneering theory of social structure, the Gini's mean difference emerges as a theoretically appropriate measure of inequality.
[8]Rigorous derivation of these and other implications of the theory is reported in the articles cited in Footnote 4.

2. The individual's number of valued goods, per unit of time, is an increasing function of reading ability and of the prevalence of electronic media.

3. Other things the same, a person will prefer to steal from a fellow group member rather than from an outsider.

4. The preference to steal from a fellow group member is more pronounced in poor groups than in rich groups.

5. When entering situations where new groups and new social hierarchies might emerge, persons carry with them goods-relevant apparatus, such as tennis racquet or chess set.

6. At the inauguration of a new housing development, when many families are moving in, there is an increase in the wearing of goods-relevant items—tennis dress, t-shirt with special logo, message buttons.

7. Persons who arrive a week late at summer camp or for freshman year of college are more likely to become friends of persons who play games of chance than of persons who play games of skill.

8. An immigrant's propensity to learn the language of the host country is an increasing function of the ratio of the origin country's per capita GNP to the host country's per capita GNP.

9. Among groups whose valued goods are N quality goods, the group's longevity is a decreasing function of group size.

10. If both spouses work full-time, marital cohesiveness increases with the ratio of the smaller to the larger earnings.

11. In a society in which the two-worker couple is the prevailing form of marriage and all husbands earn more than their own wives, the societal divorce rate increases with the dispersion in the wives' earnings distribution and with the arithmetic mean of the husbands' earnings distribution and decreases with the dispersion in the husbands' earnings distribution and with the arithmetic mean of the wives' earnings distribution.

12. In wartime, the favorite leisure-time activity of soldiers is playing games of chance.

13. In a dispute over revealing salary information, the exact preference structure depends on the salaries' distributional pattern; if this pattern follows the familiar lognormal or Pareto, then the lowest-paid and the highest-paid persons prefer to have the information revealed, forming a coalition against the middle-paid persons.

14. A society becomes more vulnerable to deficit spending as its wealth increases.

15. The phenomenon of "finding the motive" in the murderer-detection enterprise and the associated literary genre arises only in societies that value wealth.

16. Two necessary but not sufficient conditions for gender inequality to arise in a society are (1) that the society value wealth and (2) that the family wealth distributions of marriageable males and females differ.

The Social Welfare Postulate

Basic Formulas of Social Welfare

Substituting the general expression for J into formula (8) yields the basic expression for social welfare:

$$\text{Social Welfare} = E[\ln(AT/JT)], \tag{10}$$

Where AT and JT denote actual term and just term, respectively.

By algebraic manipulation, utilizing properties of logarithms and features of summation, multiplication, and exponentiation operations, we establish a connection between social welfare and the geometric means of the distributions of actual term and of just term:

$$\text{Social Welfare} = \ln \{[GM(AT)]/[GM(JT)]\}, \tag{11}$$

where GM denotes the geometric mean. The theory thus implies that social welfare increases with the geometric mean of the actual holdings of the valued good and decreases with the geometric mean of the just or expected holdings.

Invoking ceteris paribus relations among a variate's arithmetic mean, geometric mean, and dispersion $D(X)$ (see the Appendix), we can derive the first partial derivatives of $E(J)$ with respect to the arithmetic mean and the inequality of the distributions of both the actual holdings and the expected holdings:

$$[E(J)]_{E(AT)} = +[1 - D(AT)]/[GM(AT)] > 0 \tag{12.a}$$

$$[E(J)]_{D(AT)} = -[E(AT)]/[GM(AT)] \quad\quad < 0 \tag{12.b}$$

$$[E(J)]_{E(JT)} = -(1 - D(JT)]/[GM(JT)] \quad < 0 \tag{12.c}$$

$$[E(J)]_{D(JT)} = +(E(JT)]/[GM(JT)] \quad\quad > 0 \tag{12.d}$$

Hence, the theory suggests that social welfare increases with the arithmetic mean of the distribution of actual holdings of the valued good and with the dispersion of the distribution of expected holdings of the valued good and decreases with the dispersion in the distribution of actual holdings and with the mean of the distribution of expected holdings.

Using the more refined representation of the sense of distributive justice, which (1) takes account of the type of valued good (namely, quality good or quantity good) and (2) incorporates the phi factor (which captures all individual-specific influences on the just term), and working algebraically we obtain:

$$\text{Social Welfare} = \begin{cases} \ln(\delta) - \ln[GM(\phi)], & \text{quantity good} \\ \\ \ln\{[2(N!)^{1/N}]/(N+1)\} - \ln[GM(\phi)], & \text{quality good,} \end{cases} \quad (13)$$

where δ denotes the measure of inequality defined as the ratio of the arithmetic mean to the geometric mean (with inequality decreasing as the ratio approaches unity). This measure was derived by Atkinson (1970, 1975) and its connection to the sense of distributive justice described in Jasso (1980, 1982). In the quality good case, the expression $\{[(N!)^{1/N}]/(N+1)\}$ was shown in Jasso (1980) to be decreasing in the size N of the collectivity and to approach the quantity $1/e$ as its limit.

Incorporating formula (4), which describes the individual's sense of justice J in the multiple-good case as equal to the arithmetic mean of the J derived from each good, and using statistical theorems on expectation, social welfare in a society which values several goods is equal to the arithmetic mean of the set of $E(J)$ terms. Formally:

$$\text{Social Welfare} = (1/K) \, \Sigma \, E(J). \quad (14)$$

Basic Theoretical Relations Embodied in Social Welfare

Equations (13) and (14) imply a more refined expression of the theoretical relations embodied in the social welfare term. These are:

1. Universal positive effect of variability in individuals' notions of what is just for themselves. In all societies, variability in individuals' notions of the just holdings for themselves increases the social welfare.

2. Conditional negative effect of inequality in the distribution of material resources. In societies in which the set of valued goods includes at least one quantity good, reductions in the inequality of the distribution(s) of the quantity good(s) increase the social welfare.

3. Conditional negative effect of population size. In societies in which—either (1) the single valued good is a quality good, or (2) both (a) the set of valued goods includes at least one quality good, and (b) the negative quality good effects of N outweigh the positive effects, if any, of N on inequality reduction in the distributions of quantity goods—reductions in population size increase the social welfare (but note that as N increases, the effect becomes negligible).

The Basic Social Welfare Institutions Predicted by the Theory of the Distributive-Justice Force

This section begins by examining the concept of an institution and of a social welfare institution and proceeds to derive the three basic social welfare institutions predicted by distributive-justice theory.

Institutions and Social Welfare Institutions

The literature on institutions contains many definitions and many formulations. Not being nominalists, we shall make no claims concerning what is or is not a "true" institution. Nonetheless, four common elements of a useful characterization can be discerned in the literature. The first defining feature of an institution appears to be its patterning of individual and social behaviors. The second defining feature highlights the tendency of institutions to be persistent elements of the common life, albeit susceptible of considerable variation across space and over time. The third defining feature points to the focus of an institution, usually "fundamental problems of social life" (*Encyclopaedia Britannica*, Micropaedia V, 1978, p. 371) or a "fundamental human need, activity, or value occup[ying] a cardinal position within a society" (*Webster's Third New International Dictionary*, 1976). As Eisenstadt (1968a, p. 409) puts it, "the patterns of behavior which are regulated by institutions ('institutionalized') deal with some perennial, basic problems of any society." The fourth element refers to the importance of the institution for the survival of the society. In Parsons's (1951, p. 39) words, "an institution . . . is of strategic structural significance in the social system in question."

From these and similar formulations, we distilled a working definition of an institution. We define an institution as *a patterned individual and/or social behavior; a prevailing way of doing something, with variation possible across space and time.*[9]

Institutions may differ in their proximate goals, though all would have the ultimate goal of promoting the common good. To the extent

---

[9]This definition reserves characterizations of an institution's focus and purpose for the task of distinguishing among types of institutions.

that the common good may have several aspects and, indeed, that these may come into conflict with one another, it is useful to denote institutions by the particular proximate goal they serve. Within the context of the theory of the distributive-justice force, it is straightforward to denote institutions by the aspect of the J distribution that they promote. For example, an institution designed to promote social cohesiveness would be termed a social cohesiveness institution; its mission would be to increase social cohesiveness as defined in the theory (equation (9)). Similarly, one can envision a lower limit institution whose mission would be to maintain the lower limit of the J distribution as high as possible; such an institution might be given the eponymous name *Rawlsian*, after Rawls's (1971) principle of justice. In the present case, we focus on social welfare institutions, defined as an institution that promotes the social welfare, where social welfare is defined and measured as in equation (8).

It is possible that an institution may promote more than one of these proximate goals. Thus, an interesting question, but unfortunately one outside the scope of this chapter, concerns the part played in the emergence, maintenance, and elimination of institutions by shifts in the number of proximate goals they serve.

The Basic Social Welfare Institutions

We have defined a social welfare institution as an institution that promotes the social welfare—that is, which serves to increase the arithmetic mean of the society's distribution of justice evaluations. In another section, we derived three results describing the effects on social welfare of material resources, population size, and just-term variability. Hence, we can now formally derive the basic social welfare institutions predicted by the theory of the distributive-justice force. These are three, only one of which is universal; the other two are contingent on the type of good—quality or quantity—valued by the society.

Universal Institution: Variability in Individuals' Notions of What Is Just for Themselves. Because in all societies, the mean of the J distribution is an increasing function of dispersion in the ϕ distribution, as shown in equation (12.d), it follows that in all societies there will arise devices that promote variability in individuals' notions of what is just for themselves. Such devices include social differentiation, cultural pluralism, and the division of labor.

The basic subsequent question that arises is how bases of differentiation are selected, established, maintained, and discarded.

Basic Institution in a Quantity Good Society: Redistribution of Material Resources. In societies that value at least one quantity good there will arise redistributive schemes designed to achieve inequality reduction. Because within quantity good variate families, $E(J)$ is a decreasing function of inequality, the strength of the movement to redistribution is an increasing function of the magnitude of inequality. Inequality-reducing redistributive schemes are the hallmark of quantity good societies; they are absent from exclusively quality good societies, no matter how unequal the distribution of material resources.

Basic Institution in a Quality-Good Society: Limitation of Population Size. In societies that value at least one quality good, there will arise devices for population control. Such devices include policies on natural increase (natalism, family planning) and on migration (immigration, emigration). Note that although a quality-good society always seeks to limit population size, a quantity-good society may have either a positive or negative population policy, depending on the effects of population size on the distribution of material resources; thus, societies in which population growth is welcomed must be societies in which the set of valued goods includes at least one quantity good.

Selection of Valued Goods

How do individuals and societies select the good(s) they value? How do valued goods become institutionalized and deinstitutionalized? What accounts for cross-cultural and intergroup variation in valuation of money, birth, beauty, intelligence, and other goods? These questions constitute a basic element of inquiries into several distinct individual and social processes, from studies of the self and of reference groups to studies of social stratification, social institutions, and culture.

At the level of the individual, the emphasis is on the individual's choice of what in the several literatures is variously termed *dimensions of self-evaluation, attributes of self-appraisal,* or *bases of self-assessment*. The common ingredient in these literatures is the observation, noted as early as Aristotle (*Nicomachean Ethics*, Book I, Chapter 4) that there exists considerable variability across humans in the choice of attribute or possession with respect to which they experience self-evaluation, self-worth, and happiness. The classic modern statement of this observation is found in William James's analysis of the self; the profound implications of the choice of valued goods are epitomized in the celebrated passage (James 1952, p. 200): "I, who for the time have staked my all on being a psychologist, am mortified if others know much more psychology than I. But I am contented to wallow in the grossest ignorance of Greek. My deficiencies there give me no sense of personal humiliation at all."

At social levels, this question focuses on the origin, maintenance, and alteration of what in the different literatures is termed *basis of social differentiation, cultural value system*, or *national character*. It is an ancient insight that some groups value wealth, others intelligence, others physical attractiveness, and still others some weighted combination of these. It is a more modern sociological insight that these values do not appear by chance but are the product of systematic and knowable processes.[10] Understanding these social processes has come to be seen as a principal task of sociology.[11]

The two aspects—individual and social—of the goods-choice problem are densely intertwined. Contemporary approaches make explicit the connection between an attribute's relevance for self-esteem and its relevance for social status.[12] Yet the precise nature of this connection remains elusive. Virtually every commentator has noticed the swiftness with which attempts to treat one as fundamental are repelled. Aristotle's (*Politics*, Book 7, Chapter 8) inviting description, "Different men seek after happiness in different ways and by different means, and so make for themselves different modes of life and forms of government," is turned back at the door of socialization processes. And the notion that "society" inculcates the valued goods is powerless to explain either individual dissent or large-scale social change.[13]

Assessing further the importance of the question of the choice of goods of value, consider that basic statement of many social processes, including the first great micro–macro bridging concept in the study of human behavior—that of reference groups and comparison groups—

---

[10]For comprehensive review of value processes, see Albert (1968) and Williams (1968).
[11]This challenge is noted by Parsons (1951 p. 552), Sorokin (1968), and Eisenstadt (1968a, 1968b). It underlies Coleman's (1961, 1967) pioneering investigation of adolescent cultures and of the process by which high schools come to develop highly distinctive value sets, some high schools valuing athletic skill, others academic performance, still others physical attractiveness.
[12]See Zelditch (1968); Berger, Zelditch, Anderson, and Cohen (1972); and Berger, Fisek, Norman, and Wagner (1985).
[13]For example, consider the decision of individuals in a materialistic society to make a vow of poverty (Knowles 1969); or the great revolution in valued goods that replaced rents by wages.

treat as *given* the attribute regarded as the dimension-of-evaluation/
basis-of-social-hierarchies.[14] But *whence the attribute?*[15]
The theory of the distributive-justice force provides a framework
within which the problem of selection of goods of value can be
systematically investigated. The theory enables examination from at
least two perspectives: (1) an individualistic perspective, in which
members of a society act as self-interested individuals, preferring that
good under which their own *J* is highest, and (2) a collectivistic
perspective, in which individuals act as societal guardians, preferring
that good under which the social welfare is highest. In this chapter, we
formulate the collectivistic model of goods choice.[16]

Collectivistic Model of Selection of Valued Goods

Consider a model in which the objective of the societal guardians is to
maximize social welfare. Embedding this objective within the theory of
the distributive-justice force, we can state the guardian's decision rule
by:

$$\text{Guardian's decision rule: maximize } [E(J)] \tag{15}$$

Hence, the problem of selecting among several goods is solved by the
following steps:

1. Find the $E(J)$ of the J distribution arising from each good.
2. Arrange the $E(J)$ in a continued inequality. For example,

$$[E(J)]_C < [E(J)]_A < [E(J)]_D < [E(J)]_B, \tag{16}$$

where the subscripts denote the alternative goods regimes.

---

[14]Two examples of such statements are: (1)"Standing refers to the person's relative
position in a group, with regard to some attributes, and the process whereby he
determines his standing we shall call 'comparative appraisal' " (Gerard 1968, p. 464).
(2)"Social stratification . . . refers to the fact that both individuals and groups of
individuals are conceived of as constituting higher and lower differentiated strata, or
classes, in terms of some specific or generalized characteristic or set of characteristics"
(Barber 1968, pp. 288–289). See also Goldhamer (1968) on the attributes of interest in
studies of social mobility and Gusfield (1968) and Heberle (1968), in social movements.
[15]Note that if each individual had identical ranks in all potentially relevant dimensions
of evaluation or bases of stratification, then innocence of the genesis of the valued goods
would present no great cause for concern. Thus, the problem of choosing a good of value
is related to the problem of status inconsistency.
[16]The individualistic model of goods choice is formulated in Jasso (1987b).

3. The rightmost term in the continued inequality satisfies the decision rule; hence, the good associated with it is selected as valued good.

When the Guardian is considering two alternative regimes, the procedure reduces to a comparison of the two regimes' $E(J)$, for example:

$$[E(J)]_A < [E(J)]_B \qquad (17)$$

Social Welfare in Three Kinds of Goods Regimes

The Goods Component and the Phi Component. If the J distributions are observed, then formulas (2) or (3) together with formula (10) suffice for calculating the $E(J)$ for each alternative regime. However, if the J distributions are to be inferred or assigned *a priori* forms for use in theoretical analysis, then two sets of distributions must be specified, that of ϕ and that of the valued good. To prepare for using probability distributions as approximations for the distributions of the goods and of J in a collectivity, we restate expression (3) in a new form:

$$J = \begin{cases} \ln(x/\mu) - \ln(\phi), & \phi > 0, & \text{quantity good} \\ \\ \ln(2\alpha) - \ln(\phi), & 0 < \phi < 2, & \text{quality good.} \end{cases} \qquad (18)$$

In (18), the observed version of actual rank, that is, $[i/(N + 1)]$, is replaced by the corresponding parameter in a large collectivity, namely α the relative rank. Note that instantaneous J may be regarded as having two components, a *goods component* containing the magnitude and the arithmetic mean of the good, and a ϕ *component* containing the individual-specific influences on formation of the just term.

A new form of expression (13) for the social welfare follows from expression (18):

$$\text{Social Welfare} = \begin{cases} \ln(\delta) - \ln[GM(\phi)], & \text{quantity good} \\ \\ \ln(2/e) - \ln[GM(\phi)], & \text{quality good.} \end{cases} \qquad (19)$$

Like J, social welfare may be regarded as having two components, a goods component and a ϕ component. In the case of a quantity good, the goods component uses information about the arithmetic mean and the geometric mean of the good's distribution; *a priori* assignment of a distributional form to the quality good yields the goods component. In the case of a quality good, the goods component leads to a single expression, $\ln(2/e)$,[17] correct for all collectivities treated as having a large population size. The quantity $\ln(2/e)$ may be obtained in either of two ways, first, as the limit of the goods component in the quality-good branch of expression (13), or, second, as the mean of the negative-exponential distribution that arises when the justice-evaluation function is performed on the rectangular distribution of actual ranks.[18] The quantity $\ln(2/e)$, reduces to $[\ln(2) - 1]$, which is approximately equal to -0.3069.

Using Classical Probability Distributions to Model Quantity Goods. In order to achieve *a priori* expressions for the goods component in the quantity-good case, we use two families of distributional forms that are widely regarded as useful approximations for the distributions of positive quantities such as income and wealth. These are the Pareto and the lognormal variate families. Both are two-parameter families. The two parameters are a location constant, here fixed at the quantity-good's arithmetic mean μ and a shape constant (denoted c), which controls all measures of inequality and dispersion. In the Pareto, inequality is a decreasing function of c, whereas in the lognormal, inequality is an increasing function of c.

The Pareto and lognormal variate families present an interesting contrast. Although both have upper limits going to infinity, their lower-limit behavior differs dramatically, the lower limit in the lognormal going to zero, in the Pareto contained at a nonzero positive point. The Pareto is the prototype of the society with a "safety net," that is, with some minimum standard for all. The lognormal, on the other hand, represents a society in which extreme poverty may be present.

By change-of-variable techniques, we obtain the distribution of the goods component of the J distribution arising from the Pareto and lognormal families. In the case of the Pareto-distributed quantity good, the goods component of the associated J distribution is a positive exponential; in the case of the lognormally distributed quantity good, the goods component of the associated J distribution is a normal.[19]

The Method of the Inverse Distribution Function. Of the three basic functions associated with probability distributions and used to display their formulas and graphs—the probability density function

---

[17] The symbol e represents the transcendental number approximately equal to 2.7183 and used as the base of the natural logarithms.
[18] Detailed derivation is found in Jasso (1980).
[19] Detailed exposition of these derivations is found in Jasso (1980).

Table 1. Inverse Distribution Function $G(\alpha)$ for the Rectangular, Lognormal, and Pareto Variates and for the Goods Component of the Justice-Evaluation Variates Derived from Them

Variate	$G(\alpha)$	
A. Valuation of one quality good		
Rectangular	α	
J: Rectangular	$\ln(2\alpha)$	
B. Valuation of one quantity good		
Lognormal	$\mu \exp\{c[G_N(\alpha)] - (c^2/2)\}$	$c > 0$
J: Lognormal	$c\{[G_N(\alpha)] - [c/2]\}$	$c > 0$
Pareto	$[\mu(c - 1)]/[c(1 - \alpha)^{1/c}]$	$c > 1$
J: Pareto	$\ln\{[c - 1]/[c(1 - \alpha)^{1/c}]\}$	$c > 1$

Note. The notation J:aaaa denotes the goods component of the variate obtained when the justice evaluation is experienced about a good whose distribution belongs to the aaaa family, where the justice evaluation is given by $J = \ln[x/\phi\mu]$, and phi is isolated into the ϕ component. The underlying formulas for the lognormal, Pareto, and rectangular variates are restatements of formulas found in Hastings and Peacock (1974) and Johnson and Kotz (1970a). The lognormal and Pareto approximate distributional forms of quantity goods, whereas the rectangular approximates the distribution of a quality good. In the lognormal and Pareto, the shape parameter c operates as a general inequality parameter. Inequality is a decreasing function of c in the Pareto and an increasing function of c in the lognormal. The term $G_N(\alpha)$ denotes the inverse distribution function of the unit normal variate.

(pdf), the cumulative distribution function (cdf), and the inverse distribution function (idf)—we regard the idf as the most informative representational device.[20] The inverse distribution function, denoted $G(\alpha)$, expresses the value of the variate (i.e., the quantile x) as a function of α the probability that the variate takes a value less than or equal to x (i.e., α equals the cumulative distribution function $F(x)$). The probability α, much for our present purpose, can be interpreted as the relative rank corresponding to the quantile; it is approximated by its observed counterpart $[i/(N + 1)]$, where i denotes the individual's integer rank and N the population size, quantities encountered earlier. The graph of the idf has the virtue that it *simultaneously* displays both the variate's distribution as a whole, as well as two important aspects of an individual in a collectivity, namely the individual's relative rank and the individual's amount or level of the good or the magnitude of J.

Table 1 reports the idf's both for the goods component of the J distributions arising from valuation of one quality good and of one Pareto or lognormal quantity good and for the corresponding underlying goods. To accompany these formulas, Figures 1, 2, and 3 display

---

[20]Exposition of the interrelationships among these three basic functions is found in a variety of source material and encyclopedic reference texts, such as Johnson and Kotz (1970a,). For brief but comprehensive and felicitous exposition, see Hastings and Peacock (1974). For argument advancing the cause of the inverse distribution function as a superior representational device, see Jasso (1983c).

the graphs of the idf's for both the underlying good and the J distribution's goods component. As noted, in these graphs the horizontal axis represents the individual's relative rank α whereas the vertical axis represents the corresponding value of the good or the goods component of J. Thus at a glance one can learn the quantity-good amount or the goods component of J corresponding to an individual of any relative rank.

The arithmetic mean of a mathematically specified variate may be found by integrating either of two basic formulas, one based on the probability density function and the other on the inverse distribution function. The first row of Table 2 reports the arithmetic means of the goods component of the J distributions.

Solving the Guardian's Problem without Information on Phi. Of course, the basic inequality to be solved, shown in expression (17), requires $E(J)$ and not merely its goods component. Hence, procedures for handling the ϕ component must be devised. It is obvious that one could specify a distributional form for ϕ and proceed straightforwardly. Fortunately, an even simpler and more parsimonious procedure is possible, applicable in a special case that may prove to cover the majority of instances. To see this, let us examine the inequality to be solved, expression (17), replacing each mean by its fuller expression and denoting the goods component by the generic label GC:

$$GC_A - ln[GM(\phi)]_A < \{GC_B - ln[GM(\phi)]_B\} \tag{20}$$

Expression (20) makes visible the condition under which information on the goods component suffices to solve inequality (17): The two

Table 2. Arithmetic Mean, Mean of the Noncloistered, and Benefit of the Cloister to the Noncloistered, for the Goods Component of the J Distributions Arising from a Quality Good and from Pareto and Lognormal Quantity Goods

	Quality good	Quantity good	
Function	J: Rectangular	J: Lognormal	J: Pareto
A. Parameters			
$E(J)$	$ln(2/e)$	$-c^2/2$	$1/c + ln[(c-1)/c]$
UM $E(J)$	$-[\alpha ln(\alpha)]/(1-\alpha)$	$E(J) + [c/(1-\alpha)]\{f_N[G_N(\alpha)]\}$	$E(J) - c^{-2}ln(1-\alpha)$
B	$-[\alpha ln(\alpha)]/(1-\alpha)$	$[c/(1-\alpha)]\{f_N[G_N(\alpha)]\}$	$-(1/c)ln(1-\alpha)$
B. First partial derivatives			
$[E(J)]c$	—	$-c$ $\quad\quad < 0$	$1/[c^2(c-1)]$ $\quad > 0$
B_c	—	$[1/(1-\alpha)]\{f_N[G_N(\alpha)]\} > 0$	$(1/c^2)ln(1-\alpha) < 0$

Note. The terms f_N and G_N denote the probability density function and the inverse distribution function, respectively, of the unit normal variate. Inequality is a decreasing function of c in the Pareto and an increasing function of c in the lognormal.

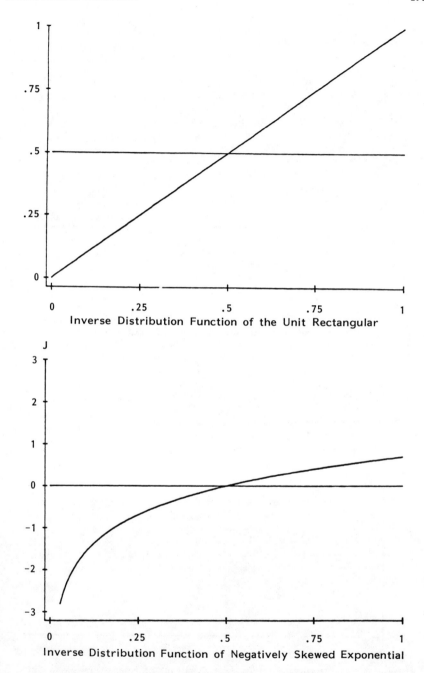

Figure 1. Distributions of quality good and of justice evaluation J derived from it.

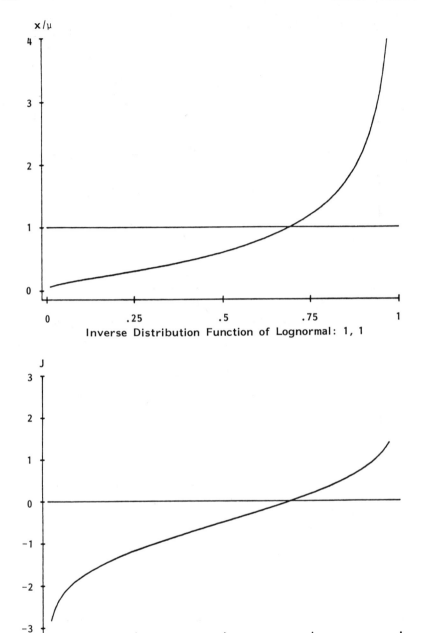

Figure 2. Distributions of lognormal quantity good and of justice evaluation J derived from it.

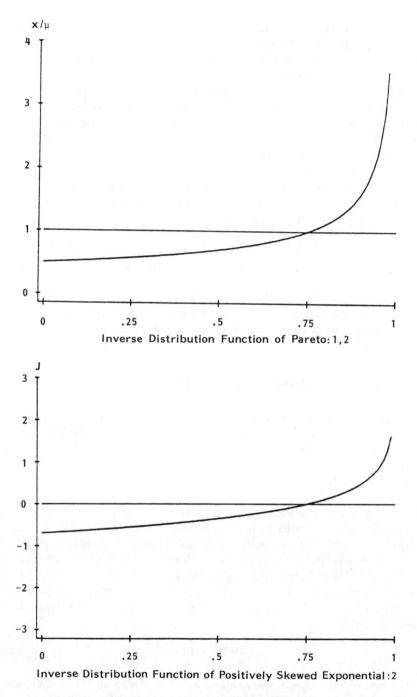

Figure 3. Distributions of Pareto quantity good and of justice evaluation J derived from it.

regimes are associated with $\emptyset$ distributions of identical geometric means, so that the GM($\emptyset$) terms on both sides of the inequality cancel each other out. It is not unreasonable to think that this condition is satisfied in the case where both of the alternative valued goods are quantity goods; in such case there is no reason to suppose that the $\emptyset$distribution would differ between them. To the extent that many goods contests involve quantity goods, this result is reassuring. Further, this condition is satisfied in an even wider set of cases, for identical geometric means are possible for many sharply different distributional forms.[21]

Thus, eliminating the GM($\emptyset$) terms permits inequality (17) to be solved by solving inequalities whose terms consist exclusively of the goods components of social welfare.

Two Quantity Goods: $[ln(\delta)]_A \overset{?}{\lessgtr} [ln(\delta)]_B$ (21.a)

Quality Good vs. Quantity Good: $[n(\delta)]_A \overset{?}{\lessgtr} [ln(2/e)]$ (21.b)

To the extent that theoretical analysis may be regarded as a search for *a* priori solutions, we focus on the problem as stated *in* expressions (21) and enabled by the sufficient condition just noted.

The Guardian Chooses a Valued Good

We now report the results of solving inequality (17), as refined in inequality (21), for three classes of contests between two goods, first, a contest between two quality goods, second, a contest between two quantity goods, and, third, a contest between a quality good and a quantity good.

Two Quality Goods. Suppose that the Guardian is considering whether society would be better off if one rather than another quality good is valued. For example, the Guardian may be weighing physical attractiveness versus intelligence or athletic prowess versus heroism in battle or noble birth versus horsemanship. In this case, the theory of the distributive-justice force predicts no winner. Because both goods are quality goods, inequality (17), for the special case of identical GM($\emptyset$) terms, yields

$$ln(2/e)_A = ln(2/e)_B$$ (22)

---

[21]The most restrictive special case satisfying the condition of equality of the GM($\emptyset$) terms arises when all persons have the same value of $\emptyset$ and that value is unity.

The goods components of the two $E(J)$'s are the same. Hence, we conclude that the Guardian will be indifferent as to a choice between two quality-good regimes and will not—on the basis of social welfare—advance an argument for one versus another quality good. This result is reported in part A of Table 3.

Two Quantity Goods. Consider the case where the Guardian is investigating the social consequences of social valuation of one versus another quantity good. For example, the candidate goods could be income versus wealth, rents versus wages, land versus livestock. In this case, inequality (17) yields

$$ln(\delta)_A < ln(\delta)_B. \tag{23}$$

From the basic theoretical relation concerning the effects of inequality on social welfare, derived previously, we know that the Guardian will choose the good whose inequality—as measured by δ—is lowest. To illustrate, we look at lognormally and Pareto-distributed goods, formally deriving this result for each variate.

Consider first the case where both goods are lognormally distributed. In this case, the goods component of the social welfare derived from them is given by $-c^2$, reported in Table 2. The first derivative of the goods component of the social welfare with respect to the general inequality parameter c, also reported in Table 2, is negative. Because inequality increases with c, SW is a decreasing function of c. Hence, in a contest between two lognormally distributed goods, the Guardian will always choose the one with the lower c, that is, the less unequal.

Next consider a contest between two Pareto-distributed quantity goods. The first derivative of the goods component of SW with respect

Table 3. The Guardian Chooses a Valued Good: Predicted Outcome by Type of Contest

Contest	Outcome
A. Quality good versus quality good	Deadlock
B. Quantity good versus quantity good	
1. Within distributional family	
Lognormal	Good with less inequality
Pareto	Good with less inequality
2. Across distributional family	Numerical solution
C. Quality good versus quantity good	
Lognormal quantity good	lognormal *iff* $c < \sqrt{[2 - ln(4)]} \approx .7834$
Pareto quantity good	Pareto *iff* $c > -1.68$

Note. Inequality is a decreasing function of c in the Pareto and an increasing function of c in the lognormal.

to the general inequality parameter c, reported in Table 2, is positive. Because in the Pareto variate, inequality is a decreasing function of c, SW is an increasing function of c. Hence, in a contest between two Pareto-distributed quantity goods, the Guardian will always choose the one with the higher c, that is, the less unequal.

Finally, consider the case where the two quantity goods come from different distributional families. In the general case, it is sometimes possible to find a symbolic solution. However, in a contest between a Pareto and a lognormal, a purely symbolic solution is not possible. Of course, a numerical solution may always be found. For example, if one candidate good is a Pareto with $c = 2$, whose goods component of $E(J)$ is given by $[\frac{1}{2} - \ln 2]$, or approximately $-.1931$, inequality (17) is set up to solve for the lognormals whose goods component of $E(J)$ is lower than the Pareto's:

$$\frac{1}{2} - \ln(2) > -c^2/2, \tag{24.a}$$

which upon algebraic manipulation yields

$$c > \sqrt{[\ln(4/e)]} \approx .6215. \tag{24.b}$$

Hence, the Guardian would prefer the Pareto ($c = 2$) to a lognormal of c greater than approximately $.6215$ and otherwise would choose the lognormal.

These results are summarized in part B of Table 3.

Quality Good versus Quantity Good. Suppose that the Guardian is evaluating the social effects of valuing one quality good versus one quantity good. Examples from the historical record would include birth versus wealth and nobility versus income. An interesting special case arises when both are aspects of the same basic good, for example, salary rank (a quality good) and salary amount (a quantity good). In all contests between a quality good and a quantity good, the equation to be solved takes the form

$$\ln(2/e) \overset{?}{\lessgtr} E(J)^{quan}. \tag{25}$$

Solving inequality (25) for the two quantity-good distributional forms we have been investigating, we obtain, for the case of a lognormally distributed quantity good,

$$[\ln(2/e) = -c^2/2] \text{ at } [c = \sqrt{[2 - \ln(4)]} \approx .7834], \tag{26}$$

and, for the case of a Pareto-distributed quantity good,

$$[\ln(2/e) = 1/c + \ln((c - 1)/c)] \text{ at } [c \approx 1.6846). \tag{27}$$

Hence, we conclude that in a contest between a quality good and a quantity good, the Guardian will prefer a Pareto of $c > 1.68$ and a lognormal of $c < .78$ to a quality good. Part C of Table 3 summarizes these results.

Thus the attractiveness of a quantity good as an alternative to a quality good increases as inequality in the quantity-good's distribution declines. This suggests that societies have a tendency to become materialistic when exogenous technological developments reduce the dispersion in the distribution of material resources. This in turn adds new meaning to Pareto's seminal work on income distribution.

Pareto (1927), in empirical analyses of the income distributions of a heterogeneous collection of societies, including such diverse specimens as fifteenth-century Augsburg and eighteenth-century Peru, found the c factor to range between approximately 1.24 and 1.79. Impressed by the narrowness of the range, Pareto concluded that there might be a universal natural constant hovering about 1.5. Twentieth-century investigators, finding values of c ranging from 1.6 to 2.4, have retained Pareto's perspective that such narrowness signals a universal constant (Lebergott 1959, 1968). The analysis reported in this chapter, on the other hand, calls attention not to the constancy in the empirical estimates of the c factor but rather to their *magnitudes*. For the theory of the distributive-justice force suggests that if income is Pareto distributed, then a crossing of the c factor, from magnitudes smaller than 1.68 to magnitudes greater than 1.68, triggers a radical social transformation—a transformation from valuation of a quality good to valuation of the quantity-good income.

This analysis of goods selection, based on the theory of the distributive-justice force, suggests that the great social transformations—such as those that replaced feudalism by capitalism and rents by wages—can be understood as the outcomes of a process in which declining dispersion in the distributions of quantity goods leads to a situation in which a higher degree of social welfare is derived from material possessions than from quality goods.

Cloister and Society: Social Welfare Effects of Monastic Institutions

In the Christian tradition, it is believed that when individuals enter a cloister, there to study, work, and pray, special benefits are conferred on those who remain in the world. That is, *the act of being cloistered—* apart from any direct service such as teaching or nursing—imparts special graces on the noncloistered, enhancing their well-being.[22] In this section, we explore the possibility that such effects are predicted by the theory of the distributive-justice force. In the spirit of Fararo (1984), we attempt to generate a salutary cloister effect from the postulates of distributive-justice theory.

Preliminary Definitions and Notation

The basic feature of the model formulated in this section is that a subgroup of the collectivity voluntarily assumes the *lowest places* in the distribution(s) of the *valued good(s)*. Assuming the lowest places in the distribution of a *nonvalued* good would confer no special benefit on society, or at least no benefit predicted by distributive-justice theory. Thus to drive the generation of the monastic effects we begin with the *J* distribution arising from the valued good(s).

Let α denote the proportion of the collectivity that is in the cloistered subgroup. The noncloistered constitute the society whose social welfare is of interest. Accordingly, there are three basic quantities to be studied:

1. The mean of the *J* distribution in the case where there is no cloistered subgroup, denoted, as before, $E(J)$
2. The mean of the censored distribution of *J*, where the censoring is from below at the point α, denoted UM (for upper mean)
3. The *benefit* that society derives from the cloistered, denoted B and given by:

$$B = UM_2 - [E(J)]_1, \qquad (28)$$

where the numerical subscripts denote temporal ordering.

It can be shown that if the two precloister distributions of $\ln(\emptyset)$— among the subsequently cloistered and among the noncloistered—have the same mean, then the quantities above reduce to the corresponding quantities for the goods components. For simplicity, we focus on this special case. Note that it is the most parsimonious case, requiring no *a priori* information on the phi component and as well imposing no *a*

---

[22]Among the many benefits believed to be associated with the monastic life, two have primacy: (1) personal sanctification and (2) redemption of the world. The first concerns what happens to the cloistered individual him-or herself, whereas the second concerns what happens to others as a result of the individual's being cloistered. To the extent that redemption has manifestations visible in this life—for individuals, happiness, and for societies, peace—one would expect such a benefit on the noncloistered to be amenable to social–scientific investigation.

priori differences between the phi components of those who enter the cloister and those who remain in the world. Note, however, that if the precloister mean of the $ln(0)$ distribution among the cloistered exceeds the mean among the noncloistered, then the benefit is greater than that given by formula (28), whereas in the opposite case, the opposite holds. Thus the benefit to society is greatest when the cloistered are disproportionately drawn from among persons with large values of phi, that is, persons with large just terms.[23]

Preliminary Results

Restricting attention to the goods components of $E(J)$, UM, and B, we invoke statistical theorems on trimmed means that show that the mean of an upper subgroup is always greater than the overall mean. In our terms, UM is always greater than $E(J)$; hence, B is always positive. These relations enable statement of the first result of the distributive-justice analysis of monastic institutions:

> CLOISTER EFFECT 1. A sufficient condition for a cloistered subgroup to confer a benefit on the noncloistered subgroup is that the cloistered subgroup occupy the lowest places in the hierarchy of the collectivity's valued good[24]

It is also known from statistical theory that the mean of the upper subgroup (the left-censored trimmed mean) increases as the censoring point moves to the right. In our terms, the mean of the noncloistered UM is an increasing function of the proportion cloistered α. Because the benefit B increases with UM, the second result is immediate:

> CLOISTER EFFECT 2. The magnitude of the benefit that the noncloistered derive from the cloister is an increasing function of the proportion cloistered of the collectivity

The Effect of the Cloister, by Type of Valued Good

We now inquire whether the salutary effect of the cloister differs across collectivities which value different kinds of goods.

---

[23] A similar mechanism may help to explain the popularity of saints whose road to the ascetic life begins with exaggerated self-indulgence.

[24] The condition is not necessary to generate the positive magnitude of the benefit B, as it is also possible for B to be positive in the case where the cloistered and the noncloistered subgroups are drawn from overlapping segments of the J distribution.

184   Guillermina Jasso

Quality-Good Regime. Consider first the case of a society that values only quality goods, for example, birth, nobility, or athletic prowess. For simplicity, we focus on the case where, though the society may value many quality goods, it does so one at a time. Thus, as shown in Jasso (1980) and discussed before, the goods component of the instantaneous distribution of justice evaluations may be approximated by a negative exponential, whose inverse distribution function $G(\alpha)$ was introduced before and appears in Table 1.

Table 2, in addition to the goods components of the $E(J)$, also reports the goods components of the mean of the noncloistered (UM) and the benefit B accruing to the noncloistered.

As expected from the formulas for the idf's and from the discussion in the immediately preceding section, the noncloistered mean and the benefit formulas represent functions of the proportion cloistered α. Figure 4 depicts the graphs of the benefit as a function of the proportion cloistered for three types of valued goods. As Figure 4 shows, when the society values one quality good, as the proportion cloistered increases, the benefit to the noncloistered increases at a decreasing rate.

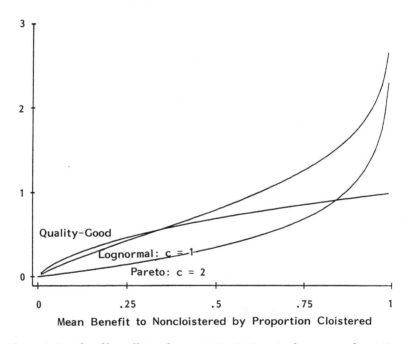

Figure 4. Social welfare effects of monastic institutions in three types of societies.

Quantity-Good Regime. Turning to the case of a society that values one quantity good, we continue investigation of two common distributional forms, the Pareto and the lognormal. For simplicity we focus on the special case in which the precloister and with-cloister quantity-good distributions are the same. Of course, formula (28) can be used to solve for more general cases.

As expected from the formulas in Table 2, shown in Figure 4, and stated in Cloister Effect 2, regardless of the quantity-good's distributional form, the benefit of the cloister is an increasing function of the proportion cloistered. What Figure 4 shows, however, that was *not* expected is the dramatic difference in the *magnitude* of the benefit across regime types, holding constant the proportion cloistered. Looking at Figure 4, the benefit conferred on the noncloistered is, for reasonable levels of cloistering (no more than a third of the population) similar in societies that value a quality good and in societies that value a lognormally distributed quantity good. The magnitude of the benefit is substantially greater than the benefit in societies that value a Pareto-distributed quantity good.

Examination of the equations and graphs of the benefit formulas across regime types and distributional forms leads to the third result of the distributive-justice analysis of monastic institutions:

CLOISTER EFFECT 3. The magnitude of the benefit of the cloister is contingent on the type and distributional form of the valued good in the society

The particular feature of the distributional form that appears to control the magnitude of the cloister benefit is the *lower limit*. Our results to date are consistent with the proposition that the level of the cloister effect is greatest in societies where the distribution of the valued good goes to zero as its lower limit—as in the quality-good distribution and the lognormal distribution. Thus a society that valued wealth and that followed the Rawlsian principles of justice would not benefit substantially from the presence of monasteries.

The benefit formulas in Table 2 reveal a further difference between quality-good regimes and quantity-good regimes: Whereas in quality-good regimes, the magnitude of the benefit is a function solely of the proportion cloistered α, in quantity-good regimes, the magnitude of the benefit is also a function of the general inequality parameter c. Thus a new question arises. Holding constant the proportion cloistered, does the benefit increase or decrease with inequality in the quantity-good's distribution? To answer this question, we differentiate partially the benefit formulas with respect to the general inequality parameter c. The first partial derivatives, reported in Part B of Table 2, indicate that the benefit of the cloister is an increasing function of the inequality in the quantity-good's distribution, enabling statement of the fourth result:

> CLOISTER EFFECT 4. Holding constant the proportion cloistered and within distributional form, the greater the inequality in the quantity-good's distribution the greater the benefit conferred by the cloister

Toward a New Perspective on Monastic Institutions

The theory of the distributive-justice force suggests that, indeed, the view that monastic institutions increase the social welfare is not without foundation. That is, under the conditions of the model we have formulated—the cloistered assume the lowest places in the distribution of the valued good—the cloister always confers a benefit on the noncloistered. However, the theory of the distributive-justice force enables derivation of new predictions concerning the *magnitude* of the cloister's benefit to society, predictions beyond anything in the monastic literature. The results reported can be stated in one general summary sentence:

> SUMMARY EFFECT OF THE CLOISTER: The precise magnitude of the cloister's benefit to the noncloistered is conditioned by three features of the collectivity: first, whether the valued good is a quality good or a quantity good; second, if a quantity good, on its distributional form, in particular, its lower-limit behavior; and third, if a quantity good, on its degree of inequality.

When is the public benefit due to the cloister greatest? Our analysis indicates that the greatest benefit occurs in two types of societies, first, a society that values a quality good, such as birth or nobility, and second, a society that values wealth and that is characterized by poverty and inequality. In contrast, prosperous societies, societies with generous "safety nets," and societies with egalitarian income distributions will not see much benefit from monasteries.

To the extent that diverse individual and social phenomena are functions of the cloister benefit, many predictions are implied concerning their connection to the societal-valued good and its distributional form.

At the individual level, consider the propensity to enter or to remain in the religious life. If this propensity is, ceteris paribus, an increasing function of the benefit to the noncloistered, then a number of predictions follow immediately. For example, a change in the society's valued good is a sufficient but not necessary condition for defections from the religious life and for a decrease in new religious vocations, as is also a societal shift in the income distribution toward less inequality. Other things the same, societies with highly unequal income distributions will have more vocations than societies with less unequal income distributions, and societies with extreme poverty will have more vocations than societies with adequate minimum incomes.

At the social level, consider the state's disposition toward monastic institutions. If this disposition is more favorable the greater the benefit to the noncloistered, then societies whose valued goods are shifting will be less favorably disposed toward monasteries, as will be societies whose distribution of material resources is shifting from, say, a lognormal type to a Pareto type.

Thus historical fluctuations in the number of monastic adherents and historical fluctuations in the state's disposition toward monasteries may be at least partly explained by the operation of the distributive-justice force.

As well, the high watermarks of the history of religious orders—the great foundations and reforms—can be understood in a new way. Our analysis suggests that the special work of the great monastic innovators and reformers was *first, to detect the valued good, and, second, persuade others to take the lowest places in the distribution of the valued good.* Because the latter is, at least in Christianity, an obvious challenge—as seen in the classic texts, such as Luke 14:7–11—we must regard detection of the valued good as the essence of their genius.

But that is not enough. Circumstances, too, must be favorable; that is, the valued good must be one amenable to making a case that taking the lowest places is feasible and godly. If the valued good is healthiness, there is not much that a religious genius can do, for it would be difficult to build a credible case for assuming the lowest places in the healthiness hierarchy. Thus monasteries can produce the salutary effect predicted by the theory of the distributive-justice force only in particular kinds of societies, societies that value a very particular kind of good, namely a good such that voluntarily taking the lowest places constitutes a religious ideal.[25]

With these insights, a reinterpretation of monastic history is possible. Though such reinterpretation lies outside the scope of this chapter, we note that the main elements would include the societal valued goods and the connection to them of the life prescribed in the

---

[25]Future work might investigate the precise character of the requisite valued good. A starting proposition might be that the valued good must be the opposite of a religious ideal. Examples of such valued goods would be (1) wealth, which is the opposite of the religious ideal of poverty; and (2) liberty, which is the opposite of the religious ideal of obedience.

monastic rules. Taking liberties with the considerable subtleties and nuances both of monasteries and societies, we hazard a preliminary look.[26]

A rereading of the lives and works of the early Fathers, especially Basil (330–379) and Augustine (354–430), and of Benedict of Nursia (480–547), suggests that they perceived in a special new way that birth and nobility were the quintessential valued goods of their time and that primacy in the rules for monastic organization must be given to equality of persons. The Rule attributed to St. Benedict, the cornerstone of what has come to be known as the Benedictine monastic ideal, stipulates absolute individual poverty and equality (Chapters 33, 34). The Rule's injunctions against "distinction of persons" (Chapter 2) and the many instructions—for rotating onerous duties (Chapter 35), for election of the abbot (Chapter 21), for the order in chapel procession (Chapter 63), and for disposition of private property upon entering the monastery (Chapters 58, 59)—leave little doubt that the monks in the Benedictine ideal were taking the lowest places in the world's hierarchies of birth and lineage (also Chapter 7). So long as the societies in which the monasteries were located valued birth and lineage, the monasteries conferred the salutary cloister effect predicted by distributive-justice theory.

The Rule of St. Benedict, however, although stipulating *individual* poverty, does not require *corporate* poverty (Chapter 32). Hence, if the societal valued good changed from birth to wealth, the monks would no longer necessarily occupy the lowest places in the new wealth hierarchy. Each monk would count, in the eyes of the world, for a 1/Nth share of the monastery's property—in some houses a sizable portion. Thus, as birth and nobility ceased to be the principal valued goods, the salutary cloister benefit would disappear. Our results would lead to the predictions that, in consequence of this shift in societal valued goods, the classical Benedictine monasteries would attract fewer monks and more state displeasure. In unambiguously wealth regimes, the religious impulse would seek new forms of expression, and activist states would dissolve the monasteries.

In the social transformations that increased the importance of money and produced new wealth hierarchies,[27] there would be two

---

[26]This section relies on the standard historical accounts of monasticism, especially Knowles (1969, 1976), on the works of Augustine, Benedict, Aquinas, Teresa de Avila, and Ignacio de Loyola, and on the biographical and textual materials in Jörgensen (1955), Brown (1958), and Tugwell (1982).

[27]The classic work of Haskins (1927) on the renaissance of the twelfth century is especially illuminating.

great new founders, Dominic (1170–1221) in Spain and Francis of Assisi (1181–1226) in Italy. Astonished by the contrasts of wealth and poverty around them, Dominic and Francis independently introduced the radical notion that it was not enough for the individual monk to be totally bereft of private property, that the new religious organization, too, must relinquish property, the new religious living, not from the income of corporate property, but by wages and alms. From the perspective of distributive-justice theory, it is no accident that the great mendicant orders arose early in the thirteenth century.

The societal transition from one valued good to another is not without trauma. Neither is the application of an unquestioned religious ideal—taking the lowest places—to the hierarchy of a new valued good. Experiment and conflict attend a new foundation.

History records Francis's first experiment with poverty, traveling to Rome where he would not be recognized, exchanging clothing with a beggar, and trying out the begging of alms outside St. Peter's. And history records the great public confrontation at which Francis, denounced by his father for giving away much of the cloth in the prosperous merchant's shop, vowed to return all his father's property—and promptly stripped himself naked.

Within 50 years, the young (some say teen-aged) Thomas Aquinas (1224–1274), educated from childhood at the great Benedictine house of Monte Cassino and intended by his parents for the Benedictine life, would rebel and choose instead the Dominican ideal, to study and to work for wages. To dissuade him form so common a a course, his family held him captive, relenting after about a year, when Thomas's determination proved unshakeable. Upon finishing his studies and for the rest of his life, Thomas Aquinas would earn his living as a university professor.[28]

Of course, not all shifts in societal valued goods are discrete and dramatic. Some may take long periods of time to complete; in different places they may occur at different times. Moreover, the seeming finality of shifts in valued goods may be deceptive, old goods returning and new goods arising. The essence of the religious genius is to detect these shifts and move to take the lowest places in the new hierarchies. For example, it is possible that the new order of Ignatius of Loyola (1491–1540) and the great reforms of Teresa de Avila (1515–1562) were linked to the intensity of wealth hierarchies newly animated by colonial revenues.

---

[28]History records that his salary at the University of Naples, a state institution, was 12 ounces of gold per year.

Summary

This chapter has described how the human sense of distributive
justice, formalized by the theory of the distributive-justice force, leads
to predictions concerning the emergence and maintenance of institutions that promote the social welfare.

We derived the three basic social welfare institutions that can be
predicted from the theory. We formulated a collectivistic model of how
societies choose the goods they value and, using tools from the study
of probability distributions, derived general predictions concerning
the choice of valued goods in two-goods contests. Finally, we derived
the theory's predictions concerning the social welfare benefit that the
cloister confers on the noncloistered.

Much remains to be done. More social welfare institutions can be
derived from the theory of the distributive-justice force. More forms of
quantity-good distributions can be investigated. The predictions derived in this chapter can be prepared for empirical testing. And the
many disparate predictions can be combined to produce an integrated
view of particular societies.

To end this initial attempt to derive institutions that promote the
social welfare from the theory of the distributive-justice force, we list
the principal predictions derived in this paper:

1. In all societies, there will arise devices that promote variability
   in individuals' notions of what is just for themselves.
2. In societies that value at least one quantity good there will arise
   redistributive schemes designed to achieve inequality reduction.
3. In societies that value at least one quality good, there will arise
   devices for population control.
4. When a societal Guardian chooses the valued good for a
   society, the decision always favors that good whose distribution is less unequal (as measured by the ratio of the geometric
   mean to the arithmetic mean).
5. In a contest between two quality goods, the Guardian is
   indifferent.
6. A sufficient condition for a cloistered subgroup to confer a
   benefit on the noncloistered subgroup is that the cloistered
   subgroup occupy the lowest places in the hierarchy of the
   collectivity's valued good.
7. The magnitude of the benefit that the noncloistered derive from
   the cloister is an increasing function of the proportion cloistered of the collectivity.

8. The magnitude of the benefit of the cloister is contingent on the type and distributional form of the valued good in the society.
9. Holding constant the proportion cloistered and within distributional form, the greater the inequality in the quantity-good's distribution, the greater the benefit conferred by the cloister.

Appendix: Relations between the Arithmetic Mean, the Geometric Mean, and the Inequality in a Distribution

Proposition 1a: Ceteris paribus, the geometric mean is a decreasing function of the dispersion in a distribution.

Proposition 1b: Ceteris paribus, the geometric mean is an increasing function of the arithmetic mean of a distribution.

Proof: Consider the measure of inequality defined as the ratio of the geometric mean to the arithmetic mean and denoted δ

$$\delta = (GM(X))/[E(X)], \tag{A1}$$

where the variate X assumes positive values, $GM(X)$ denotes the geometric mean, and $E(X)$ denotes the arithmetic mean of the variate X. This measure was derived by Atkinson (1970, 1975). Because in the distribution of a positive quantity, the geometric mean is always a positive quantity less than or equal to the arithmetic mean,

$$0 < GM(X) \le E(X), \tag{A2}$$

and because their equality obtains only in the case of an equal distribution (namely for all i, $x_i = E(X)$), it follows that the measure δ has bounds of 0 and 1, being open at zero and closed at unity:

$$0 < \delta \le 1. \tag{A3}$$

Thus, as inequality increases, the measure δ grows smaller, traveling toward zero, while as inequality decreases, the measure δ increases, attaining the value of 1 when the condition of equality obtains.

Because most measures of inequality increase as inequality increases (e.g., the variance and the Gini coefficient of concentration), it is convenient to derive a new measure of dispersion from δ. The new measure, denoted $D(X)$, is defined:

$$D(X) = 1 - \delta. \tag{A4}$$

Its domain of definition is closed at 0 and open at 1. As inequality increases, the measure $D(X)$ increases.

It is then straightforward to express the dispersion $D(X)$ as a function of the geometric mean and the geometric mean,

$$D(X) = 1 - [GM(X)]/[E(X)], \qquad (A5)$$

and, converoely, the geometric mean as a function of the dispersion $D(X)$ and of the arithmetic mean:

$$GM(X) = [E(X)][(1 - D(X)]. \qquad (A6)$$

Hence, the first partial derivative of the geometric mean with respect to the dispersion is given by

$$[GM(X)]_{D(X)} = -[E(X)]. \qquad (A7)$$

Because attention has been restricted to the distribution of a positive quantity, the first partial derivative is always negative. We conclude that the geometric mean is a decreasing function of the dispersion in a distribution.

Similarly, the first partial derivative of the geometric mean with respect to the arithmetic mean is given by

$$[GM(X)]_{E(X)} = 1 - D(X). \qquad (A8)$$

This quantity is always positive. Hence, we conclude that the geometric mean is, ceteris paribus, an increasing function of the arithmetic mean.

References

Albert, Ethel M. (1968). Values: Value systems. In David L. Sills (ed.), *International encyclopedia of the social sciences* (Vol. 16, pp. 287–291). New York: Macmillan.

Alves, Wayne M., and Peter H. Rossi. (1978). Who should get what? Fairness judgments in the distribution of earnings. *American Journal of Sociology 84*, pp. 541–564.

Alves, Wayne M. (1982). Modeling distributive justice judgments. In P. H. Rossi and S. L. Nock (Eds.), *Measuring social judgments: The factorial survey approach* (pp. 205–234). Beverly Hills CA: Sage.

Alwin, Duane F. (1987). Distributive justice and satisfaction with material well-being. *American Sociological Review, 52* 83–95.

Aristotle. (1952). *The works of Aristotle* (2 vols.; trans. by W. D. Ross). Chicago: Britannica. (Written in the fourth century B.C.)

Atkinson, Anthony B. (1970). On the measurement of inequality. *Journal of Economic Theory, 2* pp. 244–263.

Atkinson, Anthony B.(1975). *The economics of inequality*. London: Oxford.

Augustine, Saint. (1952). *The city of God* (trans. by Marcus Dods). Chicago: Britannica. (Original first published between 413 and 426 A.D.)

Augustine, Saint (1952). *The confessions* (trans. by Edward Bouverie Pusey). Chicago: Britannica. (Original first published about 400.)

Augustine, Saint (1961). *The enchiridion on faith, hope and love* (trans. by J. F. Shaw; ed. with an introduction by Henry Paolucci). Chicago: Gateway. (Original published in 421.)

Barber, Bernard. (1968). Stratification, social: Introduction. In David L. Sills (Ed.), *International encyclopedia of the social sciences* (Vol. 15, pp. 288–296). New

York: Macmillan.

Benedict, Saint. (1948). *Rule for monasteries* (trans. by Leonard J. Doyle). St. Johns Abbey: Liturgical. At least parts are believed to have been written by Saint Benedict early in the sixth century.

Berger, Joseph, Zelditch, Morris, & Anderson Bo. (1972). Introduction. In Joseph Berger, Morris Zelditch, Bo Anderson (Eds.), *Sociological theories in progress* (Vol. 2, pp. ix–xxii). Boston: Houghton Mifflin.

Berger, Joseph, Zelditch, Morris Anderson, Bo, & Cohen Bernard P. (1972). "Structural aspects of distributive justice: A status-value formulation." In Joseph Berger, Morris Zelditch, Bo Anderson (Eds.), *Sociological theories in progress* (Vol.2, pp. 119–246). Boston: Houghton Mifflin.

Berger, Joseph, Fisek, M. Hamit, Norman, Robert Z. & Wagner, David G. (1985). Formation of reward expectations in status situations. In Joseph Berger & Morris Zelditch, Jr. (Eds.), *Status, rewards, and influence: How expectations organize behavior.* (pp. 215–261). San Francisco: Jossey-Bass.

Blau, Peter M. (1977). *Inequality and heterogeneity.* New York: Free Press.

Brown, Raphael. (1958). *The little flowers of St. Francis* (trans. with an introduction by R. Brown). New York: Image.

Coleman, James S. (1961). *The adolescent society.* New York: Free Press.

Coleman, James S. (1967). Research chronicle: The adolescent society. In P. E. Hammond (Ed.), *Sociologists at work.* (pp. 213–243). Garden City, NY: Doubleday Anchor. (First published in 1964.)

Coleman, James S. (1973). *The mathematics of collective action.* London: Heinemann. Constitution of the United States. (1952). Chicago: Britannica. (Original document finalized in 1787.)

Eisenstadt, Shmuel N. (1968a). Social institutions: The concept. In David L. Sills (Ed.), *International encyclopedia of the social science* (Vol 14, pp. 409–421). New York: Macmillan.

Eisenstadt, Shmuel N. (1968b). Social Institutions: Comparative study. In David L. Sills (Ed.), *International encyclopedia of the social sciences* (Vol. 14, pp. 421–429). New York: Macmillan.

Fararo, Thomas J. (1984). Neoclassical theorizing and formalization in sociology. In T. J. Fararo (Ed.), *Mathematical ideas and sociological theory: Current state and prospects. A special issue of the Journal of Mathematical Sociology* .(pp. 143–175) New York: Gordon & Breach.

Festinger, Leon. (1954). A theory of social comparison processes. *Human Relations, 7,* pp. 117–140.

Gartrell, C. David. (1985). Relational and distributional models of collective justice sentiments. *Social Forces, 64,* pp. 64–83.

Gartrell, C. David. (1987). "Representing justice sentiments with blockmodels (Rejoinder to Markovsky and Ford)." *Social Forces, 65,* pp. 1149–1152.

Gerard, Harold B. (1968). Social psychology. In David L. Sills (Ed.), *International encyclopedia of the social sciences* (vol. 14, pp. 459–473). New York: Macmillan.

Goldhamer, Herbert. (1968). Social mobility. In David L. Sills (Ed.), *International encyclopedia of the social sciences* (vol. 14, pp. 429–438). New York: Macmillan.

Gusfield, Joseph. (1968). Social movements: The study of social movements. In David L. Sills (Ed.), *International encyclopedia of the social sciences* (Vol. 14, pp. 445–452). New York: Macmillan.

Haskins, Charles H. (1927, 1957). *The Renaissance of the twelfth century.* New York: Meridian.

Hastings, N. A. J., & Peacock, J. B. (1974). *Statistical distributions:A handbook for students and practitioners.* London: Butterworth.

Heberle, Rudolf. (1968). Social movements: Types and functions . In David L. Sills (Ed.), *International encyclopedia of the social sciences* (Vol. 14, pp. 439–444. New York: Macmillan.

Homans, George Caspar. (1974). *Social behavior: Its elementary forms.* (Rev. ed.). New York: Harcourt, Brace, Jovanovich. (First published in 1961.)

Hyman, Herbert H. (1968). Reference groups. In David L. Sills (Ed.), *International encyclopedia of the social sciences* (Vol. 13, pp. 353–361). New York: Macmillan.

Ignacio de Loyola, San. (1963). *Obras completas* (Ed. by I. Iparraguirre & C. de Dalmases). Madrid: Espasa-Calpe. Items written between 1521 and 1556.

James, William. (1952). *The principles of psychology.* Chicago: Britannica. (First published in 1891).

Jasso, Guillermina. (1978). On the justice of earnings: A new specification of the justice evaluation function. *American Journal of Sociology, 83,* 1398–1419.

Jasso, Guillermina. (1980). A new theory of distributive justice. *American Sociological Review 45,* 3–32.

Jasso, Guillermina. (1981). Further notes on the theory of distributive justice (Reply to Soltan). *American Sociological Review, 46,* 352–360.

Jasso, Guillermina. (1982). Measuring inequality by the ratio of the geometric mean to the arithmetic mean. *Sociological Methods and Research, 10,* 303–326.

Jasso, Guillermina. (1983a). Fairness of individual rewards and fairness of the reward distribution: Specifying the inconsistency between the micro and macro principles of justice. *Social Psychology Quarterly, 46,* 185–199.

Jasso, Guillermina. (1983b). Social consequences of the sense of distributive justice: Small-group applications. In David M. Messick & Karen Cook (Eds.), *Equity theory: Psychological and sociological perspectives.* (pp. 243–294). New York: Praeger.

Jasso, Guillermina. (1983c). Using the inverse distribution function to compare income distributions and their inequality. *Research in Social Stratification and Mobility, 2,* 271–306.

Jasso, Guillermina. (1986). A new representation of the just term in distributive-justice theory: Its properties and operation in theoretical derivation and empirical estimation. *Journal of Mathematical Sociology, 12,* 251–274.

Jasso, Guillermina. (1987a). Distributive-justice effects of employment and earnings on marital cohesiveness: An empirical test of theoretical predictions.In Murray Webster & Martha Foschi (Eds.), *Status generalization: New theory and research*(pp. 123–162, 490–493). Palo Alto, CA: Stanford University Press.

Jasso, Guillermina. (1987b). Choosing a good: Models based on the theory of the distributive-justice force. *Advances in Group Processes; Theory and Research, 4,* 67–108.

Jasso, Guillermina. (1988b). Principles of theoretical analysis. *Sociological Theory 6,* pp. 1–20

Jasso, Guillermina. (1989a). Notes on the advancement of theoretical sociology (reply to Turner). *Sociological Theory 7,* pp. 135–144.

Jasso, Guillermina. (1989b). The theory of the distributive-justice force in human affairs: Analyzing the three central questions. In J. Berger, M. Zelditch, Jr., and B. Anderson (Eds.), *Sociological theories in progress: New formulations.* (pp. 354–387). Newbury Park, CA: Sage.

Jasso, Guillermina. (1990a). Methods for the theoretical and empirical analysis of comparison processes. In C. C. Clogg (Ed.), *Sociological Methodology 1990.* Washington, DC: American Sociological Association.

Jasso, Guillermina. (1990b). Cloister and society: Analyzing the public benefit of monastic and mendicant institutions. (1990). Paper presented at the annual meeting of the Society for the Scientific Study of Religion, Virginia Beach,

Virginia, November.

Jasso, Guillermina, & Rosenzweig Mark R. (1986). What's in a name? Country-of-origin influences on the earnings of immigrants in the United States. Research in Human Capital and Development, 4, 75–106.

Jasso, Guillermina, & Rossi Peter H. (1977). Distributive justice and earned income. American Sociological Review, 42, 639–651.

Johnson, Norman L., & Kotz Samuel (1970a). Distributions in statistics: Continuous univariate distributions—1. Boston: Houhgton Mifflin.

Johnson, Norman L., & Kotz Samuel. (1970b). Distributions in statistics: Continuous univariate distributions—2. Boston: Houghton Mifflin.

Jörgensen, Johannes. (1955). St Francis of Assisi: A biography (First published in 1912). Garden City, NY: Image.

Kelley, Harold H. (1952). Two functions of reference groups. In G. Swanson, T. M. Newcomb, & E. L. Hartley (Eds.), Readings in social psychology (pp. 410–414). New York: Holt.

Kidder, Louise H. (1986). There is no word for "fair"—Notes from Japan. Paper presented at the International Conference on Social Justice in Human Relations, Leiden University, The Netherlands.

Knowles, David. (1969). Christian monasticism. London: Cambridge.

Knowles, David. (1976). Bare ruined choirs: The dissolution of the English monasteries. London: Cambridge.

Lebergott, Stanley. (1959). The shape of the income distribution. American Economic Review, 49, 328–347.

Lebergott, Stanley. 1968. Income distribution: Size. In David L. Sills (Ed.), International encyclopedia of the social sciences (Vol. 7, pp. 145–154). New York: Macmillan.

Markovsky, Barry. (1985). Toward a multilevel distributive justice theory. American Sociological Review, 50, 822–839.

Markovsky, Barry, Ford Thomas W. (1987). Testing justice theories with blockmodels (Comment on Gartrell, SF 1985). Social Forces, 65, pp. 1143–1149.

Merton, Robert K. (1957). Continuities in the theory of reference groups and social structure. In R. K. Merton, (Ed.), Social theory and social structure, Second edition (pp. 281–386). New York: Free Press.

Merton, Robert K. & Rossi, Alice S. (1950). Contributions to the theory of reference group behavior. In R. K. Merton & P. Lazarsfeld (Eds.), Continuities in social research: Studies in the scope and method of "The American Soldier" pp. 40–105). New York: Free Press.

Mirowsky, John. (1987). The psycho-economics of feeling underpaid: Distributive justice and the earnings of husbands and wives. American Journal of Sociology, 92, 1404–1434.

Pareto, Vilfredo. (1927). Cours d'Economie Politique Professé à l'Université de Lausanne (2nd ed., 2 vols). Paris: Giard & Brière. (First published in 1896–1897.)

Parsons, Talcott. (1951). The social system. New York: Free Press.

Rawls, John. (1971). A theory of justice. Cambridge: Harvard.

Ridgeway, Cecilia, & Berger Joseph, (1986). Expectations and legitimation in groups. American Sociological Review, 51, 603–617.

Rossi, Peter H. (1951). The application of latent structure analysis to the study of social stratification. Unpublished PhD dissertation, Columbia University.

Rossi, Peter H. (1979). Vignette analysis: Uncovering the normative Structure of complex judgments. In Qualitative and quantitative social research: Papers in honor of Paul F. Lazarsfeld (ed. by Robert K. Merton, Coleman, James S. & Rossi Peter H., pp. 176–186. New York: Free Press.

Rossi, Peter H., & Anderson Andy B. (1982). The factorial survey approach: An introduction. In *Measuring social judgments: The factorial survey approach*. (pp. 65–67). Beverly Hills: Sage.

Rossi, Peter H., & Berk Richard A. (1985). Varieties of normative consensus. *American Sociological Review, 50,* 333–347.

Shepelak, Norma J., & Alwin, Duane F. (1986). Beliefs about inequality and perceptions of distributive justice. *American Sociological Review, 51,* 30–46.

Sherif, Muzafer. (1968). "Self Concept." In David L. Sills (Eds.), *International encyclopedia of the social sciences* (Vol. 14, pp. 150–159). New York: Macmillan.

Soltan, Karol Edward. (1981). Jasso on distributive justice (comment on Jasso. *ASR,* February 1980. *American Sociological review* 46, pp. 348–352.

Sorokin, Pitirim A. (1968). Social differentiation. In David L. Sills (Ed.), *International encyclopedia of the social sciences* (Vol. 14, pp. 406–409). New York: Macmillan.

Teresa de Avila, Santa. (1982). *Obras completas* (Annotated and with an introduction by Luis Santullano. Based on the text edited and annotated by P. Silverio). Madrid: Aguilar. (Items written between 1546 and 1582.)

Thomas Aquinas, Saint. (1952). *Summa theologica* (2 vols., translated by Fathers of the English Dominican Province. Revised by Daniel J. Sullivan). Chicago: Britannica. (Written between 1267 and 1273.)

Tugwell, Simon (Ed.). (1982). *Early Dominicans: Selected writings.* New York: Paulist.

Wagner, David G., & Berger Joseph. (1985). Do sociological theories grow? *American Journal of Sociology, 90,* pp. 697–728.

Williams, Robin M., Jr. (1968). Values: The concept of values. In David L. Sills (Ed.), *International encyclopedia of the social sciences* (Vol. 16, pp. 283–287). New York: Macmillan.

Zelditch, Morris, Jr. (1968). Status, social. In David L. Sills (Ed.), *International encyclopedia of the social sciences* (Vol. 15, pp. 250–257). New York: Macmillan.

9

Criteria for Distributive Justice in a Productive Context

Bert Overlaet and Erik Schokkaert

Introduction

In 1977, the Center for Community Psychology started a research program on the attitudes toward redistribution of income. In 1981, we presented an analysis and interpretation of questionnaire data of 180 subjects (Lagrou, Overlaet, & Schokkaert, 1981). We questioned our subjects on how they perceived and evaluated the existing income distribution. In general, there appeared a strong tendency to redistribute incomes by reducing the span between high and low-income groups. The structure of the income distribution was left unchanged. These results were further elaborated into a formal mathematical model (Overlaet & Lagrou, 1981; Schokkaert & Lagrou, 1983).

The purpose of this research program was to identify the relevant criteria used by people to justify income differences. We proposed three criteria: merit, need, and compensation for work conditions. The results attributed an overwhelming importance to "merit" considerations in ethical judgements on the income distribution. When we asked our subjects whether it would be equitable if "John earns more than Peter because . . . (e.g.) John has more responsibility in his job," 80% to 90% agreed or strongly agreed with such an income difference

Bert Overlaet • Department of Psychology, K. U. Leuven, 3000 Leuven, Belgium
Erik Schokkaert • Center for Economic Studies and Center for Economics and Ethics, K. U. Leuven, 3000 Leuven, Belgium.

198 Bert Overlaet and Erik Schokkaert

if it was due to responsibility, risk taking, competence, effort, or leadership. Factor analysis revealed that these criteria could be considered as reflecting one factor, which we called "managers' ethos," expressing an overall ideology of merit. Other criteria as need or compensation were more controversial. We also examined the judgments of equitable incomes for 12 well-known occupations, taking into account perceived job characteristics of those occupations. The evidence from this indirect method was similar to the evidence drawn from direct questioning. Our results confirmed previous research (e.g., Alves & Rossi, 1978; Hermkens & Van Wijngaarden, 1977) indicating merit as a generally applied and accepted justification for income differences.

However there were two major shortcomings: (1) Since we did not ask our subjects to *compare* criteria, we could draw no conclusions as to the judgment of our subjects in situations where different criteria interact, whereas in real life this is almost always the case. (2) The clusters *merit* or *desert* contain dissimilar criteria that often conflict in real-life situations. The diversity of merit criteria threatens to reduce our conclusion to a self-fulfilling prophecy[1] because one can always find some "merit" to justify income differences. We concluded that further differentiation was necessary and that we needed a method that allows for comparison and simultaneous application of different criteria.

Method

The methodology we used in this study is well known in social psychology. We adapted it from Yaari and Bar-Hillel (1984). Subjects are presented simple but concrete cases in which a specific distributional problem is demonstrated. They are asked to give a judgment on how a certain amount of goods is to be distributed among parties. They can choose between a number of given distributions that are based on theoretical models, or they can (if they prefer) add their own solution.

Very few people are in a position to influence the income distribution at large. However, many people find themselves confronted with the problem of dividing a limited sum (be it a premium, a raise, or a loss) in a way that may possibly reduce or reinforce the income

---

[1]Yaari and Bar-Hillel (1984) state that the use of the terms *merit* and *desert* should be avoided because they are too close to being synonyms for "attributes possibly justifying a departure from equality." In our interpretation, "merit" and "desert" are related to productive contribution.

difference between the people involved. By formulating our cases as similar to such real-world situations as possible, we tried to increase the immediate social relevancy of our work.

A basic idea of Yaari and Bar-Hillel that we followed was to construct a series of variants slightly modifying a common basic situation. These variants were presented to different, comparable groups of respondents. By systematically manipulating the information provided in the variants and by comparing the responses to this manipulation, it becomes possible to assess effects of certain conditions or variables. For this reason this method can be considered as quasi-experimental.

In May 1986, we presented a first list of cases to 243 first-year university students taking a course in economics. Twelve sets of cases were constructed in such a way that no one contained variants of the same case. The sets were randomly distributed among the students. Each student responded to one set of cases. There was no interaction among the respondents. In comparing responses between sets, we found patterns that were remarkably consistent and stable. We therefore consider our data as reliable.

In the next section, we will present some results. First we describe how respondents distribute a bonus in a productive context when different merit criteria are in conflict. Second, we discuss the problem of effort versus result, and finally we compare the distribution of gains with the distribution of losses. Because we consider our results as exploratory, no sophisticated statistical tests were applied.

Results

Income Differences in a Productivity Context

In economic organizations, wage differences are almost exclusively determined by merit criteria. People are paid according to their acknowledged contribution to the overall result of the organization. Four criteria are generally used in determining the personal productivity of each individual worker: seniority (experience), educational level, job content (position), and output. Wage scales and extra provisions are linked to the persons position on these four criteria.

Seniority, educational level, and hierarchical position can be considered as "acquired rights": They refer to a position one has built up by effort and competence shown in the past. Output, on the other hand, refers to *actual* efforts. In practice, the first three criteria dominate: Effort has only a marginal impact on income differences, although for some jobs it may provide an important incentive. As effort is an important criterion determining promotion to a higher (and better paid) position, we may conclude that effort is remunerated mostly in an indirect way.

This system works well as long as sufficient promotion possibilities exist to reward meritorious junior employees. In a context of austerity programs, however, aimed at reducing wage cost or government spending, it leads to conflict between senior and junior employees. Senior workers consider their vested titles as postponed pay: They have been earned in the past so they cannot be modified. This argument puts the weight of cost reduction on the youngest and weakest shoulders. The young employees see their promotion deferred and their effort unsufficiently rewarded. In this way, recent economic experience has shown that the original principle of "each according to his merit" cannot be easily applied.

The first case examines how our respondents solve this problem.

> In a government agency, a permanently appointed clerk who has 15 years service, earning 50.000 BF a month, and a probational employee[2] earning 30.000 BF a month, work in the same office. They do the same work and *work equally hard* . An extra amount of 8.000 BF must be divided between the two of them. What would you consider to be a fair distribution?

For this case we expected the subjects to choose between four different answers. The first two possibilities respect or reinforce the vested interests claimed by the senior employee. The two remaining answers compensate for the differences in earning and try to establish a more equal treatment.

1. A distribution proportional to the existing differences in pay (5.000–3.000)
2. An equal distribution (4.000–4.000) because both employees do the same job and produce the same effort
3. A distribution inversely proportional to the differences in earning (3.000–5.000)
4. A distribution that compensates stronger (from 2.000–6.000 to 0–8.000) because the amount to be distributed is relatively small compared to the differences in earning.

The first column of Table 1 shows the responses of our subjects: An overwhelming majority (89.7%) do not interfere with the existing claims. On the average, the senior employee gets 7% more of the extra

---

[2]In Belgium, organizations are legally obliged to hire a certain number of unemployed on probation. As a consequence, many young employees start their career as probationers.

Table 1. Distribution of Responses and Average Responses for Case 1 (Seniority versus Effort)

Distribution	Equal effort	Unequal effort
1. Equal 4.000–4.000	46.6%	17.2%
2. Proportional 5.000–3.000	43.1%	10.3%
3. Inversely proportional 3.000–5.000	3.4%	46.6%
4. Extreme compensation > 5.000	6.9%	25.9%
Average part senior employee	4.284 BF	2.740 BF
Average part junior employee	3.716 BF	5.260 BF
Number of respondents	58	58

provision than a younger colleague, who does the same job. Equal and proportional distribution are approximately equally supported.

The answer pattern changes dramatically when the statement in italics in the text is replaced by the indication that the probationer works harder than his senior colleague. In this condition, the number of subjects reinforcing the existing seniority rights drops from 43% to 10%. Even when we add those advocating an equal distribution, only a large quarter of our respondents take seniority into account. Seventy-two percent on the other hand try to restore the balance by compensating. In this case, the probational employee receives on the average two-thirds of the extra. We conclude from this comparison that seniority is viewed by the majority of our respondents as a right justification for income differences, as long as both parties show comparable effort. However, when a significant unbalance of effort arises, considerations of seniority rights are overwhelmed by a much stronger need to reward effort.

A second case examines whether the same effect can be produced when seniority is replaced by hierarchical position or by educational level, and when the reward to be divided is substantially bigger. In the "educational degree/equal effort" condition, the case runs as follows:

> Two salesmen from the same company are working on a trade fair. Johnson has a university degree and earns 50.000 BF a month, whereas Peters has no degree and earns 30.000 BF a month. Their collective success raises an extra premium of 240.000 BF. What do you consider to be an equitable distribution when you know that both men have equally contributed to the success?

In the "hierarchical condition," the first paragraph is replaced by

> On a trade fair, salesman Johnson and his assistant Peters are doing a great job. Normally Johnson earns 50.000 BF a month, whereas Peters earns 30.000 BF a month.

In both versions the last phrase was replaced in the "unequal effort" condition by

. . . when you know that Peters has been twice as much on the stand than Johnson.

In this case we expected the subjects to choose between four answers:

1. An equal distribution reflecting the efforts in the "equal effort" conditions, while constituting a tentative compensation in the "unequal effort" conditions
2. A distribution proportional to the existing pay difference (150.000–90.000) that reinforces the claims of hierarchical position or educational level
3. An inversely proportional distribution (90.000–150.000) that compensates for the pay difference, trying to establish final equality
4. A distribution proportional to the efforts in the "unequal effort" conditions (80.000–160.000) that rewards effort without taking into consideration the other criteria.

The results are shown in Table 2. In the "equal effort" conditions, approximately two-thirds of our subjects opt for an equal distribution, the remainder of our sample advocating a distribution proportional to the earnings. As in the previous case, educational level and hierarchical position are viewed as legitimate justifications for income differences, although here the support for a proportional distribution is smaller.

In the "unequal effort" conditions, however, claims based on hierarchical position and past educational efforts are again swept away by the need to reward actual dedication. In both instances, almost two-thirds of the subjects compensate for the existing pay differences

Table 2. Distribution of Responses and Average Response for Case 2 (Education and Hierarchy versus Effort)

	Educational level		Hierarchical position	
	Equal effort	Unequal effort	Equal effort	Unequal effort
Distribution[a]				
1. Equal (120.000–120.000)	70.7%	20.0%	66.7%	21.1%
2. Proportional (150.000–90.000)	22.0%	12.5%	28.2%	13.2%
3. Inversely Proportional (90.000–150.000)	2.4%	30.0%	2.6%	10.5%
4. Proportional to effort (80.000–160.000)	—	30.0%	—	52.6%
Average premium Johnson (high level)	126.220	105.750	127.950	100.000
Average premium Peters (low level)	113.780	134.250	112.050	140.000
Number of respondents	41	40	39	38

[a]Thirteen subjects (8%) chose other distributions. Because for 6 of them the difference from those postulated was minimal, they were added to the frequency distribution.

and in the "hierarchical" condition more than half of the subjects divide the extra according to the efforts shown. Only 13% stick to the existing unequality whereas 21% divide the premium equally: This means that they give a small compensation for effort or are just avoiding taking clear positions.

The general conclusions from our data are obvious: Our respondents tend to respect seniority, hierarchical position, and educational level and thus honor the claims for a higher pay. *But*, and this is important, *only if efforts are comparable*. In unequal effort conditions, people do not consider acquired rights in favor of rewarding actual efforts. It thus appears that people attach more importance to the reinforcement of output than is current practice in industrial and governmental organizations.

Effort versus Output

If effort is so dominant in justice evaluations, this attitude possibly rests on the assumption that effort leads to desired results. It is possible that our respondents associate effort with output and distribute income proportionally with the output assumed. The cases presented are vague in this respect and may suggest that for example, the probational employee produces more or better results than his senior colleague.

The question then raises what exactly our subjects value: the effort shown or the results produced. This distinction is far from academic and not restricted to the context of income distribution. Anyone who has ever evaluated student papers reflecting enormous effort, but with little meaningful result, knows how painful and difficult this distinction can be.

On the other hand, some people produce results with seemingly little effort: They are talented. Rephrasing the question, we can ask whether all individual characteristics leading to a higher output (ceteris paribus) should be valued in the same way. In general, philosophers as well as social psychologists[3] seem to agree that according to social justice (and efficiency), effort should be rewarded more than ability or talent. The next case examines the ethical intuitions of our respondents to this problem.

A cosmetic firm has two salesman: Mr. Jeckill and Mr. Hyde. Both do the same work. They both do what they can, they work hard, but, because of

---

[3]See, for example, Roscam Abbing (1978), Cohen (1974), Greenberg (1979), and Larwood, Lewin, Shaw, and Hurwitz (1979).

natural charm Mr. Jeckill gets 60 orders a month, whereas Mr. Hyde brings
in 40.
Both earn 40.000 BF a month. A monthly bonus of 10.000 BF is to be
divided between the two them.
What would you consider to be a just distribution?

We call this variant the "60/40 variant," where the surplus orders are
obtained by natural talent. A second variant inverses the number of
orders (40/60), and the surplus orders now stem from a difference in
effort. The relevant passage reads as follows:

Both men do the same work, but as Mr. Hyde puts in some extra effort from
time to time, he brings in more orders, that is 60 a month, whereas Mr.
Jeckill gets 40 orders a month.

A third variant combines both cases so that the number of orders is the
same for both salesman: 50/50.

Mr. Jeckill has a natural charm, but Mr. Hyde sometimes puts in a little
more effort, so both of them bring in the same number of orders, that is, 50
a month.

The answers in this case are much more complex than the answers to
the previous cases:

1. An equal distribution (5.000–5.000) reinforces the acquired
    equal position of both men, whereas in the 50/50 variant, it can
    also mean a distribution according to output
2. An unequal distribution (6.000–4.000) is proportional to output
    in the unequal variants and can indicate an extra reward for the
    effort or for the charm in the 50/50 condition
3. Finally, it is possible to divide even more unequally (more than
    6.000 for one of the men), indicating a strong need to compen-
    sate for charm or effort.

The results for our sample are shown in Table 3. Both natural talent
and effort are rewarded by our respondents but to a different degree. In
the first (60/40) variant, Mr. Jeckill is awarded proportional compensation for his charms by 56% of the sample. About 40% of the
respondents do not want to compensate for output differences, if they
only follow from innate characteristics. In the second 40/60 variant, the
wish to compensate for the effort of Mr. Hyde is much stronger: Only
15% of the sample do not give him a larger part of the bonus, and more
than a quarter of the subjects give him a more than proportional
compensation for his effort.
These observations lead to the hypothesis that effort will be extra
rewarded in the 50/50 case. Indeed, 17% of our respondents advocate
an extra bonus as a reward for the efforts of Mr. Hyde, whereas no one

Table 3. Distribution of Responses for Case 3 (Talent versus Effort)[a]

Output (Jeckill/Hyde)	60/40	40/60	50/50
Distribution			
1. >6.000 for Hyde	—	27.5%	—
2. 4.000–6.000	(2.6%)[a]	57.5%	16.7%
3. 5.000–5.000 (Equal)	41.0%	2.5%	83.3%
4. 6.000–4.000	56.4%	(7.5%)[a]	0.0%
5. 6.000 for Jeckill	0.0%	(5.0%)[a]	—
Average distribution between			
Jeckill and Hyde	55/45	36/64	48/52
Number of respondents	39	40	42

[a]Numbers in parentheses refer to answers not accounted for in the test.

rewards the natural charms of Mr. Jeckill in this situation. The overwhelming majority of respondents, however, stick to an equal distribution of the bonus, that is, proportional to output. These results suggest that effort is highly rewarded but only if it leads to a substantial difference in output.

Distribution of Profits versus Distribution of Losses

The results presented have one major drawback concerning social relevance: There is little room for extras to be divided in an economic context of scarcity. Private as well as public organizations are trying to reduce labor cost, facing severe competition and financial crises. As mentioned before, this produces a conflict between better paid senior workers defending their vested interests and younger and unexperienced employees. We already demonstrated how our subjects solve this conflict when there is a bonus to divide. We will now examine whether the solution is similar when there is a loss to divide.

In our previous research (see Overlaet & Lagrou, 1981), we found that the current income position is an important reference point in the judgment of income distributions. For the average respondent, what is considered as a just income lies slightly above his actual income level. This means that the income legitimation of most people presumes the existence of a bonus margin. We can hypothesize from this finding that, when labor cost has to be reduced, people are reinforced by their ethical judgment to defend their vested interests against each other, even if this results in an income distribution that they would consider unfair on itself.

This paradox is demonstrated by the next case that illustrates the meaning of the expression *acquired rights*. In the first version there is still a bonus to divide.

> John and Peter are glass blowers and set up a business together. John works 5 days a week and Peter only 4. Their work is complementary, and they are both indispensable. John has a net income of 500.000 BF a year, and Peter earns 400.000 BF. After a year they have got a sales revenue of 990.000 BF, so that they, after deduction of their wages, have realized a profit of 90.000 BF. What would you consider to be a just distribution of this profit?

So far this case is similar to those from the previous section. Three answers are plausible:

1. A 50.000–40.000 distribution, reinforcing the proportionality between earnings and effort
2. An equal distribution (45.000–45.000) for those who feel that the present compensation is sufficient
3. Those who think that the present earnings differential overcompensates the difference in the number of working days can give a larger part of the profit to Peter.

The results are summarized in the first column of Table 4. Given the results described in the first sections, it is not surprising that a very large majority prefers a proportional distribution of the profit. No one gives a higher bonus to Peter.

But consider the same case, with the last two sentences replaced by

> After a year they have got a sales revenue of 810.000 BF, so that, after deduction of their wages, they have incurred a loss of 90.000 BF. What is a just distribution of this loss?

The results for this variant are given in the second column of Table 4. Here also a proportional distribution might seem the most obvious choice, placing the greatest burden on the strongest shoulders. However, this possibility is only chosen by 41% of our respondents. About half of our sample prefers an equal distribution of the losses and 10% even impose a larger burden on poor Peter.

These results suggest that the notion of acquired rights is predom-

Table 4. Distribution of Responses for Case 4 (Profits versus Losses)

	Profit	Loss
Proportional (50.000–40.000)	85%	41.0%
Equal (45.000–45.000)	15%	48.8%
Inversely proportional (40.000–50.000)	0%	10.3%
Number of respondents	40	39

inant in the ethical judgments of many people. Although acquired rights can be overruled by effort when a bonus has to be divided, they remain influential in distributing a loss of income. This asymmetry supports the idea that the fairness of a distribution should not be judged by the end state as such but depends on the fairness of the distributional processes that have determined this specific end state. In this interpretation, the notion of justice appears as a historical one, in contrast to most existing social psychological theories.

Conclusion

Notwithstanding the exploratory nature of our results, they already indicate directions for further research on social justice. In the first place, the "effort" criterion must be specified further. The answers of our respondents suggest that the ethical intuitions of the workers (at least of future workers) are in conflict with common practice in industry. This should be checked while including senior employees in the sample to avoid a systematic bias.

Second the notion of acquired rights has proven to be essential in the construction of a theory of justice. The notion is a complex one. It gives support to a more "historical" notion of fairness, challenging not only theories that restrict themselves to end state principles but also research programs that restrict themselves to single distributional processes. It may be that people do not judge the fairness of a distribution in simple terms of equity, equality or need, but in complex combinations of these principles. This would explain for example, why no universal proportionality rule applies symmetrically for income increases and income decreases.

In general, all our cases, no matter how simple they may seem at first glance, have elicited complex judgments, reflecting several specific factors. It appears that simple theories and models, although attractive from a scientific point of view, cannot represent the complexity of the fairness judgments of our respondents.

References

Alves, W. M., & Rossi, P. H. (1978). Who should get what? Fairness judgments of the distribution of earnings. American Journal of Sociology 84, 541–564.

Cohen, R. L. (1974). Mastery and justice in laboratory dyads: A revision and extension of equity theory. Journal of Personality and Social Psychology, 29, 464–474.

Greenberg, J. (1979). Protestant ethic endorsement and the fairness of equity inputs. Journal of Research in Personality, 13, 81–90.

Hermkens, P., & Van Wijngaarden, P. (1977). *Inkomensongelijkheid en recht vaardig-heidscriteria* Den Haag.

Lagrou, I., Overlaet, B., & Schokkaert, E. (1981). Beoordeling van inkomens verdeling. *Psychologica Belgica, 21,* 123–147.

Larwood, L. et al. (1979). Relation of objective and subjective inputs to exchange preference for equity or equality reward allocation. *Organizational Behavior and Human Performance, 23,* 60–72.

Overlaet, B., & Lagrou, L. (1981). Attitude toward a redistribution of in come. *Journal of Economic Psychology, 1,* 197–215.

Roscam Abbing, P. J. (1978). The ethical justification of income inequalities. In W. Krelle & A. Shorrocks (eds.), *Personal income distribution:* (pp. 59–77). Amsterdam: North-Holland.

Schokkaert, E. & Lagrou, L. (1983). An empirical approach to distributive justice. *Journal of Public Economics, 21,* 33–52.

Yaari, M. E. & Bar-Hillel, M. (1984). On dividing justly. *Social Choice and Welfare, 1,* 1–24.

10

Social Distance on the Income Dimension

Bernard M. S. van Praag and Nico L. van der Sar

Introduction

Social justice refers, according to Jasso (1980), to a distribution of goods. As long as we may assume that all citizens have the same distribution in mind, we may concentrate on the definition of a social justice index. Preliminary to that problem is the question whether all citizens perceive the same distribution of goods. In this chapter, we show that different people at different levels of society will have different perceptions of the distribution. This is due to the fact that there exists a varying social distance between citizens.

One of the most elusive sociological concepts is the one of social distance. Apart from being hard to describe in objective terms, this phenomenon also is difficult to treat in a quantitative way. Our feeling that we perceive less distance to one person than to another does not automatically provide us with an empirically measurable social distance concept. Devising a method of measuring attitudes on disputed social issues has never been a matter of course (see, e.g., Thurstone & Chave, 1929). It is often felt (see Krech, Crutchfield, & Ballachey, 1962, Katz, 1960, Katz & Stotland, 1959) that an attitude consists of various components: an action-tendency or conative component that refers to the behavioral aspects of the attitude or put in other words to the

Bernard M. S. van Praag • Econometric Institute, Erasmus University, P.O.Box 1738, 3000 DR Rotterdam, The Netherlands   **Nico L. van der Sar** • Department of Business Finance, Erasmus University, P.O. Box 1738, 3000 DR, Rotterdam, The Netherlands.

potential or readiness to respond, an affective or feeling component that relates to the emotional aspects of the attitude, and a cognitive or belief component that concerns the interpretations, expectations, and evaluations of an individual with regard to an object. A similar distinction is made in AIO which stands for activities, interests, and opinions and is used interchangeably with psychographics (see Reynolds & Darden, 1974). Our manner of treating the social distance concept will be in a *cognitive-evaluative* sense. We are interested not only in the way things are, say the objective element, but especially in the way people think things are, the subjective element. Perception of things and persons, the determinants of people's opinions and their frame of reference concerning certain objects and subjects are important to us.

The concept of social distance has very often been used for the study of intergroup relations and is associated with research on social stratification (see, e.g., Westie, 1959). Jackson and Curtis (1968) describe stratification as the study of units (roles, individuals, families, groups, or whatever a given theorist wishes to specify) distributed along one or more rank systems (dimensions of value, facilities, or evaluation); they use rank to mean the location of a unit along a rank system and status to mean some (specified) composite of unit's ranks. Following conventions in the literature of social stratification (see, e.g., Barber, 1957), the social status of a household chosen as the basic unit of social stratification is its evaluation in the eyes of other members of society. In our research, the ranking of households and the weight assigned to them are not important from a societal point of view. What counts is the weight other people carry for a person and the influence they exert on him when forming an opinion concerning certain objects and subjects, or put in other words, which people are part of a person's frame of reference and to what extent. We do not restrict our concept to person-to-person relationships but also concentrate on person-to-group and group-to-group relationships like Bogardus (1947) did. McFarland and Brown (1973) who gave a short history of social distance made a distinction between two types of social distance:

- An interaction notion (see, e.g., Bogardus, 1933, 1955) that is related to the chance of social interaction between individuals or groups, like, for example intermarriage.
- A similarity notion (see, e.g., Sorokin, 1927) that has to do with the degree of similarity of individuals or groups on certain attributes like, for example, income.

In this chapter, we introduce a different type of social distance for which we use the term *reference notion*.

In Section 2 we discuss the concepts in a general setting. In Section 3 we describe an empirical tool, the income evaluation question (IEQ). In Section 4 we describe the theory of the social filter process (SFP), first proposed in Van Praag (1981) that may be thought to generate the responses to the IEQ. In Section 5 we operationalize the sociological concepts described in the second section. In Section 6, we describe our dataset and specify the notions to be measured. In Section 7, we present the empirical results. In the eighth section, we discuss the results and draw some conclusions.

The Concepts

In this chapter, we are not interested in particular individuals but in social types. Social types will be described by a vector of social characteristics x, the dimensions of which may correspond to income, age, religion, and the like. Generally the vector x is defined on a space of social characteristics x.

Let us now consider the social distance between two persons, described by $x^{(1)}$ and $x^{(2)}$. The distance is denoted by $d(x^{(1)};x^{(2)})$. Let us assume that the first person is the owner of a mansion and the second person his servant. What may be the intuitive meaning of social distance between the two? In our view, we call a person "near" to us, if he has a strong influence on our value pattern, our judgments, and our resulting social behavior. If the other person has practically no influence, we call him "socially far away" from us. It follows that the mansion owner is socially near to the servant but most probably not inversely. It follows that $d(.;.)$ is in general not symmetric. More precisely if $d(x^{(1)};x^{(2)})$ reflects the social distance between owner $x^{(1)}$ and servant $x^{(2)}$ as perceived by the servant, we most probably find that $d(x^{(1)};x^{(2)})$ is large but that $d(x^{(2)};x^{(1)})$ is much larger.

Is it true that people feel minimal distance to their own type, for example, after suitable normalization $d(x;x) = 0$? We do not believe that people as a rule are mostly influenced in their pattern by their social equals, hence as a rule $d(x;x) \neq 0$. If the value range of $d(.;.)$ is $[0,\infty)$, for a type x we may find a social type $x_0(x)$, such that $d(x_0;x) = 0$. The $x_0(x)$ is the type that has most influence on the pattern of x. We call $x_0(x)$ the social focal point of the social type x. In general $x_0(x) \neq x$. That is, x has not itself as social focal point. If x is the social focal point of y, it is also not necessary that y is the social focal point of x. If $d(x;x) \neq 0$, it implies that people assign more social weight to other types than to their own kind. We call this social schizophrenia and $d(x;x)$ is a measure for it.

Let us now consider a hypothetical *social distance* table (Table 1). In Table 1 we split up society according to one social dimension, income. We consider four income brackets of $10,000, $20,000, and so on. We assume here that each income bracket has the next higher bracket as its social focal point. For instance, the $10,000 bracket assigns zero distance to the $20,000 bracket, as $d(20;10) = 0$. Inversely, the $20,000 bracket perceives a considerable distance between themselves and the $10,000 bracket as $d(10;20) = 2$. The columns stand for the distance concept just defined.

From the table it is obvious that there are actually *two* distance concepts. The *passive* distance concept, reflecting the influence other social types exert on us and an *active* distance concept, reflecting in how far our own social type is able to exert influence on others. The latter one is reflected in the table by considering it rowwise. We see for instance that the $30,000 bracket exerts most influence on the $20,000 bracket for which it serves as social focal point, an equal but smaller influence on the $10,000 bracket and on the own bracket, and still less influence on the $40,000 bracket. Notice that each type has the same schizophrenia $d(x;x) = 1$.

The limiting case clearly is that where $d(x^{(1)};x^{(2)}) = \infty$. In that case, $x^{(2)}$ is not directly influenced by $x^{(1)}$. This does not imply that there is no indirect influence by $x^{(1)}$ on $x^{(2)}$. For instance, let $x^{(1)}$ be the $50,000 bracket, $x^{(2)}$ be the $20,000 bracket, and $x^{(3)}$ be the $40,000 bracket; then it may very well be that the $50,000 bracket has influence on $x^{(3)}$ and $x^{(3)}$ on $x^{(2)}$. This is the well-known phenomenon that norms and values trickle down through society from the upper class through the middle class to the lower class.

Let us now consider the idea of a *social reference group* (SRG). We say that type $x^{(1)}$ belongs to $x^{(2)}$'s social reference group, if $d(x^{(1)};x^{(2)}) < \infty$. If all social types $x^{(1)}$ have finite distance to $x^{(2)}$, it would imply that the whole society acts as social reference group to $x^{(2)}$. Although this is true in a sense, we may assume that some types $x^{(1)}$ carry more weight for $x^{(2)}$ than others, and this is reflected by the fact that $d(x^{(1)};x^{(2)})$ is not constant in $x^{(1)}$. Then it follows quite naturally that the social reference group of $x^{(2)}$ may be defined as the

Table 1. A Hypothetical Social Distance Table

$x^{(1)}$ $x^{(2)}$	10	20	30	40
10	1	2	3	4
20	0	1	2	3
30	1	0	1	2
40	2	1	0	1

set in X with $\{x^{(1)} \epsilon X | d(x^{(1)};x^{(2)}) < \alpha\} = SRG(\alpha;x^{(2)})$. The *radius* of the SRG is α. Notice that if X is more dimensional, $SRG(\alpha;x^{(2)})$ will be a more dimensional set. Another way of defining the concept may be in terms of percentile definition. Let the percentage of the population belonging to $SRG(\alpha;x^{(2)})$ be denoted by $\pi_R(\alpha;x^{(2)})$, then we may solve the equation $\pi_R(\alpha;x^{(2)}) = 0.90$ for α yielding a $\alpha_{R,0.90}$. In such a way we get a more practical delineation in terms of social characteristics. We notice that, due to the asymmetric distance definition, it follows that, if $x^{(1)}$ belongs to $x^{(2)}$'s SRG, this does not automatically imply that $x^{(2)}$ belongs also to $x^{(1)}$'s SRG.

The SRG is derived and defined by the *passive* distance definition, where we look at Table 1 column-wise. In a similar way, we may define the *social* (direct) *influence group* (SIG) of social type $x^{(1)}$ by looking at Table 1 row-wise. We define

$$SIG(\alpha;x^{(1)}) = \{x^{(2)} \epsilon X | d(x^{(1)};x^{(2)}) < \alpha\}$$

and likewise $\alpha_{I,0.90}$ as the solution of $\pi_I(\alpha;x^{(1)}) = 0.90$.

We considered a social distance table $D = [d_{ij}]$ where $d_{ij} = d(i;j)$ stands for the influence i exerts on j. The matrix D is asymmetric. If d_{ij} stands for the passive distance, d_{ji} stands for the active distance between i and j. It is now easy to define the distance concept between groups A and B in the population. We define the *passive* distance between A and B

$$d_{AB} = \frac{1}{N_A N_B} \sum_{i \epsilon A} \sum_{j \epsilon B} d_{ij}$$

where N_A and N_B stand for the number of people in A and B. Analogously we define the *active* distance between A and B as d_{BA}. It may be that A is identical with B. In that case, we get the average schizophrenia in group A, say d_{AA}. It is the average passive *and* active distance of members of A among themselves. We may call it also the schizophrenia in group A.

In this section we dealt with the concepts, assuming that $d(.;.)$ is a known function. In the following sections, we shall try to define a measurement procedure in order that we can specify the function $d(.;.)$.

The Income Evaluation Question as a Tool

In the introduction, we suggested that social distance between persons may be measured by the impact one person has on the norms or value patterns of another person. This may correlate with geographical nearness or with frequent communication but that is not necessarily so. The Queen of the Netherlands, for example, has a strong influence on the value patterns of Dutch citizens, but perhaps not vice versa.

If someone may dictate more or less what type of *clothing* I am wearing, I have a short distance to that person with respect to *clothing* norms. If my ethical or religious norms are influenced to a large extent by what another person thinks, that person is socially near to me on the *ethics* dimensions. The same holds for music, for food, for children, for education, and for my perception of what is a good income. Then it follows that social distance perception *depends* on the *aspect of life* the value pattern refers to. This gives a somewhat schizophrenic character to the idea of social distance. Two individuals may be buddies in sport, but professionally they may belong to different classes.

However, if we take the value pattern to a rather fundamental issue, the social distance concept derived from it may be considered important too. We shall not consider in this chapter the possibility of how to derive a (simultaneous) social distance concept based on several aspects of life. The aspect of life we shall consider here is *net household income*. Properly speaking, this chapter deals with the social distance concept on the income dimension only. We shall assume that someone's value pattern may be described by his or her response to the so-called income evaluation question (IEQ) that runs as follows:

> Please try to indicate what you consider to be an appropriate amount for each of the following cases? Under my (our) conditions I would call a net household income per week/month/year of:

>> About_____ very bad
>> About_____ bad
>> About_____ insufficient
>> About_____ sufficient
>> About_____ good
>> About_____ very good

> Please enter an answer on each line, and underline the period you refer to.

The response to this battery of attitude questions may be denoted by the vector $c = (c_1, \ldots, c_6)$ where c_1 stands for the response to what income level amounts to a "poor" situation and c_6 to a "prosperous" situation. Obviously the response to the IEQ describes the respondent's value pattern with respect to income. The IEQ has been posed in many oral and written questionnaires since 1969, and it appears to be a very handsome and reliable tool of research. We refer to Van Praag (1971,

1985), Van Praag and Van der Sar (1988). In Van Praag (1985), a review of the main results thus far has been given.

The response variation between individuals is wide. The variation may be due to two factors. First, it may be that individuals give different answers, because they are in different circumstances. For instance, one respondent may have a large family and another may be single. Second, it may be that two individuals in identical circumstances respond differently because the verbal labels *very bad* to *very good* may have different emotional connotations between them. In other articles (Van Praag & Van der Sar, 1988, Van der Sar, Van Praag, & Dubnoff, 1988, Van Praag, 1990, Van Praag, 1990) we show that there is much evidence that the connotation difference is not important. We briefly summarize the arguments.

First, there is the general reason that words are information transmitters and that the very essence of a language for a community is that words convey the same meaning to different members of the language community. It is obvious, although hard to show, that this ideal is not completely realized in the real world, but this is far from saying that that ideal is not even approximately realized. It is hard to believe that a language that serves well in courts, business, love affairs, and philosophy would not serve well in conveying a concept in interview questions.

A second argument yielding the same conclusion is more empirical. Let us consider per individual n his answers c_{in}. As usual to free ourselves from the money-unit dimension we consider from now on the natural logarithm of the answers, their log-average μ_n and their log-variance σ_n^2. Let us now consider the log-standardized answers

$$u_{in} = \frac{\ln c_{in} - \mu_n}{\sigma_n},$$

where

$$\mu_n = \frac{1}{6} \sum_{i=1}^{6} \ln c_{in} \text{ and } \sigma_n^2 = \frac{1}{5} \sum_{i=1}^{6} (\ln c_{in} - \mu_n)^2.$$

We have

$$\ln c_{in} = \sigma_n u_{in} + \mu_n.$$

If u_{in} would be constant over respondents n (or random but not dependent on characteristics of respondent n), we would have separated the *label* effect from the respondent's characteristics.

Table 2. Average and Sample Standard Deviation of u_i and $N(u_i)$

Label	u_i	ssd(u_i)	$N(u_i)$	ssd($N(u_i)$)	Equal interval
1	−1.291	0.236	0.104	0.041	0.083
2	−0.778	0.190	0.222	0.059	0.250
3	−0.260	0.241	0.400	0.091	0.417
4	0.259	0.239	0.600	0.091	0.583
5	0.760	0.190	0.773	0.061	0.750
6	1.311	0.229	0.899	0.040	0.917

In Table 2 we present the average

$$\bar{u}_i = \frac{1}{N} \sum_{n=1}^{N} u_{in}$$

over a sample of about 500 individuals in an American sample survey, which is described more precisely in another section. We present behind it its sample standard deviation (ssd)

$$ssd\,(u_i) = \sqrt{\frac{1}{N-1} \sum_{n=1}^{N} (u_{in} - \bar{u}_i)^2}.$$

We see from Table 2 that the standardized answers u_i are nearly symmetric about zero and that the ssd's are of the same order of magnitude over the six levels and relatively small. We could find no interdependency between u_{in} and characteristics of n. Although the choice of the six verbal labels has an impact on the values of μ_n and σ_n, it is obvious that μ_n and σ_n are only weakly dependent on the response to a specific level i and if it would have been possible to offer more than six levels that specific influence presumably would have been reduced even further. So it may be assumed that μ_n, σ_n depend on the individual characteristics of the respondent n, whereas u_i stands for the specific level and depends only on the verbal label i. We have

$$\ln c_{in} = u_i \sigma_n + \mu_n.$$

It follows that the verbal labels very bad to very good are translated on a numerical scale on $(-\infty, +\infty)$ into numbers $u_1, \ldots, u_6$. Obviously, this numerical scale may be subjected to a second order-preserving transformation $\hat{U}_i = N(u_i)$. As evaluations by individuals are always performed on bounded scales, say a (0,10)-scale or a letter scale $A, \ldots, F$, where the endpoints stand for the best and the worst evaluation possible, this suggests that we should select $N(.)$ to be a distribution function on $(-\infty, +\infty)$ and with a view on the symmetry of the u_i's about zero, the standard-normal distribution lies at hand. The values $N(u_i)$ with their standard deviations over the sample have been tabulated in Table 2 as well. It follows then that the "evaluation" of c_{in} is

$$U(c_{in}) = N \left(\frac{\ln c_{in} - \mu_n}{\sigma_n} ;0,1\right).$$

We notice that our procedure is a noncardinal one; although the function $U = N(.)$ may be interpreted as a cardinal utility function of income, that is not necessary (cf. Van Praag, 1971, 1975, 1985).

The main points that emerge from this section are that the six responses to the IEQ are basically explained by two individual parameters (μ_n, σ_n), that the values $u_1, \ldots, u_6$ are symmetric about zero and that $\hat{U}_1, \ldots, \hat{U}_6$ maybe interpreted as values on a 0–1 scale attached by individual n to income levels $\{c_{in}\}_{i=1}^6$. In the next section, we shall discuss whether this finding is just an empirical regularity or whether it can be put into the perspective of a theoretical model context.

The Social Filter Process

In the previous section we discovered a surprising regularity in the response pattern to the IEQ that may be described as if the individual answers to a verbal label i by solving the equation

$$N \left(\frac{\ln c_{in} - \mu_n}{\sigma_n} ; 0,1\right) = \hat{U}_i \qquad (i=1,\ldots,6)$$

for c_{in}. In this section we shall try to interpret this result in the context of a model. It is well-understood that norms on nearly any subject are acquired through life by comparing situations with others. This holds as well for how *sweet* a cup of tea is or how *tasty* our food is, as for questions on a more abstract level, as whether a human being is "young" or "old" or what income level corresponds to "very bad" or "very good." If nearly everybody in our environment is less than 30 years old, a person older than 30 will be called "old." If nearly everybody in our environment earns more than $60,000 a year, an income of $30,000 amounts to being "poor." This is a relative definition of poverty. More specifically, with a view on incomes, we may operationalize the idea as follows. Let the income distribution of our environment be described by an income distribution function $F(y)$ or a density function $f(y) = \dfrac{dF(y)}{dy}$. Then a specific income level y is associated with poverty, say, if 20% of our environment earns *less* than $y_{0.20}$, where $y_{0.20}$ is the solution of $F(y) = 0.20$. Indeed, this is the poverty line definition advocated by some authors (Miller & Roby, 1970). Similarly, you may have 25% poverty, and so on. In this approach the poverty concept is purely relative; it depends on the threshold percentage accepted and the income distribution perceived. Similarly the concepts of *old* and *young* may be defined with reference to the age distribution.

In some form or another, this theory has been proposed inter aliis by Layard (1980), Kapteyn (1977), Duesenberry (1949), Scitovsky (1976), Van Praag (1981), and Frank (1985). We follow and develop here the theory proposed by Van Praag (1981). The consequence of identifying verbal qualifications of income levels with specific quantiles in the income distribution is that every individual would say the same income level when asked "what is poor." If this is not found in practice, it implies that people have different perceptions of the income distribution in their environment. Consider a rich man B and a poor man A with corresponding environmental income distribution depicted in Figure 1. As they refer themselves to different income distributions, $F_A(y)$ and $F_B(y)$, they answer with different estimates $y_{poor\ A}$ and $y_{poor\ B}$ of what is poor. The perceived by individual n,

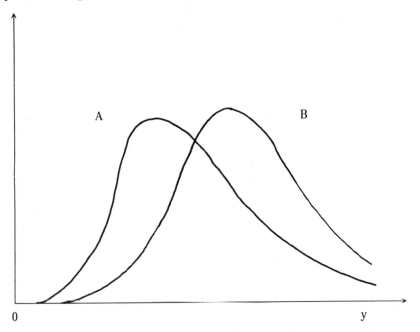

Figure 1. The perceived income density functions of persons A and B.

income density $f_n(y)$ will now be set equal to the density of the evaluation function $U_n(y) = N(\frac{\ln y - \mu_n}{\sigma_n};0,1)$ in the previous section. It follows that the observed response behavior may be a clue to deriving the income distribution the respondent refers to.

Let us denote the objective income density by $f(y)$ and let us assume the density perceived by n to be $f_n(y)$, then we may define $\phi_n(y)$ by

$$f_n(y) = \phi_n(y)f(y).$$

Let us now interpret $f(y_0)\Delta y$ as the real fraction of the population in the income bracket of width Δy about y_0 and $f_n(y_0)\Delta y$ as the perceived fraction in that same bracket. Then the interpretation of the factor $\phi_n(y)$ is straightforward. If $\phi_n(y) > 1$, it implies n exaggerates the numbers in that bracket by a factor $\phi_n(y)$ and if $\phi_n(y) < 1$, it implies that the size of that bracket is perceived as less than there really is.

We call $\phi_n(y)$ the *social filter* applied by n on the income distribution. If $\phi_n(y) = 1$, there is no distortion of our perception. The reason that $\phi_n(y)$ differs from one may be due either to the fact that people are actually "not seen" by n or that they are seen but do not carry special weight. We cannot distinguish between both. The function $\phi_n(.)$ is the sum result of both phenomena. If $f_n(y)$ is set equal to $\frac{dU_n(y)}{dy}$ and $f(y)$ is known by observation, $\phi_n(y)$ is directly assessed as well. We have

$$\ln f_n(y) = \ln \phi_n(y) + \ln f(y),$$

Let us assume that the income distribution $F(y)$ is lognormal as is approximately true and that $F_n(y)=U_n(y)$ is a lognormal distribution function as well, with (μ_0, q_0^2) being the log median and the log variance of the income distribution.

Then we obtain

$$+ \frac{1/q_n^2}{\sigma_0^2}(\ln y - \mu_n)^2 \propto (\frac{1/q_n^2 - 1}{\sigma_0^2})(\ln y - \hat{\mu}_n)^2 + \frac{1}{\sigma_0^2}(\ln y - \mu_0)^2$$

where $\sigma_n^2/\sigma_0^2 = q_n^2$ and where $\hat{\mu}_n$ is implicitly defined, and $\propto$ means "neglecting constants."

Consider now the interpretation of $\ln \phi_n(y)$. If $1/q_n^2 - 1 = 0$, it is constant. If $q_n^2 < 1$ it implies that $\ln \phi_n(y)$ (do not forget the minus!) is maximal at $\ln y = \hat{\mu}_n$ and vanishes to the tails. Or in more plain terms, it assigns most social weight to people with income equal to $\exp(\hat{\mu}_n)$, and it reduces the importance of individuals away from $\hat{\mu}_n$. Actually the social filter may be interpreted as an optical lens with *focal point* at $\hat{\mu}_n$ and *myopia factor* q_n^2. In general $q_n^2 < 1$, or $v_n^2 < \sigma_0^2$, that is, the perceived distribution is more concentrated than the real one. We also see that the perceived log-median μ_n is a weighted mean of the social focal point $\hat{\mu}_n$ and the true log-median μ_0. If $q_n^2 = 1$, the filter is constant, and the perceived median coincides with the true one. If $q_n^2 = 0$, the perception does not bear any relation to reality and $\mu_n = \hat{\mu}_n$; the myopia is complete.

We notice that q_n^2 and $\hat{\mu}_n$ differ among individuals. In the next section we shall consider the empirical results.

Operationalization and Estimation

First, we introduce some notations. Let sc_n stand for the years of schooling of individual n, pex_n for his or her potential years of labor market experience, defined as $(age_n - sc_n - 6)$, i.e., age minus years at school minus, infant years, and fs_n for family size. Our dataset is a sample of about 500 heads of households in the Boston area (USA) that was collected in 1983. The survey was designed and carried out by Steve Dubnoff and was created for methodological purposes only; it is not exactly representative for the Boston population, although it covers the whole population.

Let us now make some remarks on the empirical results, borrowed from Van der Sar, Van Praag, and Dubnoff (1988), where the social filter function $\phi_n(.)$ and the utility function of income $U_n(.)$ are estimated.

1. The Myopia Factor

   - q_n^2 varies positively with sc_n, which reflects the fact that better educated people have more fantasy concerning income than the less educated.
   - q_n^2 varies negatively with pex_n, which may have to do with the fact that "much experienced" people are more or less set in their income habits, left with only a small income sensitivity.
   - In general, $q_n^2 < 1$, that is, individual n is short-sighted.

2. The Social Focal Point

   - Since on average, $q_n^2 < 1$, the social filter function generally peaks and has a maximum at $\hat{\mu}_n$.
   - $\hat{\mu}_n$ varies positively with own income, which reflects the fact that the mode of the social filter function shifts with shifting income.

- $\hat{\mu}_n$ is positively correlated with family size, indicating that the larger fs_n the higher the income level needed.
- Generally $\hat{\mu}_n > \ln y_n$, which shows people's tendency to focus their attention especially on people earning more than themselves; it may be explained, by the fact that people are trying "to keep up with the Joneses," their mind is put on people being somewhat more fortunate; this view stresses the relative aspect.

3. The Parameter μ_n

The larger one's μ_n, the larger the income one needs in order to reach a specific income evaluation; μ_n may be interpreted as an individual want parameter; assuming that $q_n^2 < 1$ we have

- The preference drift rate, which reflects the well-known tendency of people to adapt their income judgments to their own income circumstances (see Van Praag, 1971), is about 0.66; as distinct from earlier research results it varies among individuals: The higher q_n^2, the smaller the preference drift rate that may be explained by a broader view on incomes.
- The family size elasticity, which is indicative of the influence of one's family size on one's income needs, is about 0.11; it varies among individuals with q_n^2 in the same way as the preference drift rate.
- If society's income and thus μ_0 rises, then because of interdependency one's needs also rise; the effect depends on the value of q_n^2: the larger q_n^2, the broader one's income horizon and the bigger the effect of a rise of μ_0 on μ_n; there is, however, no reason that the effect should be proportional ($q_n^2 = 1$).

Considering the individual's social filter function with respect to income, we derive the following propositions on the individual's social reference group loosely defined as the income class to which the social filter function assigns considerable importance

1. It especially contains those people with an income (somewhat) bigger than one's own.
2. The width of the group is positively correlated with one's years of schooling and negatively with one's potential labor market experience; the effect of the latter being smallest in absolute terms.

The Social Distance Concept

Now we return to the concept of social distance as loosely defined in the second section. What is the relationship between the social distance and the social filter? We defined the (passive) social distance between a person and another as small, if the other has a strong Influence on the person considered. In filter terms, this is equivalent to saying that the social weight of the other person is high, so its corresponding filter value and social distance are two sides of the same coin. Let us write $d(y;y_n)$ for the passive social distance, that is, the distance individual n perceives between himself and a person earning income level y, then we define

$$d^2(y;y_n) = (\frac{1/q_n^2 - 1}{\sigma_0^2}) (\ln y - \hat{\mu}_n)^2.$$

As we saw that $(\hat{\mu}_n, q_n^2)$ depends on (y_n, fs_n, sc_n, pex_n), we see that we may tabulate $d^2(y; y_n, fs_n, sc_n, pex_n)$ like in Table 1. Such social distance tables are presented later for various decompositions of the sample population. The most interesting point is clearly the asymmetry of this distance. Let there be two individuals n and n' with incomes y_n and $y_{n'}$, respectively. Then in general

$$d^2(y_{n'}; y_n) \neq d^2(y_n; y_{n'})$$

and also the social focal point $\hat{\mu}_n$ generally does not coincide with y_n. If we call an income bracket self-centered if it perceives distance to the own bracket as smaller than to any other, an income bracket is only self-centered if $\hat{\mu}_n = \ln y_n$.

This is only true for special cases. For instance, for $fs_n = 4$ we find $y_n^* = \$15,962$; for $fs_n = 2$ we have $\$35,446$.

In Figure 2 we draw $\hat{\mu}_n$ as a function of $\ln y_n$. It follows that rather poor people look to the poorer as their social focal point and rich people to the richer. People with income below y_n^* look downward, and those above y_n^* look upward. We notice that family size has a surprisingly strong influence on y_n^*. We did not perform a similar analysis on European datasets, so we do not have any basis for comparison. However, as a preliminary interpretation, we see that family size is a social characteristic of major importance. If people have a large family, they are more inclined to look upward than a couple without children with the same income. The reason may be that the latter household, although it has a large income due to two breadwinners, socially belongs to a lower class than its total household income suggests.

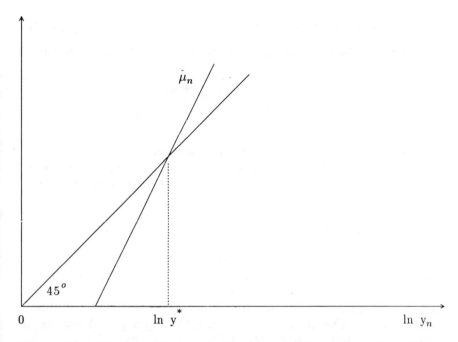

Figure 2. The social center y* is determined by the intersection of the social focal point $\hat{\mu}_n$ as a function of log-income and the 45° line.

Obviously, the fact that classes are *not* self-centered implies a certain social schizophrenia. One's most important example for the derivation of norms and values is not one's own class but another one. There are several other distance measures of interest. What is the average passive distance *APD* of *n* to society Ω? It is $d_{\Omega,n} = \dfrac{1}{N} \sum_{i \in \Omega} d(i;n)$.

It can be shown that the average passive distance increases when $(\mu_0 - \hat{\mu}_n)^2$ increases; that is, the social focal point $\hat{\mu}_n$ is farther away from the median μ_0. The distance decreases if $1/q_n^2$ decreases, that is, if myopia reduces. Average passive distance is felt to be minimal, q_n kept constant, at the median bracket $\hat{\mu}_n = \mu_0$ where it equals $(1/q_n^2 - 1)$. By means of this concept it is also possible to compute the passive/active distance between subgroups in the population. In the second section, we distinguished a *passive* distance concept, corresponding to columnwise comparison in Table 1 and an *active* distance concept. If d_{ij} stands for the passive distance between *i* and *j*, d_{ji} stands for the active distance.

The *average* active distance is then $d_{n,\Omega} = \frac{1}{N} \sum_{j \in \Omega} d(n;j)$. Finally, we may calculate the average of AAD and of APD over n. We obtain

$$\overline{AAD} = \frac{1}{N^2} \sum_{i \in \Omega} \sum_{j \in \Omega} d_{ij}^2$$

$$= \overline{APD}$$

where we interchanged the order of summation.

The measure $\overline{APD} = \overline{AAD}$ may be seen as an *overall stratification measure for the society as a whole*. For our sample, it equals 2.84.

Empirical Results

In this section we present some empirical results, with respect to social distance. For an "average" respondent, that is a household with $22,500 net income, a family size of 2.6, a schooling of 14.4 years, and labor experience of 22.1 years, that is an average age of $22.1 + 14.4 + 6 = 42.5$ years, we find a $\exp(\hat{\mu})$ of $24,146 and a q^2 of 0.563. Let us now consider the social distance table for schooling (see Table 3); the population is decomposed into three subgroups, namely schooling $\leq$ 12 years, schooling between 12 and 16, schooling > 16 years.

First we consider the diagonal terms that describe the average social distance within the group, the schizophrenia. In the population as a whole, it is 2.84. In the low-schooling subgroup, it is much higher, namely 3.24, whereas in the two higher education groups, it is lower than the average figure. The ($sc > 16$) group that consists of university graduates and the like is knit together with an average distance of 1.89.

Consider now the distance of the lowest group to the higher groups. The passive distance to the ($12 < sc \leq 16$)-group is 4.00 and the active distance is 2.63. It follows that the low-schooling group exerts more influence on the high-schooling groups than inversely. The average passive distance to the whole society is 3.88 whereas the active distance is 2.83. Social distance seems to be more strongly perceived by low schooling classes than by people with higher education. Consider now Table 4 computed in the same way as Table 3.

We see that schizophrenia is much less in the group PEX $\leq$ 10 than in the low-schooling group in Table 4. This is not true for the groups with intermediate and long labor experience. The passive distance of a group increases with labor experience. As PEX has much to do with age, it reflects the fact that older people seem to be less susceptible to influences from other people. On the other hand their

Table 3. Social Distance between Schooling Groups

		$sc \leq 12$	$12 < sc \leq 16$	$sc > 16$	AAD
$sc \leq 12$	(149)	3.24	2.63	2.62	2.83
$12 < sc \leq 16$	(200)	4.00	2.27	1.98	2.78
$sc > 16$	(99)	4.59	2.35	1.89	2.99
APD		3.88	2.41	2.17	2.84
					$(\overline{AAD} = \overline{APD})$

Table 4. Social Distance between Labor Experience Groups

		$PEX \leq 10$	$10 < PEX \leq 30$	$PEX > 30$	AAD
$PEX \leq 10$	(130)	2.09	2.79	3.40	2.75
$10 < PEX \leq 30$	(197)	2.35	2.63	4.10	2.95
$PEX > 30$	(121)	2.05	3.02	3.16	2.78
APD		2.19	2.78	3.64	2.84

active distance to others is on the average 2.78 that is caused by their strong influence on young people (2.05) with short labor experience. On the whole young people are more susceptible than older people.

From Table 5 we see that the average distance within each subgroup is not large but that the distance between the extreme subgroups is very large. It is somewhat less for the upper income group than for the low income group but the difference is not spectacular. The influence of the top income bracket on other income brackets is not large except for the adjacent lower bracket. The passive distance is 0.84, which is even smaller than within the top group itself. It is interesting that this is not reciprocated by the upper income group that sees an average passive distance of 3.44.

Discussion and Conclusion

In this chapter, we make a first attempt to operationalize the concept of social distance. The crucial point seems to be that such a concept, unlike to what is suggested by its geometric background, is asymmetric. The distance between Peter and Paul is not necessarily equal to that between Paul and Peter. The social distance concept is measured in terms of *influence*. Paul may have a lot of influence on Peter, in which case we call Peter socially near to Paul, but Peter may have no influence on Paul in which case we call Peter far away from Paul. So it is better to speak about *passive* and *active* distance, say d(Peter;Paul) and d(Paul;Peter). The concept is operationalized on the basis of the

Table 5. Social Distance Between Income Classes

	INC ≤ 10000	10000 < INC ≤ 20000	20000 < INC ≤ 40000	40000 < INC	AAD
INC ≤ 10000 (92)	1.75	1.06	4.51	12.79	3.46
10000 < INC ≤ 20000 (149)	4.82	0.35	1.24	6.60	2.11
20000 < INC ≤ 40000 (171)	8.82	1.40	0.29	3.44	2.66
40000 < INC (36)	15.74	4.54	0.84	1.24	5.16
APD	6.59	1.23	1.52	6.23	2.84

social filter function that translates the objective income distribution into the subjective norm on incomes as reflected by the IEQ response. On the basis of this measured concept, we defined the concepts of average active and passive distance, the social focal point of an individual, and a general social stratification measure. These concepts have been evaluated for a moderate sample of less than 500 respondents. The main virtue of this chapter is its methodological contribution. The sample that is used is not created for deriving valid conclusions on the Bostonian society. It is evident that there is much to do in this field. Although norms on income are a major aspect of the complete norm pattern, it is not the only one. So it seems possible to construct a similar theory on different aspects of life as well. Will we then find similarity between the filters and how can we construct more dimensional filters? A second issue is the validity of the IEQ. How sensitive are our constructs to modifications in the IEQ?

Finally we do not deny that in building this apparatus, we have *defined* the primitive metaphysical concept of social distance by a *measurement* method. By doing so, we have applied a Procrustean bed on a fine and elusive concept; many people may feel that their view on the social distance concept does not conform to our empirical definition. We cannot prove or disprove that we are right, nor can they. The only thing we require from those who are nonbelieving is that they offer an empirically operational rival definition, such that two or more measured concepts may be compared.

Postscript. A more detailed version of this chapter containing the technical aspects of the model and its estimates is available from the authors. They express their gratitude to Steven Dubnoff, who created the dataset with financial support of the National Science Foundation. They like to thank Wil Arts for his stimulating advice. The authors take sole responsibility for all remaining errors and the opinions expressed.

References

Barber, B. (1957). *Social stratification.* New York: Harcourt, Brace & World Inc.

Bogardus, E. S. (1933). A social distance scale. *Sociology and Social Research, 17,* 265–271.

Bogardus, E. S. (1947). The social distance differential. *Sociology and Social Research, 32,*, 882–887.

Bogardus, E. S. (1955). *The development of social thought.* New York: Longmans, Green and Co.

Duesenberry, J. S. (1949). *Income, saving and the theory of consumer behavior.* Princeton: Princeton University Press.

Frank, R. H. (1985). *Choosing the right pond: Human behavior and the quest for status.* New York:Oxford University Press.

Jackson, E. F., & Curtis, R. F. (1968). Conceptualization and measurement in the study of social stratification. In H. M. Blalock & A. B. Blalock (Eds.), *Methodology in social research* (pp. 112–149). New York: McGraw-Hill Book Co.

Jasso, G., (1980). A new theory of distributive justice. *American Sociological Review, 45,* 3–32.

Kapteyn, A. (1977). *A theory of preference formation.* PhD thesis, Leiden University, Leiden.

Katz, D. & Stotland, E. (1959). A preliminary statement to a theory of attitude structure and change. In S. Koch (Ed.), *Psychology: A study of a science* (Vol. 3, pp. 423–475). New York: McGraw-Hill Book Co.

Katz, D. (1960). The functional approach to the study of attitudes. *Public Opinion Quarterly, 24,* 163–191.

Krech, D., Crutchfield, R. S., & Ballachey, E. L. (1962). *Individual in society.* New York: McGraw-Hill Book Co.

Layard, R. (1980). Human satisfaction and public policy. *The Economic Journal, 90,* 737–750.

McFarland, D. D., & Brown, D. J. (1973). Social distance as a metric: A systematic introduction to smallest space analysis. In E. O. Lauman (Ed.), *Bonds of pluralism: The form and substance of urban social networks* (pp. 215–252). New York: John Wiley & Sons.

Miller, S. M., & Roby, P. (1970). *The future of inequality.* New York: Basic Books.

Reynolds, F., & Darden W. (1974). Construing life style and psychographics. In W. D. Wells (ed.), *Life Style and Psychographics* (pp. 71–96). Chicago: American Marketing Association.

Scitovsky, T. (1976). *The joyless economy.* Oxford: Oxford University Press.

Sorokin, P. A. (1927). *Social mobility,* retitled *Social and cultural mobility* and reprinted in 1959. New York: Free Press.

Thurstone, L. L. & Chave, E. J. (1929). *The measurement of attitude.* Chicago: University of Chicago Press.

Van der Sar, N. L., van Praag, B. M. S., & Dubnoff, S. (1988). Evaluation questions and income utility. In B. Munier (Ed.), *Risk, decision and rationality* (pp. 77–96). Dordrecht, Holland: D. Reidel Publishing Co.

Van Praag, B. M. S. (1971). The welfare function of income in Belgium: An empirical investigation. *European Economic Review, 4* 33–62.

Van Praag, B. M. S. (1975). Utility, welfare and probability: An unorthodox economist's view. In D. Went & C. Vlek (Eds.), *Utility, probability and human decision making* (pp. 279–295). Dordrecht, Holland: D. Reidel Publishing Co.

Van Praag, B. M. S. (1981). *Reflections on the theory of individual welfare functions,* Report 81.14, Center for Research in Public Economics, Leiden University, Proceedings of the American Statistical Association.

Van Praag B. M. S. (1985). Linking economics with psychology. An economist's view. *Journal of Economic Psychology, 6,* 289–311.

Van Praag, B. M. S. (1990). Ordinal and cardinal ability: An intergration of the two dimensions of the welfare concept. Forthcoming in the *Journal of Econometrics.*

Van Praag, B. M. S. (1990). The relativity of the welfare concepts. In A. Sen & M. Nussbaum (Eds.), *Quality of life.* Forthcoming at Clarendon Press, Oxford.

Van Praag, B. M. S. & van der Sar, N. L. (1988). Household cost functions and equivalence scales, *Journal of Human Resources, 23,* 193–210.

Westie, F. R. (1959). Social distance scales, *Sociology and Social Research, 43,* 251–258.

11

Explaining Variation in Attitudes toward Income Equality

A. Szirmai

Introduction

This chapter presents some results of a larger study on attitudes toward income inequality in The Netherlands. This study is based on a national survey held in The Netherlands in October 1980.[1] One of its conclusions was that, in 1980, members of the economically active population were characterized by highly egalitarian attitudes with regard to the distribution of income. In all ranges of the income hierarchy, there was a clear preference for smaller income differentials.

In this chapter the focus is on the explanation of variation of attitudes toward inequality. Questions to be examined in this context are: Why are some people more egalitarian than others and how can such differences be explained theoretically?

The dependent variable in this chapter is a measure of an individual's tendency to equalize the income distribution as he perceives it. This measure TEQ has been constructed from data gathered with the so-called income ruler technique (Bunjes et al., 1977; Overlaet & Lagrou, 1981; Schokkaert Lagrou, 1983; Szirmai, 1982, 1988). The income ruler technique can be described as follows. First, respondents

---

[1] A representative sample of the economically active population, working more than 25 hours a week, older than 22 years and younger than 65 years, was interviewed. 952 interviews were completed. For a discussion of the questionnaire, the sampling procedures and the representativeness of the sample, I refer to Szirmai (1988).

A. Szirmai • Department of Economics, University of Groningen, P.O. Box 800, 9700 AV Groningen, The Netherlands.

are given 15 small cards with well-known occupations or positions printed on them, plus one card with the legend *Yourself*. Each of the occupations or positions is selected in such a way that it represents important groups in the (working) population. For instance, skilled workers are represented by the car mechanic or the plumber, public employees are represented by the secondary schoolteacher or the policeman, people outside the laborforce are represented by the old age pensioner or by the welfare recipient. The complete list of occupations and positions is as follows: director of large company, prime minister, general practitioner, head of a personnel department, secondary schoolteacher in a HAVO (higher general secondary education), self-employed plumber, typewriter salesman, car mechanic, small shop-keeper without employees, construction worker, policeman, typist, unskilled factory worker, person with a state old age pension (AOW), and person receiving welfare.

First, the respondents are asked to rank the 16 cards according to income level. The card with the highest estimated income should be placed at the top; the card with the lowest income at the bottom. The interviewer makes a note of the rank numbers and then hands respondents an income ruler with income levels running from 0 to 300,000 guilders.[2] He gives the following explanation:

> On the income ruler I am giving you, you see a whole series of figures. These figures represent gross yearly incomes. By gross income we mean yearly earnings before taxes and social premiums have been deducted. Would you make an estimate of the average yearly income belonging to each of the cards. You can do this by positioning the cards on the left-hand side of the income ruler. When trying to estimate the incomes, think of someone of about 40 years old.

When the respondent has placed the cards along the income ruler—in doing so he is allowed to change the rank order—the interviewer writes down the income amounts and gives the respondent a second set of 16 cards identical to the first set, which remains on the table as positioned by the respondent. The interviewer says:

---

[2]Between 0 and 100,000 guilders, the income amounts printed on the income ruler increase in steps of 5,000 guilders. Between 100,000 and 200,000 guilders, the income amounts increase in steps of 10,000 guilders. Between 200.000 and 300,000 guilders, the income amounts increase in steps of 20,000 guilders. This increase in the size of the steps was necessary to avoid an unmanageable size of the income ruler. Between the printed income amounts, there are small lines, so that estimated and preferred incomes can be indicated in thousands of guilders. At the top, the income ruler is open, so that people whose estimates of top incomes are higher than 300,000 guilders can make this clear to the interviewer.

> I am giving you another set of cards. They have the same occupations and positions printed on them as before. If it were up to you to decide, what would a fair income for each of these occupations or positions be? Which income would you give them? You can show this by positioning the cards on the right hand side of the income ruler.

These procedures result in a wealth of information about how people perceive the distribution of incomes and about the differences between their perceived and their preferred or just distribution of incomes. Per respondent, we get three sets of figures: 16 rank numbers for the occupations and positions according to estimated income level, 16 estimated income levels for each position and occupation, and 16 fair or just incomes for each position and occupation. The analysis concentrates on the changes people make in the income distribution as they perceive it: changes in the degree of inequality, changes in the rank order of occupations and positions, changes in absolute income levels of specific occupations or positions, and changes in the relative income levels of specific occupations or positions. The great advantage of the income ruler technique is that we have acquired all this detailed information about distributive preferences, without having to ask a single direct question about income distribution or about distributive policy. Thus the danger of socially desirable responses is minimized.

The variable Tendency to Equalize (TEQ) has been constructed from the income ruler data as follows. The 16 estimated income levels are taken to represent respondents' perceptions of income inequality. The 16 just income levels represent respondents' just income distributions. For both these distributions measures of dispersion can be calculated such as the Gini-coefficient, the variance, the relative average deviation, and the Theil-coefficient. In this chapter I have chosen the Theil-coefficient. Thus estimated inequality is measured by the Theil-coefficient of the estimated income levels (TEST). Just inequality is measured by the Theil-coefficient of the just income levels (TJUST). The percentage difference between TEST and TJUST is interpreted as the tendency to equalize the perceived income distribution (TEQ).[3]

One could also defend an alternative interpretation of TEQ as an indicator of the cognitive dissonance with regard to income inequality. In this view, TEQ measures the discrepancy between perceived and

----

[3]The Theil-coefficient is the measure of the degree of inequality of a distribution, most frequently used in publications about the inequality of incomes in The Netherlands. For a discussion of the Theil-coefficient see G. R. Mustert (1976). As all the—16—incomes in each distribution are known, I have made use of the formula for ungrouped data in calculating the Theil-coefficients (Mustert, 1976, p. 100). For a discussion of distributive measures, see D. G. Champernowne (1974) ; A. J. Vermaat (1975); and Mustert (1976).

preferred inequalities of income. Because the income ruler technique involves respondents actually changing the positions of cards on the income ruler, thereby increasing or decreasing the incomes attached to given positions and occupations, I prefer the interpretation of TEQ that stresses the active tendency to change the distribution.

A second important indicator of attitudes toward income inequality is the scale variable measuring the degree of inequality aversion (INEQAV). The items making up this scale have been selected with help of factor analysis. With exception of the first item that is of the *in favor of*–opposed to type, all items are of the *agree–disagree* type (Likert). The following items have been included in the scale: Raising the minimum wage (V146); I would like to live in a society with less inequality (V192); if income differentials are smaller, people are less jealous of each other (V197); the common man in The Netherlands does not have it all that good;, income restraint is not fair to him (V199); if income differentials in The Netherlands are not made smaller, social tensions will increase (V200); people are equal in principle, large income differences are unjust (V204); a society with less inequality is a more happy society (V308). Scale scores are summations of item scores. The highest possible scale value is 35, the lowest value 7. Cronbach's alpha is .84.

Comparing the Inequality Aversion scale INEQAV with TEQ, I interpret INEQAV as measuring evaluative aspects of the attitude toward inequality and TEQ measuring the more conative aspects of these attitudes.

On average, the Theil-coefficient for the just distribution is no less than 37.2% lower than the Theil-coefficient of the estimated distribution. The data suggest that the respondents have a powerful tendency to equalize the income distribution as they perceive it. It must be stressed that here I am interested in the variation in the tendency to equalize rather than its average strength. Elsewhere, I have shown that all social groups in the sample, even upper income groups and top occupational groups, are characterized by strong tendencies to equalize (Szirmai, 1988, Chapter 4). I have also demonstrated that people tend to leave the rank ordering of income groups on the income ladder unchanged. In this respect, there seems to be consensus concerning the criteria for the distribution of incomes (Szirmai, 1988, Chapter 4; see also Hermkens, 1983). However, I found considerable differences in the degree to which people reduce perceived income differentials. The question why different people react in a different manner to a given degree of income inequality in society is the central topic of this chapter.

Theoretical Approaches to the Study of Egalitarian Tendencies

In this section I will present a set of research questions and hypotheses. The research project from which these derive was, however, of a more inductive nature, examining which theories and which operationalizations contributed most to explained variation of the dependent variable. Three articles in particular have been a fruitful source of both hypotheses and operationalizations, namely "Class as Conceived of by Marx and Dahrendorf," by R. V. Robinson and J. Kelley (1979); "Equality, Success and Social Justice in England and the United States," by R. V. Robinson and W. Bell (1978), and "The Structure of Egalitarianism," by R. Della Fave (1974). These three articles have in common that they summarize large bodies of literature and research on subjective aspects of social inequality and attempt to synthesize them.

Before discussing specific research questions and hypotheses, I want to bring some order into the discussion by distinguishing six different complexes of theories that are of relevance for the understanding of attitudes toward inequality: (1) theories of absolute deprivation, (2) status theories, (3) class theories, (4) cognitive theories, (5) theories of relative deprivation, and (6) theories of long-run changes in attitudes toward inequality.

Theories of Absolute Deprivation

In theories of absolute deprivation, egalitarian tendencies are linked with the degree of absolute deprivation. The lower people's incomes or standards of living are, the more they are in favor of equalization. (Della Fave, 1974, pp. 201 ff.; Hermkens & Van Wijngaarden 1977, p. 49; Robinson & Bell, 1978). Such theories are straightforward theories of self-interest. People with low incomes are in favor of equalization because they think they stand to gain from such equalization. People with higher incomes who objectively benefit from the existing stratification are more likely to judge its inequalities to be just (Robinson & Bell, 1978). They will tend to be less in favor of equalization because they are afraid they will lose out. Such interest theories leave little room for idealistic motives with regard to the distribution of incomes.

Status Theories

Status theories focus on the relationships between egalitarian tendencies and indicators of low prestige such as low occupational or educational level. Low educational and occupational levels are hypothesized to be associated with strong tendencies to equalize. Equalizing tendencies are interpreted as attempts to improve one's own status and decrease status differences in general. Status theories are also interest theories. One's interest lies in increasing one's status rather than one's material resources. The dividing line between status theories and theories of absolute deprivation cannot be clearly drawn, as low income is also an indicator of low status. For instance, under the heading of the underdog hypothesis, Robinson and Bell discuss both low income and low status as explanations of egalitarian attitudes (Robinson & Bell, 1978).

With regard to one of the often used indicators of status, educational level, Robinson and Bell have formulated an alternative hypothesis, the enlightenment hypothesis. This hypothesis suggests that well-educated people will be more likely to favor equality as fair than less educated people (Robinson & Bell, 1978, p. 129).

Location in Structures of Class and Authority

The Marxian tradition stresses the importance of the location in the structure of production, as opposed to factors such as degree of absolute deprivation or indicators of social status such as education or occupation. People's locations in the structure of production determine their objective interests, and in due course they become subjectively conscious of their objective interests and act accordingly. Relating class position to attitudes toward equalization means stretching the Marxian position considerably. The Marxian tradition focuses on revolutionary consciousness and revolutionary mobilization. Income equalization is regarded as a despicable form of petty bourgeois reformism. Nevertheless, I will try to relate equalizing tendencies to class position and hypothesize that members of subordinate classes have a stronger tendency to equalize than members of dominant classes. In contrast with deprivation and status theories, class theories suggest sharp conflicts of interest between members of different classes and therefore also conflicting attitudes with regard to income inequality.

The Dahrendorfian tradition considers class relations and class conflict as a special case of the ever-existing conflict relations between people in positions of authority and people in subordinate positions (Dahrendorf, 1959). This tradition suggests clear-cut differences of opinion with regard to income inequality between members of "command classes" and members of "obey classes."

Cognitive Theories

Cognitive theories of the tendency to equalize tend to stress people's definitions of the inequality situation, rather than their objective locations in hierarchies of income or status or in structures of class or authority. Such theories suggest that differences in perceptions of income and inequality are more important in explaining attitudes toward income inequality than objective differences in income, class, or social position. Self-interest is not necessarily less important in cognitive theories than it was in the other theoretical categories discussed. Cognitive theories only emphasize that what people perceive to be in their interest depends on their often warped perceptions of reality.

Under the heading of cognitive theories fall all theories with regard to relationships between perceived inequality and the tendency to equalize. Such theories predict that the greater the degree of perceived inequality, the greater perceived increases in inequality and the lower one's perceived position on the income ladder, the stronger the tendency to equalize. Other cognitive theories stress the relationships between perceived consequences of equalization and egalitarian tendencies. Perceived negative consequences make for weaker tendencies to equalize.

An interesting example of cognitive theory is the application of the theory of mental incongruities as formulated by Tazelaar and Wippler (Tazelaar & Wippler, 1981; Tazelaar, 1981) to attitudes toward income inequality. This theory focuses on how individuals react to discrepancies between cognitions and standards.

In simplified terms, the theory of mental incongruities runs as follows. According to Tazelaar and Wippler, a discrepancy (incongruity) between a person's perception of a situation (Tazelaar and Wippler use the term *cognition*) and his normative standard concerning that situation gives rise to a tendency to reduce this discrepancy (incongruity, dissonance) in one way or another. This formulation differs in little from older formulations of the theory of cognitive dissonance (Festinger, 1957). What is new about Tazelaar and Wippler's contribution is the idea of secondary incongruities. A distinction is made between the primary area of a mental system, the secondary area, and the tertiary area. What the primary area is depends on the question or problem the researcher is interested in. Attempts to reduce incongruities in the primary area can have positive or negative consequences in other areas of the mental system. For instance, other incongruities may be increased when primary incongruities are reduced. That area of the mental system that is in some way affected by changes in the primary system is called the secondary area. The tertiary area is defined as the area where changes in the primary area have no consequences at all. The relationships between the primary and the secondary area of the mental system are formed by so-called subsidiary cognitions (Hilfscognitionen). Such subsidiary cognitions consist of perceptions of the relationships between changes in one area and changes in another area. For instance, the reduction of a primary incongruity in the sphere of one's political behavior might be conceived of as causing conflicts with friends and relatives with other political preferences. This can create a secondary incongruity with regard to the normative standard "consensus with relevant others."

The importance of the idea of secondary incongruities is that mental incongruities can never be completely reduced, whether by changes in behavior or by changes in perceptions or normative standards. Reduction of incongruities in one sphere always leads to an increase of incongruities in some other spheres. Therefore the central hypothesis is not that people tend to eliminate primary incongruities but that mental systems tend to reduce the sum total of all primary and secondary incongruities to a minimum. The theory is further elaborated in a large number of abstract postulates and hypotheses, which among others definitely throw new light on the much debated relationships between attitudes and behavior. However, the theory is far too refined for my purposes and will only be operationalized in highly simplified form.

In terms of this chapter the primary sphere is, of course, the income distribution. Perceptions of income inequality are the "primary cognitions." The "primary normative standard" is the attitude toward income inequality as measured by the Inequality Aversion Scale (INEQAV). The tendency to reduction of incongruities is finally seen as being operationalized by our dependent variable, the Tendency to Equalize (TEQ). Other things being equal, the theory of mental incongruities predicts that the combination of a strong inequality aversion and a perception of great income inequality results in the strongest tendency to reduce the incongruity between standard and perception by equalizing the perceived income distribution.[4] The

---

[4]One could argue that it is not permissible to regress TEQ on INEQAV as the two variables do not measure different aspects of the attitude toward income inequality. TEQ is defined as the percentage difference between the inequality of the estimated and just incomes on the income ruler. As just income levels represent respondents' normative standards with regard to income levels, TEQ represents normative standards just like INEQAV.

I do not agree with this argument. There is a clear difference between normative standards with regard to inequality—for example, there should be complete income

greater the perceived degree of inequality, the stronger the tendency to equalize will be (see also Bunjes et al., 1977, p. 40; Hermkens, 1983, p. 46).

The interview schedule includes various questions dealing with perceptions of negative consequences of income equalization. All the variables derived from these questions can be taken as operationalizations of secondary mental incongruities. The theory of mental incongruities predicts that such secondary incongruities dampen the tendency to equalize. Secondary mental incongruities are also operationalized in a more indirect fashion, by distinguishing individuals for whom monetary incentives play an important role in their work and labor market behavior, from people for whom monetary incentives are less important. The hypothesis is that people for whom financial incentives are important are less prone to equalize.

Finally, the theory of mental incongruities states that the more dominant a normative standard is in the mental system, the stronger the tendency toward reduction of incongruities. In this case, this implies that the more importance people attach to questions concerning the distribution of incomes, the stronger their tendency toward reduction of inequalities. The importance of salience is also stressed by many other authors writing about mental incongruities, cognitive dissonance, or relative deprivation (see, e.g., Gurr, 1970).

In an interesting review of the literature on attitudes toward inequality, Richard Della Fave has made a comprehensive attempt to identify the factors that "lead some people to support the idea of economic equality and others to oppose it" (Della Fave, 1974, p. 199). The question Della Fave is interested in answering is why most people, even most poor people, are usually not in favor of complete income equality. His explanation for this is that the belief that present gross inequalities of income and wealth should be sharply curtailed or even eliminated will only be held if many other supporting beliefs are held simultaneously. Because of Della Fave's emphasis on the structure of beliefs, it makes sense to discuss his contribution under the heading of cognitive theories.

According to Della Fave, the structure of beliefs supporting

---

inequality, incomes should be distributed according to need, according to age, or according to effort—and fair or just income levels that are the result of the application of normative criteria to the distribution of rewards. In this respect, it makes good sense to relate the amount of change respondents make in their perceived income distribution to their normative standards and their perceptions with regard to income inequality.

It is worth noting that the correlation between INEQAV and the inequality of just incomes on the income ruler (TJUST) is .28 which is much lower than the correlation between TEQ and INEQAV (.41).

egalitarianism can be broken down into five components: (1) a feeling
of deprivation; (2) blaming the organization of society, "the system,"
for the deprivation; (3) a belief that social justice requires equality; (4)
a belief that human nature is sufficiently flexible to accommodate
equality in a complex society; and (5) a belief that the transition from
the present society to an egalitarian one is both feasible and worth the
effort. (Della Fave, 1974, p. 200.)

Under the heading of deprivation, Della Fave discusses both
absolute and relative deprivation. Absolute deprivation has been
discussed. Relative deprivation, described as a state of subjective
dissatisfaction with one's present situation, will be dealt with in the
following paragraph. Deprivation is a necessary but not a sufficient
condition for egalitarianism. Instead of striving to change an unsatisfactory situation, people may redefine it in less unsatisfactory terms.[5]
And even if people do want to change their situation, such changes are
not necessarily egalitarian ones. A further condition for egalitarianism
is system blaming. Attempts to improve one's situation will only be of
an egalitarian nature, if people explicitly blame their deprivation on
society in general. They have to feel that not only they themselves but
also identifiable groups to which they belong are discriminated against
and unjustly treated. They have to relate their private and group
dissatisfactions to the way their society is organized.

System blaming will only lead to demands for equality of results
(true egalitarianism, according to Della Fave) if people also have an
egalitarian conception of justice. In itself, system blaming can just as
well give rise to demands for preferential group treatment or to
demands for a more open society, for more equality of opportunity.

Finally Della Fave identifies two sets of factors that can impede
egalitarianism, even when the previous conditions are met. Under the
heading "Conceptions of Human Nature" Della Fave argues that
popularly held conceptions of human nature can be incompatible with
egalitarianism. One such conception is that people cannot be motivated to perform arduous and demanding tasks in society if they are not
motivated to do so by financial incentives. Della Fave calls this popular
functionalism. A second conception is that there are always unscrupu-
lous individuals and groups who subvert an egalitarian system and
profit from it. It is this conception, which Della Fave calls the *jungle
view of human nature*, which underlies most prisoners' dilemma types
of analysis. Under the heading of "transition costs" to an egalitarian

---

[5]Implicitly, Della Fave treats relative deprivation as a situation of cognitive dissonance.
The similarities between cognitive theories and relative deprivation theories are discussed in the second section of this chapter.

society, Della Fave refers to the fears people may have about the costs associated with a major and perhaps revolutionary restructuring of society. He mentions not only transition costs proper but all fears of negative consequences of egalitarianism: less prosperity, unemployment, a loss of individual freedom, monotony, and so forth.

There are some interesting parallels between Della Fave's treatment of the structure of egalitarianism and the theory of mental incongruities. For instance, Della Fave makes a distinction between the "belief that social justice requires inequality" and the "belief that inequalities of income and wealth should be curtailed." This directly mirrors the distinction made here between a normative standard with regard to inequality (INEQAV) and the tendency to reduce perceived income inequality (TEQ). Also, Della Fave's discussion of the role of beliefs concerning human nature and beliefs concerning the costs of transition to egalitarianism is none other than a discussion of secondary mental incongruities in another guise. If reduction of primary incongruities with regard to income inequality leads to an increase in secondary incongruities, this will weaken the tendency to equalize. Rephrased in Della Fave's terms, this implies that when people conceive of human nature as incompatible with egalitarianism or are afraid of the costs of equalization, they will be less prone to equalize (TEQ).

Theories of Relative Deprivation

Whereas absolute deprivation, status, and class theories stress the objective situation of an individual, theories of relative deprivation, like cognitive theories, focus on individuals' subjective experience of inequality relationships.

In discussions of relative deprivation, two traditions can be distinguished. One tradition of which T. R. Gurr is an important exponent conceives of relative deprivation as any situation in which there is a discrepancy between what a person has and what he feels he should have (Gurr, 1970). In terms of this study, those people are relatively deprived whose perceived actual income is lower than the income they think they should be receiving. As applied to income inequality, the theory predicts that the greater the degree of relative deprivation, the stronger the tendency to change the income distribution in one's favor. In other words, this implies that the strength of the tendency to equalize is influenced by the direct financial gain or loss that one associates with equalization, irrespective of the height of one's income. This formulation is a straightforward interest theory of the tendency to equalize.

In an elaboration of his conceptual apparatus, Gurr suggests than relative deprivation does not only depend on the individual's perception of his situation at a given moment. It also depends on his past experience, his future expectations, and on his perception of the development of the overall situation in his society. Translated into terms of income and tendencies to equalize, the hypothesis states that people who have experienced income increases in the past, who expect income increases in the future, and who perceive the overall standard of living to be improving have weaker tendencies to equalize. Very similar is Robinson and Bell's treatment of "perception of monetary success" as an intervening variable contributing to the explanation of the variation of egalitarian attitudes (see Robinson & Bell, 1978, p. 133).

Gurr only discusses the effects of relative deprivation. But people's actual rewards can also be higher than the rewards they feel they deserve. Homans and Jasso have argued that such situations of overreward or relative privilege can be experienced as inequitable just as well as situations of underreward (Homans, 1961; Jasso, 1978). In Robinson and Bell's models, relative deprivation surfaces as one of the intervening variables under the heading, "Sense of Personal Equity" (Robinson & Bell, 1978 p. 133 ff.).

Jasso has developed a formula for the justice evaluation of rewards, which states that the justice evaluation is a function of the logarithm of actual reward divided by just reward (Jasso, 1978, 1980). According to this formula, the justice evaluation of a reward has zero value if actual earnings equal just earnings; it has a positive value when actual rewards exceed just rewards. It has a negative value when actual rewards are less than just rewards. Also, because of the logarithmic nature of the formula, underreward is felt more keenly than overreward. The Jasso formulation fits within the relative deprivation tradition à la Gurr because it also takes a discrepancy between an actual and a preferred situation as its point of departure.

If similar relationships obtain between our relative deprivation variables and the tendency to equalize, this would mean that the more deprived people feel, the stronger their tendencies to equalize, but also that the more people feel relatively privileged, the stronger their tendency to equalize. In this case, the relationship between relative deprivation and the tendency to equalize would be curvilinear.

The second tradition with regard to relative deprivation is associated with the name of Runciman. Runciman defines relative deprivation as a feeling of deprivation people can experience when they compare themselves with other people (Runciman, 1966). Though *Why Men Rebel* is a fruitful source of operationalizations, Gurr's concept of relative deprivation is theoretically not very satisfying. It exists in a social vacuum: Any discrepancy between what one wants and what one has is considered to be a form of relative deprivation. Runciman's conception of relative deprivation is more sociological. He emphasizes that the essence of the concept of relative deprivation lies in people' comparisons with other relevant individuals or social groups.

In terms of the income inequality, this means that one should not look at the difference between what a respondent earns and what he feels he should be earning but at the difference between what respondents earn compared to other people and what they feel they should be earning compared to other people. In this formulation, respondent's interest lies in improving his relative income position, rather than his absolute income level.

In the Runciman version of relative deprivation, it is not only of interest with whom or with which group one compares oneself but also to which group one feels one belongs (membership reference group). One may hypothesize that individuals who subjectively identify with or feel they belong to lower classes, groups, or occupational levels will tend to have stronger tendencies to equalize. In both traditions, what a person "has" is not some objective level of reward but some subjective perception of the existing state of affairs.

It is hard to draw a clear boundary line between theories of absolute deprivation and status theories on the one hand and theories of relative deprivation on the other. People with low incomes may be in favor of equalization, not so much because they think they will gain financially, but because they feel jealous, relatively deprived, or because they feel income differentials are unjust. The same holds for people with low status positions. Nevertheless, there is a difference. Theories of absolute deprivation and status theories tend to focus on objectively measurable rewards. Theories of relative deprivation focus on the subjective side of deprivation. Theories of relative deprivation allow for the possibility that people with higher incomes sometimes feel more deprived than people with lower incomes.

Theories of relative deprivation could also have been classified under the heading of cognitive theories. One might well argue that feelings of relative deprivation represent discrepancies between standards of what one should have and perceptions of what one has. This holds in particular for the Gurr version of relative deprivation, which is none other than a reformulation of the theory of cognitive dissonance. I have chosen to discuss theories of relative deprivation under a separate heading for three reasons. First, there is a large body of specialist literature on relative deprivation. Second, in its more sociological versions, the theory of relative deprivation refers not so much to discrepancies between perceptions of reality and standards but to comparisons between the social rewards of different groups in society. Third, most theories of relative deprivation have been explicitly formulated to explain how people react to inequality relationships. Thus Runciman's study tries to answer the question why objectively deprived individuals and groups are not always deeply dissatisfied with their situation. Most cognitive theories, on the other hand, are general theories that analyze how people react to discrepancies between preferred and perceived situations, of which inequality relationships are a special instance.

Long-Run Changes in Attitudes toward Inequality

Many authors have suggested that in the long run, more egalitarian attitudes have developed in Western societies (see Lenski, 1966; Beteille, 1973; Elias, 1970; Szirmai, 1988, Chapter 6). In the field of income inequality, this should manifest itself in a long-run shift toward a preference for a more equal income distribution. This hypothesis can only be tested by longitudinal research, some of which is now coming available but which usually does not yet cover a very long time span (Social and Cultural Report, 1986).

Robinson and Bell have formulated an "egalitarian Zeitgeist principle" that predicts that younger people will be more in favor of equalization than older people (Robinson & Bell, 1978, p. 129). They argue that if attitudes toward inequality are changing over time and that people have become more egalitarian than they used to be, such changes should be reflected in differing attitudes among people of different ages.

Research Questions

Apart from several specific hypotheses that have already been touched upon, the six classes of theories introduced in the previous section give rise to a number of interesting questions that will be examined in the empirical analysis.

One of these questions pertains to the relative importance of objective versus subjective factors in explaining the tendency to equalize. Is this tendency primarily influenced by one's location in the structure of inequality of positions and rewards (class, occupation, education, income) or rather by subjective factors? If subjective factors turn out to be important, are they primarily determined by individuals' locations in the social stratification system—in other words, are they intervening variables mediating the influence of objective variables, or are they unrelated to objective background characteristics? Absolute deprivation, status, class, authority refer to objective factors; cognitive theories and relative deprivation theories to subjective factors.

A second question, related to the first, is the question of social consensus. If objectively defined social groups differ significantly in their attitudes toward income inequality, one may conclude that there is a lack of social consensus concerning distributive questions. If, however, objective variables turn out to be unimportant, one may conclude that there are no fundamental clashes of opinion in this area. Answers to these questions bear on the discussion between function-alist and conflict theories of social stratification. Theories of class and group conflict predict diametrically opposed attitudes toward inequal-ity, status theories predict gradual differences of degree, whereas the extreme functionalist position predicts a high degree of consensus about the existing distribution of financial rewards.

A third question has to do with the role of self-interest in explaining tendencies to equalize. Absolute deprivation, status, and class theories all suggest that those people are in favor of equalization who think they will profit from it. In the case of relative deprivation à la Runciman, interest is conceived of in a relative sense, but disinter-ested motives of justice or equity are also involved. The notion of a fair reward can also give rise to feelings that one earns too much. The same holds for relative deprivation in the Gurr tradition. Nevertheless, usually relative deprivation implies that a situation in which an individual receives more reward is seen as fairer than the existing situation.

A fourth question refers to the relative importance of class and status variables in the explanation of the variation of attitudes toward inequality. In "Class as Conceived of by Marx and Dahrendorf," Robinson and Kelley (1979) try to bridge the gap between empirical research on status attainment in the Blau–Duncan tradition and theo-retical analyses of class and authority structures associated with Marx and Dahrendorf. Though attitudes toward income inequality are not explicitly included in their analysis, their article suggests various hypotheses and operationalizations with regard to the influence of social status and class position on the tendency to equalize.

In the Blau–Duncan interpretation, social stratification consists of a finely graded hierarchy of people with differing amounts of education, educational prestige, and occupational prestige (Blau & Duncan, 1967). Marx and Dahrendorf stress the importance of sharp dichotomies and conflicts of interests between owners of the means of productions versus nonowners, or between groups with authority who are in a position to command versus groups without authority who have to obey. Using data from surveys in the United States and Great Britain, Robinson and Kelley try to explain variation in income, class identification, and political preference by regressing them on variables derived from both *class* and *status* traditions. They claim that in this way they can demonstrate that "there are two distinct stratification systems in modern society, one the familiar status system centering on education and occupational status and the other a class system rooted in ownership of the means of production and authority" (Robinson & Kelley, 1979, p. 309). Robinson and Kelley also argue—rather convincingly—that the Marxian and Dahrendorfian analyses of class are both incomplete. Marxian analyses of class tend to disregard authority structures with the absurd consequence that managers of a company and workers of a company are treated as members of one and the same class. Dahrendorfian analyses tend to disregard differences of class, thus making it impossible to distinguish members of command classes who own the means of production from managers who are employees. Elaborating on Wright and Perrone's reinterpretation of Marxist class categories (Wright & Perrone, 1977), Robinson and Kelley combine operationalizations of Marxian categories with operationalizations of Dahrendorfian categories in their regression analysis.

Robinson and Kelley show that in regression analysis, Blau–Duncan variables and Marx-Dahrendorf variables together explain far more variation than either the Blau–Duncan variables or the Marx–Dahrendorf variables separately. I will attempt to explain the variation in the tendency to equalize (TEQ) in a similar fashion, by regressing it on both Blau–Duncan variables and Marx–Dahrendorf type variables.

Operationalizations[6]

Dependent Variable

The dependent variable in the analysis is the Tendency to Equalize (TEQ). This variable is operationalized as the percentage difference between the Theil-coefficient of estimated incomes and the Theil-

---

[6]Variable names and numbers correspond to those used in Szirmai (1988, Annex F).

coefficient of the just incomes on the income ruler. (See the first section).

Inequality Aversion

The operationalization of the normative standard with regard to inequality is the Inequality Aversion scale discussed in the first section.

Perceptions of Income Inequality

The following variables operationalize various aspects of the perception of income inequality: the Theil-coefficient of the estimated distribution of incomes on the income ruler (TEST), the estimated percentage of income recipients earning more than respondent (V108), perceived changes in the degree of income inequality (V119) and expected changes in the degree of income income inequality (V122).

Secondary Incongruities

The interview schedule includes a large number of questions dealing with perceptions of various negative consequences of income equalization or with the perceived importance of monetary incentives: V160, V161, V215, V219, V220, V221, V226, V231, V233, V234, V235, V236, V237, V238, V239, DMOB and PERF and DISCON. DISCON is a factor analytically derived scale created from Likert-type items referring to negative consequences of equalization.

Relative Deprivation

Relative deprivation à la Gurr is operationalized by the difference between respondents estimated and just income on the income ruler (RDEP). Relative deprivation in the Jasso formulation is operationalized by the logarithm of the ratio of respondent's estimated income to respondent's just income on the income ruler (LOGQUOT). An alternative operationalization of the feeling of over- or underreward derives from a direct question (V109).

Variables related to the relative deprivation discussion are Perceived changes in the standard of living (V050), Past changes in respondent's income level (V041), and Expected changes in respondent's income level (V049). Four variables operationalize different aspects of the salience of income inequality.

Relative deprivation à la Runciman is operationalized with help of the income ruler. This operationalization is found by taking respondent's estimated income as a fraction of the average of estimated incomes and subtracting it from respondent's just income as a fraction of the average of the just incomes on the income ruler (RELDIF).

A person's subjective estimate of his own position in the occupational structure is operationalized by the variable Self-rated occupational level (V048A). His identification with higher or lower social groups or classes is operationalized by three dummy variables REFGR1, REFGR2, and REFGR3 that refer to identification with lower, middle, and higher groups or classes respectively.

Income

Income is taken as the operationalization of the degree of absolute deprivation. The income concept used is respondent's net yearly income, including holiday allowance and additional income from secondary sources, but excluding children's allowances.

Class and Authority

The ownership of means of production is operationalized by the dummy variable for self-employed–not self-employed (DV018). The question whether a respondent belongs to the obey or the command class (Dahrendorf) is operationalized by the question whether or not respondent supervises other people in his work (V021). In addition, V018 and V021 have been combined to create a dummy variable EMPLOYER (EMPL) of which Code 1 represents self-employed persons who have subordinates working for them or employed persons who have subordinates working for them (managers).

Status Variables

As status variables, occupational level (V017) and educational level have been included in the analysis.

System Blaming

Three questions refer to whether people blame capitalism for their problems (V194), whether they would prefer to transfer power to a strong working class party (V296), and whether they feel that class relationships are antagonistic (V293A). These questions are taken as operationalizations of Della Fave's concept of system blaming. Variable V293A has also been transformed into a dummy variable.

Empirical Results

In this section, a path model explaining the variation of the tendency to equalize will be presented. This path model is the end result of a series of partial analyses in which specific hypotheses or models have been examined and that subsequently have been synthesized into this larger model. For reasons of brevity, only the final model can be presented. For a more extended treatment the reader is referred to Szirmai (1988, chapter 5). The basic correlation matrix is reproduced in Appendix 1 to this chapter.

The statistical analysis proceeded as follows. On the one hand the dependent variable was regressed on the whole pool of relevant items, which could be considered as operationalizations of the concepts discussed in the second section (73 items). The stepwise procedure served to select those variables that were likely candidates for inclusion in the final regression equations. The variables with clearly nonsignificant coefficients were subsequently dropped from the analysis. On the other hand, TEQ was regressed on subsets of items, each consisting of items forming alternative operationalizations of theoretical concepts such as relative deprivation, system blaming, and conceptions of human nature. For instance, a series of stepwise regressions was performed, taking all possible operationalizations of relative deprivation as the independent variables.[7] One of the main functions of the regressions over these subsets of variables was to select those operationalizations that contributed most to explained variation of the dependent variable TEQ. Once a smaller set of candidates for inclusion in the final regression equation was available, a series of regressions

---

[7]The procedure used in this study is the SPSS stepwise regression procedure. In this procedure, independent variables are entered in the order of their respective contributions to explained variation. The 5% level of significance was set as the minimum level for inclusion. In the option chosen, inclusion of successive variables is combined with deletion of variables that no longer meet the preestablished criterion at each successive step (Nie et al., 1975, p. 345).

were run over selected clusters of variables in order to find the equation that explained most variation of the dependent variable and in which all the coefficients were significant at the 5% level.[8] The resulting final equation can be found in Table 1.

Next—using the same combination of stepwise and nonstepwise regression—TEQ was regressed on all variables measuring objective background characteristics of respondents such as income, age, sex, and occupational level. The resulting equation is presented in Table 2. By comparing the equation in Table 1 with the equation in Table 2 one can better assess the relative importance of objective versus subjective variables for the explanation of TEQ.

In the third place, the four most interesting variables in the regression equation explaining the variation of TEQ (Table 1) were in turn regressed on the remaining variables, in order to establish secondary effects of variables on TEQ, which are mediated by intervening variables. The relevant equations are reproduced in Tables 3 to 6. In the following paragraphs, the regression equations will first be discussed one by one. Next, the whole path model will be presented (see Figure 1). On the basis of this path model, the theoretical conclusions will be summarized.

It should be stressed that the path model consisting of the equations in Tables 1, 3, 4, 5, and 6 is an incomplete model. Not all path coefficients have been computed—the model would have become unmanageable—only those that are of theoretical interest. All equations have been estimated using ordinary least squares regression, the assumption being that the path model is a recursive model. As most of the variables in the model are attitude variables that have been measured simultaneously, this assumption cannot be proved. If one finds a correlation between two variables, it is hard to say which way

---

[8]This combination of stepwise regression with nonstepwise regressions over smaller numbers of variables is the standard procedure followed throughout this study. As each variable has a certain number of missing cases, stepwise regressions over a large number of variables can lead to the deletion of a great number of cases, when the listwise deletion of missing cases option in SPSS is used. In some instances, this effects the significance of the coefficients. Therefore, stepwise regression is only used as a first step in the analysis, to see which variables are likely candidates for inclusion in the final regression equations. Subsequently, the regressions are rerun over smaller clusters of variables from which unlikely variables have been excluded. These clusters include variables the coefficients of which approached the 5% level but that were not included in the regression equation resulting from the stepwise procedure. Other variables are included in the cluster because of their theoretical importance or on basis of high first-order correlations with the dependent variable. In this manner, some of the theoretical objections against an indiscriminate use of stepwise regression are met (see Wonnacott & Wonnacott, 1970, pp. 309–312).

the causal path should run, other than on theoretical grounds or on grounds of plausibility. In this model, the ordering of the variables has been determined by the theoretical discussions in the preceding sections.

The main point in discussing the regression equations of the intervening variables is to see whether theoretically important variables that have no significant coefficients in the regressions explaining the variation of TEQ have some secondary effects via one or more of the intervening variables. The term *intervening variables* is used to indicate the endogenous variables in the path model. Strictly speaking the use of the term *intervening variable* implies that the partial correlations between the dependent variable and the exogenous variables, controlling for intervening variables, should not deviate significantly from zero (Gadourek, 1972). As the model is incomplete and not all possible path coefficients have been computed, in a few cases partial correlations between TEQ and the exogenous variables, controlling for the relevant intervening variables, are in fact not equal to zero. However, if one controls for all variables in the regression equation explaining TEQ (Table 1), the partial correlations disappear without exception.

Direct Determinants of the Tendency to Equalize

The final results of the regressions of TEQ on the whole pool of variables are represented in the following table.

The regression equation in Table 1 accounts for 47% of the variation of the tendency to equalize. For an analysis based on individual-level data, this is not unsatisfactory. Though the equation contains no less than 12 variables, 41.5% of the variation of the dependent variable is explained by three variables: RELDIF, INEQAV, and V219. The remaining 5% of variation is explained by the other 9 variables. Nevertheless, these 9 variables all have significant coefficients, are theoretically relevant and have signs that are in line with hypotheses formulated in this chapter.

Of the 12 variables, two are operationalizations of relative deprivation: RELDIF and DUMQUOT1. The most important variable is Relative deprivation à la Runciman (RELDIF). Alone it explains 27.8% of the variation of TEQ. People who feel their relative income position is too low, as manifested by their tendency to improve their relative income position on the income ruler, are the people with stronger tendencies to equalize. DUMQUOT1 is the dummy variable for fair income level. Other things being equal, people whose just income

Table 1. Determinants of the Tendency to Equalize

Variable		Lowest and highest value	Standardized beta coefficient	t-value
Dependent				
TEQ	Tendency to equalize			
Independent:				
RELDIF	Relative just income minus relative estimated income		+.42	+13.45
DUMQUOT1	Dummy fair income level	0. 1. Just equals estimated income	−.08	−2.56
INEQAV	Inequality aversion	7. Lowest value 35. Highest value	+.22	+6.23
V122	Expected changes in income inequality	1. Great decrease in inequality 7. Great increase in inequality	+.07	+2.29
CLASS2	Dummy perception of class society	0. No mention of class society 1. Mention of class society	+.07	+2.25
V219	Willingness to sacrifice income for more pleasant work	1. certainly 5. certainly not	−.16	−5.49
V221	Negative effects of social security on mobility of labor	1. certainly 5. no	+.06	+2.18
V239	Effects of equalization on unemployment	1. Less unemployment 3. More unemployment	−.07	−2.44
DISCON	Discontent with equalization	7. Lowest value 35. Highest value	−.08	−2.51
DGEREF	Dummy "Gereformeerde Kerk"	0. Not a member 1. Member	−.08	−2.78
EDMOB	Intergenerational educational mobility	−7. Downward mobility +7. Upward mobility	+.07	+2.26
EMPL	Dummy employer	0. Not an employer 1. Employer	−.07	−2.41
			$R^2 = .47$	$N = 682$

equals their estimated income have lower tendencies to equalize than either people who feel overrewarded or underrewarded.

The variables INEQAV, V122, V219, V221, and V239 derive from the theory of mental incongruities. The greater the discrepancy between people's inequality aversion (INEQAV) and their expectations with regard to income inequality in the future (V122), the stronger their tendency to equalize. The greater the secondary incongruities created by equalization as measured by variables V219, V221, and V239, the more the tendency to equalize is dampened. All the signs are in the expected directions.

System blaming is represented in the equation by dummy variable CLASS2. People who see Dutch society as a class society have stronger tendencies to equalize than people who do not.

Objective Determinants of the Tendency to Equalize

It is striking that only three of the 12 variables in Equation 1 measure objective characteristics of the respondents: Membership of the "Gereformeerde Kerk" (DGEREF), Dummy Employer (EMPL), and Intergenerational Educational Mobility (EDMOB). Members of the strict Protestant *gereformeerde kerk* have weaker tendencies to equalize than other people, as have respondents who employ other people. With regard to educational mobility, upwardly mobile respondents have stronger tendencies to equalize than downwardly mobile respondents. The contribution of these three variables to explained variation is modest. Together, they add only some 1.4% to explained variation. Neither educational level nor occupational level has significant coefficients. Not even absolute deprivation as measured by income (V373) has a significant effect on TEQ.

It is conceivable that objective variables have secondary effects on TEQ, which are mediated by intervening subjective variables. If these secondary effects were important, a regression of TEQ on objective variables only should give a R^2 not much lower than that found in Equation 1.

If we compare Table 2 in which the results of regressions of TEQ on the pool of objective background variables are reproduced, with Table 1, the insignificant role of objective variables becomes immediately obvious. Together the five variables with significant coefficients—Income, Experience of Promotion, Church Membership, Membership of the "Gereformeerde Kerk and Union Membership"—explain only 10% of the variation of TEQ, compared with 47% in Equation 1. Only two of the variables have any relevance for my

Table 2. Objective Determinants of the Tendency to Equalize

Variable		Lowest and higest value	Standardized beta coefficient	t-value
Dependent				
TEQ	Tendency to equalize			
Independent				
V373	Income		−.20	−5.87
DGEREF	Membership of	0. Not member		
	"Gereformeerde Kerk"	1. Member	−.12	−3.49
V319	Church membership	0. Not member of church		
		1. Member	−.10	−2.76
V246	Union membership	0. Not member of union or professional organization		
		1. Member	+.11	+3.30
DV036	Experience of	0. Not promoted recently		
	promotion	1. Promoted recently	−.09	−2.67
			$R^2 = .10$	$N = 811$

hypotheses, namely Income, the coefficient of which is in line with the absolute deprivation hypothesis and Experience of Promotion which is a weak operationalization of Gurr's concept of value loss. Finally none of the objective variables measuring class, status, age, or sex have significant coefficients.

Intervening Variables

Variables of theoretical interest, which have no significant direct effects on TEQ, may have secondary effects via intervening variables. For instance, income does not figure in Equation 1. But, before rejecting the absolute deprivation hypothesis which states that low income is associated with strong tendencies to equalize, one should ascertain whether income does not have a significant effect on one or more of the variables in that equation. Ideally, one should interpret all the variables in Table 1 as potential intervening variables and regress them on all remaining variable discussed in this chapter, in order to identify secondary effects on the dependent variable. However, most variables in this table contribute so minimally to the explanation of the variation of TEQ that it is not worthwhile to explore all secondary effects via these variables.

Four variables from Equation 1 have been selected as intervening variables: RELFDIF, INEQAV, DUMQUOT1, and V219. RELDIF and

INEQAV are the variables that contribute most to R^2 and that have the highest standardized beta coefficients. DUMQUOT1 does not contribute so much to explained variation, but it is of theoretical interest as an operationalization of relative deprivation à la Gurr, and it has a fairly high first-order correlation with TEQ. V219 measures the importance of monetary incentives for respondents. It has been selected as intervening variable because of its relatively high beta coefficient and because it contributes most to explained variation, once RELDIF and INEQAV are held constant.

On the basis of the theory of mental incongruities and Della Fave's discussion of the role of an egalitarian conception of justice, the inequality aversion scale INEQAV is interpreted as the crucial variable mediating the influence of other variables on TEQ. Therefore, INEQAV was regressed on all remaining objective and subjective variables in the model, including the other three intervening variables. Subsequently, RELDIF, V219, and DUMQUOT1 were regressed on all remaining variables (but not on each other). In the following paragraphs, I will discuss the regression equations for the intervening variables, focusing on the secondary effects of theoretically interesting independent variables on TEQ, via the intervening variables.

In the TEQ model, INEQAV is considered to be an intervening variable. However, as a variable measuring aspects of attitudes toward inequality, it is also interesting for its own sake. Many of the hypotheses concerning egalitarian attitudes that I have formulated with regard to the tendency to equalize are applicable to inequality aversion as well. Therefore, in the discussion of the regression equation for INEQAV, I will not only focus on secondary effects on TEQ via INEQAV, but I will also check whether hypotheses that had to be rejected for TEQ can be maintained for INEQAV and vice versa.

Comparison between Equations 3 and 1 makes it clear that relative deprivation à la Runciman (RELDIF), the most important variable in the equation explaining the tendency to equalize, also has a significant coefficient in the equation explaining INEQAV. In terms of contribution to explained variation, the importance of RELDIF is considerably less than in the TEQ equation. But the importance of the relationship between relative deprivation and attitudes toward inequality is confirmed by the fact that not only RELDIF, but also three other operationalizations of relative deprivation have significant coefficients and signs in the expected directions. These variables are the operationalization of Gurr's concept of Past Experience of Value Loss (V049), the operationalization of Gurr's concept of Perception of Value Stocks Available to All People in Society (V050), and a second operationalization of Relative Deprivation à la Runciman (V109). In addition, the salience variable V038 has a significant effect on inequality aversion (see Table 3).

The most striking difference between the Equations 3 and 1 lies in the role of variables measuring objective and subjective social status. The coefficients of occupational level (V017), educational level (V011), and self-rated occupational level (V048A) all offer support for the social status version of Robinson and Bell's underdog hypothesis. People with lower social status tend to have stronger feelings of inequality aversion. None of these variables figured in Equation 1.[9]

As before, the absolute deprivation hypothesis, which predicts that lower income recipients are more egalitarian than high income recipients, is not confirmed. Of course there are correlations between income and the status variables (the correlation between V373 and V011 is .40, between V373 and V017 .46, and between V373 and V048A -.50; see Appendix 1), which implies that income has secondary effects on INEQAV via status variables. But in any case, when V011, V017, and V048A are included in the regression equation, V373 does not have a significant coefficient.

As in Equation 1, age has no significant coefficient. This result contradicts Robinson and Bell's egalitarian Zeitgeist hypothesis. By and large, the other results are also comparable to the TEQ equation. Significant coefficients are found for the variable operationalizing system blaming (CLASS2), for perceptions of changes in income inequality (V119), and for variables measuring various dysfunctions of equalization (V221, V223, and V239). When the scale variable Discontent with Equalization (DISCON) is included among the regressors along with the variables in Equation 3, R^2 jumps from .42 to .49 whereas all the variables of Equation 3 retain their significant coefficients and their signs. However, it seems tautological to regress one scale variable measuring attitudes toward income inequality on another scale variable measuring attitudes toward income inequality. Therefore, DISCON has not been included in the regression equation explaining INEQAV.

---

[9]As mentioned in the introduction to this section, the ordering of variables in the path model has a certain element of arbitrariness. On theoretical grounds discussed elsewhere, I have chosen to interpret TEQ as the dependent variable in the path model and INEQAV as an intervening variable. Other researchers could have defended a reverse sequence.

If one includes TEQ among the regressors of INEQAV, the resulting regression equation becomes: INEQAV = .23 TEQ − .10 V017 + .15 V119 − .13 V233 + .11 V050 − .15 V239 + .07 V109 + .10 V048a + .09 V221 + .07 CLASS2 − .08 V038 − .10 V011 + .06 V049. All coefficients are significant at the 5% level. R^2 is .45. The only difference between this equation and equation 3 is that RELDIF has been replaced by TEQ. All other variables have retained their significant coefficients and their signs.

Table 3. Determinants of the Intervening Variable Inequality Aversion

Variable		Lowest and highest value	Standardized beta coefficient	t-value
Dependent				
INEQAV	Inequality aversion	7. Lowest value 35. Highest value		
Independent				
RELDIF	Relative just income minus relative estimated income		+.08	+2.66
V109	Fairness of relative income position	1. Fair income 3. Too much	+.08	+2.83
V119	Perception of changes in income inequality	1. Great decrease in inequality 7. Great increase in inequality	+.16	−5.04
V038	Salience of income comparisons	1. Often compares incomes 3. Hardly ever compares incomes	−.09	−2.90
V049	Expected changes in own real income	1. Substantial improvement 5. Substantial deterioration	+.07	+2.31
V050	Perception of changes in standard of living	1. Great improvement 5. Great deterioration	+.11	+3.63
V048A	Self-rated occupational level	1. Businessmen, company directors 8. Unskilled laborers	+.13	+3.21
CLASS2	Dummy perception of class society	0. No mention 1. Mention of class society	+.10	+3.45
V221	Negative effects of social security on mobility of labor	1. Certainly 5. No	+.12	+4.14
V233	Effects of equalization on enjoyment of work	1. Enjoyment of work will increase 3. Will decrease	−.15	−4.86
V239	Effects of equalization on unemployment	1. Less Unemployment 3. More unemployment	−.17	−5.77
V011	Educational level	1. Primary school 8. University degree	−.10	−2.29
V017	Occupational level	1. Unskilled laborers 6. Higher professions	−.09	−1.94
			$R^2 = .42$	$N = 719$

The regression equation for intervening variable Relative Deprivation (RELDIF) is represented in Table 4. It is interesting to note the
effects of Age (V005), Dummy Self-Employment (DV018), and Income
(V373). The sign of the coefficient of age is in line with the egalitarian
Zeitgeist principle. Younger people have stronger feelings of relative
deprivation à la Runciman and—as we have seen before—relative
deprivation à la Runciman is positively related to the tendency to
equalize. The secondary effect of income on TEQ via RELDIF is in line
with the absolute deprivation hypothesis. Self-employed people feel
more deprived than employed people. This contradicts the Marxian
hypothesis of the effects of class position as operationalized by Rob-

Table 4. Determinants of the Intervening Variable RELDIF

Variable		Lowest and highest value		Standardized beta coefficient	t-value
Dependent					
RELDIF	Relative just minus relative estimated income				
Independent					
V005	Year of birth	16.	1916		
		57.	1957	+.09	+2.47
DV018	Dummy self-employed	0.	Not self-employed		
	nonself-employed	1.	Self-employed	+.17	+4.94
V373	Income			−.12	−3.20
V246	Union membership	0.	Not member of union or professional organization		
		1.	Member	+.13	+3.71
V214	Income satisfaction	1.	Very satisfied		
		7.	Very dissatisfied	+.27	+7.67
TEST	Theil-coefficient estimated distribution			+.20	+5.74
V239	Effects of equalization on unemployment	1.	Less unemployment		
		3.	More unemployment	−.07	−2.16
POL	Political preference	1.	Small right-wing parties		
		7.	Small left-wing parties	+.08	+2.27
V119	Perception of changes in income inequality	1.	Great decrease in inequality		
		7.	Great increase in inequality	+.08	+2.29
				$R^2 = .26$	$N = 679$

inson and Kelley. It is not the exploited employees who feel most deprived but people who own their own (small) businesses. Other variables of theoretical interest are Perceived Income Inequality (TEST) and Perceived Changes in Income Inequality (V119). Relative deprivation is positively associated with the degree of perceived inequality and with perceived increases in inequality. Via RELDIF these variables have positive secondary effects on TEQ.

Turning to the intervening variables, DUMQUOT1 and V219, the following effects are worth noting. Perceptions of inequality have significant effects on both intervening variables. The signs of TEST in Equation 6 and of V119 in Equation 5 are as hypothesized. However, the signs of V119 and TESTLOW (the slope shift dummy of estimated income inequality for the bottom 40% of income recipients) in Equation 6 are contrary to my expectations. I have hypothesized that the greater the degree of perceived inequality, the stronger the tendency to equalize. Here, greater degrees of perceived inequality and perceived increases of inequality are associated with a greater emphasis on monetary incentives (V219), which in turn is associated with weaker

Table 5. Determinants of the Intervening Variable DUMQUOT1

Variable		Lowest and highest value	Standardized beta coefficient	t-value
Dependent				
DUMQUOT1	Dummy fair income level	1. Just equals estimated income		
Independent				
V214	Income satisfaction	1. Very satisfied 7. Very dissatisfied	$-.21$	-5.60
TESTLOW	Slope shift dummy TEST (Theil coefficient estimated distribution for bottom 40%		$-.14$	-3.68
DISCON	Discontent with equalization	7. Lowest value 35. Highest value	$+.09$	$+2.55$
V119	Perception of changes in income inequality	1. Great decrease in inequality 7. Great increase in inequality	$-.09$	-2.47
V038	Salience of income comparisons	1. Often compares incomes 3. Hardly ever compares incomes	$+.11$	$+3.14$
			$R^2 = .14$	$N = 725$

Table 6. Determinants of the Intervening Variable V219

Variable		Lowest and highest value	Standardized beta coefficient	t-value
Dependent				
V219	Willingness to sacrifice income for more pleasant work	1. Certainly 5. Certainly not		
Independent				
V011	Educational level	1. Primary education 8. University degree	−.19	−4.79
POL	Political preference	1. Small right-wing parties 7. Small left-wing parties	−.11	−2.92
V221	Negative effects of social security on mobility of labor	1. Certainly 5. No	−.09	−2.56
V119	Perception of changes in income inequality	1. Great decrease in inequality 7. Great increase in inequality	+.11	+3.08
DISCON	Discontent with equalization	7. Lowest value 35. Highest value	+.10	+2.76
TEST	Theil coefficient estimated inequality		−.10	−2.71
TESTLOW	Slope shift dummy TEST for bottom 40%		+.09	+2.34
			$R^2 = .12$	$N = 763$

tendencies to equalize. Interesting are the secondary effects of educational level on TEQ, via V219. The higher the educational level, the greater the willingness to sacrifice income for more pleasant work, which in turn is associated with stronger tendencies to equalize. Finally, the salience variable has a secondary effect on TEQ via DUMQUOT1, as predicted (see Tables 5 and 6).

In the interpretation of these secondary effects, it should be stressed that all secondary effects of variables via DUMQUOT1 and V219 are very weak. DUMQUOT1 and V219 only contribute modestly to explained variation of TEQ, whereas the amount of variation of these intervening variables explained by the variables in Equations 5 and 6 is less than 15%.

Conclusions

The path model is finally summarized in Figure 1. It must be stressed once more that this model, complicated as it is, is only a partial model. Not all possible relationships between variables have been explored. Only four of the variables with a direct effect on the tendency to equalize have been regressed on other variables. Of course it would have been interesting to regress variables such as Self-Rated Occupational Level (V048A), Estimated Inequality (TEST), Political Preference (POL), or Income Satisfaction (V214) on other variables—some of these regressions have indeed been discussed in the previous sections—but the secondary and tertiary effects of these variables on TEQ are so weak that it is not worthwhile to pursue these lines of analysis further.

Figure 1 enables us to review our findings in the light of the theoretical categories introduced in the second section and the more specific hypotheses formulated in the subsequent sections. The following general conclusions can be drawn:

1. Feelings of relative deprivation are among the most important determinants of the tendency to equalize. Relative deprivation à la Runciman, as measured by variable RELDIF, contributes most to the explanation of the variation of the dependent variable TEQ. It has both a strong direct effect on the tendency to equalize and a secondary effect mediated by inequality aversion.

The significant coefficient of the dummy variable Fair Income Level (DUMQUOT1), one of the operationalizations of relative deprivation à la Gurr, indicates that other things being equal, the tendency to equalize will be at its weakest when people feel fairly rewarded. Higher values for the tendency to equalize are found both in the case of underreward and in the case of overreward.

A second operationalization of relative deprivation à la Runciman, namely Fairness of Relative Income Position (V109), has a significant coefficient in the equation explaining INEQAV and thus a secondary effect on the tendency to equalize. As in the case of DUMQUOT1, respondents who feel their relative income position is fair, have the weakest feelings of inequality aversion and the weakest tendencies to equalize.

In the equation of INEQAV there are two other variables that derive from Gurr's discussion of relative deprivation. Expected Changes in Own Real Income (V049) is the operationalization of Gurr's concept of "value potential." Perception of Changes in the Standard of Living (V050) is the operationalization of Gurr's concept of "perception of value stocks." According to Gurr these variables should affect the degree of relative deprivation. In the path model, V049 and V050 do not have significant coefficients in the equation explaining relative deprivation (RELDIF), but they do have secondary effects on the tendency to equalize, mediated by inequality aversion.

The effect of intergenerational educational mobility on TEQ is intriguing. Strictly speaking, it would be consistent with theories of relative deprivation that people who have experienced downward educational mobility feel more deprived than people who have experienced upward mobility. In the model in Figure 1 the opposite is the case. People whose educational level is lower than their father's are less in favor of equalization than people who have experienced upward educational mobility. One should remember, however, that the contribution of educational mobility to explained variation of the tendency to equalize is very small.

Finally, the secondary effects of the salience variable V038 on TEQ mediated by INEQAV and DUMQUOT1, are as hypothesized by Gurr. People for whom income differences are more salient have stronger tendencies to equalize than people who never think about income differences.

2. The absolute deprivation hypothesis finds far less support than one would expect. Income (V373) has no direct influence on the tendency to equalize or on inequality aversion. The only effect worth noting is a secondary effect on TEQ via RELDIF. This effect is as hypothesized. The lower one's income, the stronger the feeling of relative deprivation and the stronger the tendency to equalize.

3. Status variables turn out to be of somewhat greater importance in explaining attitudes toward inequality. Three of the variables operationalizing social status—Educational Level (V011), Occupational Level (V017), and Self-Rated Occupational Level (V048A)—have a direct effect on inequality aversion and thus a secondary effect on the tendency to equalize. In addition, education has a secondary effect via V219. One may conclude that people with lower social status are more likely to equalize on the income ruler than people with higher social status. The enlightenment hypothesis that predicts a positive relation between the level of education and egalitarian attitudes has to be rejected.

Of course, the status variables are correlated with income, so that the effects of status variables also reflect the effects of income level. But the correlations between income and the status variables are not so high that there is serious multicollinearity, and when the effects of the status variables are held constant, income has no significant coefficient in the equations of TEQ, and INEQAV.

4. The effects of class position on attitudes toward income ine-

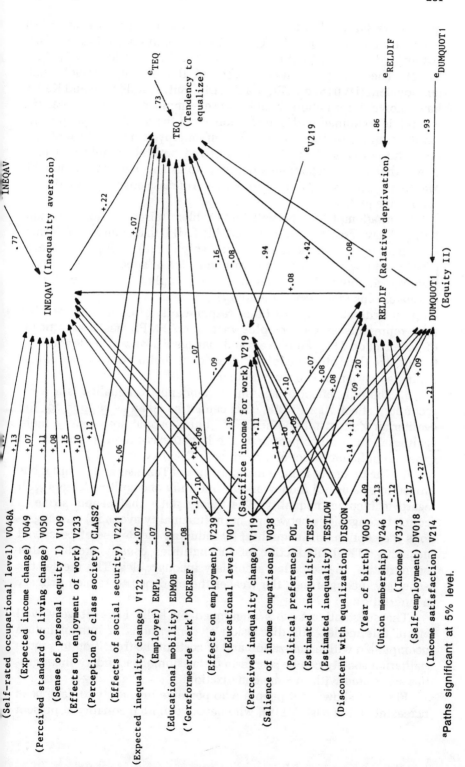

Figure 1. Determinants of the Tendency to Equalize[a]

[a]Paths significant at 5% level.

quality are far weaker than one would expect. There are no direct effects on either TEQ or INEQAV of the operationalizations of class according to Marx (DV018) or of class according to Dahrendorf (V021, V022). There is a secondary effect of the dummy variable self-employment (DV018) on TEQ via RELDIF. But, as Robinson and Kelley have shown, information about being self-employed is only interesting when it is combined with information about the number of people one employs. In my sample, most of the self-employed are small shopkeepers, who consistently feel more deprived both absolutely and relatively, than other respondents in the sample. This has little to do with Marxian hypotheses about the importance of class position for attitudes toward inequality.

In an attempt to cope with the problem raised by Robinson and Kelley, I have created a dummy variable EMPL that combines information about type of employment relationship (V018), occupational level (V017), and whether or not a respondent has subordinates (V021). Dummy variable EMPL distinguishes self-employed people with subordinates plus members of the higher professions in the private sector with subordinates from all other respondents. This dummy variable thus represents employers plus managers. EMPL has a significant direct effect on TEQ. Employers and managers have weaker tendencies to equalize than other people. But the contribution of this variable to explained variation is only marginal.

5. The only effect of age on the tendency to equalize is a weak secondary effect via RELDIF. This cannot be taken as support for the egalitarian Zeitgeist hypothesis. If young people were really more egalitarian than older people as the hypothesis predicts, one would expect significant direct effects on both INEQAV and TEQ.

6. The theory of mental incongruities of Tazelaar and Wippler has proved to be a useful framework for the study of cognitive factors with regard to income inequality. The theory states that people strive to reduce incongruities between a norm (inequality aversion) and cognitions (perceptions of inequality) by reducing the degree of perceived inequality (TEQ). Reduction of incongruities usually creates other incongruities, the so-called secondary incongruities. The greater the secondary incongruities, the weaker the tendency to reduce primary incongruities.

The substantive factors mentioned by Della Fave fit very well within this model. His discussion of conceptions of human nature incompatible with equalization and of costs of the transition to a more egalitarian society can be seen as a discussion of secondary incongruities associated with income equalization.

Figure 1 shows that people who perceive inequality to have been increasing in the past (V119), who perceive more inequality at present

(TEST), and who expect inequality to increase in the future (V122) have a stronger tendency to equalize. V122 has a direct effect on TEQ. V119 has secondary effects via INEQAV, RELDIF, DUMQUOT1, and V219. The secondary effects of V119 via V219 run counter to the hypothesis. All other effects are consistent with the hypothesis. Estimated inequality has secondary effects on TEQ via RELDIF, V219, and DUMQUOT1. These effects are as hypothesized. Nevertheless, on the basis of earlier research one would have expected perceptions of inequality to have more powerful direct effects on the tendency to equalize than can be observed in the path model.

Secondary incongruities of various kinds clearly affect attitudes toward inequality. People who perceive various dysfunctions of equalization (V219, V221, V233, V239, DISCON) have weaker tendencies to equalize than people who perceive no such dysfunctions. Effects on TEQ are both direct and secondary.

7. A more general conclusion to be drawn from the preceding analysis is that a considerable part of the variation of attitudes toward inequality can be explained by respondent characteristics. This would seem to contradict the conclusion drawn in another research tradition, namely that respondent characteristics explain hardly anything of the variation of the fairness judgments of incomes. Using a vignette technique, Jasso, Alves, Rossi, and Hermkens have asked respondents to evaluate the fairness of incomes of households with various characteristics (Alves & Rossi, 1978; Jasso Rossi, 1977; Hermkens, 1983). When these household characteristics are held constant in regression analysis, respondent characteristics add no more than 1% to explained variation. These authors conclude that there is widespread concensus in the population concerning the criteria by which people judge the distribution of incomes.

The contradiction turns out to be only apparent. As we saw elsewhere in this study, respondents also tend to leave the ordering of occupations in the income hierarchy unchanged, when given the chance to redistribute incomes. This means that, by and large, they agree on the criteria for distributing incomes over occupations and positions. What they do not agree about is the degree of inequality that should exist between various rungs in the income hierarchy. On the contrary, people differ greatly in their tendencies to equalize the income distribution as they perceive it.

8. A second general conclusion regards the role of objective versus subjective characteristics in explaining the tendency to equalize. Throughout the analysis, one finds that objective variables play a very minor role. Objective variables taken alone explain but 10% of the variation of the dependent variable, and of these variables only income is a social stratification variable. One may conclude that there are no

deep cleavages between identifiable groups in Dutch society in 1980, with regard to their attitudes toward income inequality.

Neither functionalist nor conflict theories of social inequality can satisfactorily account for these results. Functionalist theories of social stratification assume that there exists consensus concerning both the criteria by which rewards are distributed and the resulting degree of inequality in reward. As we saw, there is a certain consensus concerning the preferred criteria for distributing incomes, but great differences of opinion exist concerning the preferred degree of income inequality. Conflict theories, on the other hand, predict sharp clashes of opinion between the haves and have-nots in society, with the haves, however defined, defending the existing types and degrees of inequality and the have-nots wanting to change them. No such clashes were found.

What I found was that, on average all groups in the sample, from low to high, would prefer less income inequality. The degree to which inequality should be decreased differs greatly from person to person, but this is more influenced by subjective factors such as relative deprivation than by their objective locations in the structure of inequality and privilege.

9. Perhaps the most important conclusion of this chapter is that the tendency to equalize is associated with self-interest in relative terms. Objective factors such as income or class position have little effect on TEQ. The variable with the greatest contribution to explained variation in the regression equation of the tendency to equalize is the relative deprivation variable RELDIF. This variable represents the changes respondents make on the income ruler in their own incomes relative to the average income level.[10] Elsewhere I have noted that high

---

[10]There is an unresolved inconsistency is this chapter between my interpretation of the income ruler variables as representing changes made by respondents in the perceived distribution of incomes on the one hand and my interpretation of these variables as representing discrepancies between existing and preferred situations. When the focus is on relative deprivation, variables such as RDEP, RELDIF, and LOGQUOT have been interpreted as discrepancies between preferred and existing states. When the focus is on the tendency to equalize or on self-interest, the variable TEQ is interpreted as a tendency to change the income distribution, and RELDIF is interpreted as a change in relative income position.

As I prefer to link my empirical analyses of the tendency to equalize to theoretical discussions concerning relative deprivation, I have chosen to leave this inconsistency of which I became conscious at the final stage of the analysis unresolved.

Empirically there is less of a problem. Whether one speaks of discrepancies or changes, it is interesting to find out to what extent differences between just and perceived income distributions are related to difference between respondents' just and perceived absolute income position and relative income positions.

income recipients who are in favor of income equalization seldom realize that such equalization entails income sacrifices on their part (Szirmai, 1984, 1988). Here we see that people in favor of equalization generally think that equalization will improve rather than worsen their relative income position.

References

Alves, W. M., & Rossi, P. H., (1978). Who should get what? Fairness judgements of the distribution of earnings. American Journal of Sociology, 84(3), 541–564.

Béteille, A. (1973) The decline of social inequality. In A. Béteille (Ed.), Social inequality (pp. 362–380). Harmondsworth: Penguin.

Blau, P., Duncan O. D., (1967). The American occupational structure. New York: The Free Press.

Bunjes, A. M., van Geffen, L. M. H. J., Keuzenkamp, T. M., Lijftocht, S. G., Wijga, W. (1977). Inkomens op tafel [Incomes above Board]. Nederlandse Stichting voor Psychotechniek. Alphen a/d Rijn: Samsom.

Champernowne, D. G. (1974). A comparison of measures of inequality of income distribution. The Economic Journal, No. 336, Vol. 84, December, 787–816.

Dahrendorf, R.(1959). Class and class conflict in industrial society. Stanford: Stanford University Press.

Della Fave, R., (1974). The structure of egalitarianism. Social Problems, December 1974, Vol. 22.2 199–213.

Della Fave, R., (1980). The meek shall not inherit the earth: Self-evaluation and the legitimacy of stratification. American Sociological Review, 955–971.

Elias, N. (1970). Was ist Soziologie?. München: Juventa Verlag.

Festinger, L. (1957). Theory of cognitive dissonance. New York:

Gadourek, I. (1972). Sociologische onderzoekstechieken [Techniques of sociological research]. Deventer: Van Loghum Slaterus.

Gurr, T. R. (1970). Why men rebel. Princeton NJ: Princeton University Press.

Hermkens, P & van Wijngaarden, P. (1977). Inkomensongelijkheid en rechtvaardigingskriteria [Income inequality and criteria of justification]. Sociologisch Instituut, Utrecht.

Hermkens, P., & van Wijngaarden, P. (1977). Rapport inkomensongelijkheid en rechtvaardigingskriteria [Report on income inequality and criteria of justification]' Sociale Zaken, Verslagen en Rapporten, 1977–1983, Den Haag.

Hermkens. P J. J. (1983). Oordelen over de rechtvaardigheid van inkomens [Judgments on the fairness of incomes] Utrecht, Dissertation.

Homans, G. C. (1961) Social behavior: Its elementary forms. New York: Harcourt Brace and World.

Homans, S. C. (1967). Fundamental social processes. In N. J. Smelser (ed.), Sociology: An introduction. New York, Wiley.

Jasso, G. (1978). On the justice of earnings: A new specification of the justice evaluation function. American Journal of Sociological, 83, 1398–1419.

Jasso, G. (1980). A new theory of distributive justice. American Sociological Review, 45,3–22.

Jasso, P., & Rossi, P. (1977). A new theory of distributive justice and earned income. In American Sociological Review, 42 (August), 639–651.

Appendix 1. Correlations and Standard Deviations of the Most Important Variables[a]

		1	2	3	4	5	6	7	8	9	10	11	12
1. TEQ	Tendency to equalize	26.1											
2. INEQAV	Inequality aversion	.40	5.6										
3. RELDIF	Relative Deprivation à la Runciman	.53	.27	.17									
4. V219	Income vs. attractive work	−.12	.08	.07	1.44								
5. DUMQUOT1	Dummy fair income level	−.28	−.24	−.32	−.02	.50							
6. V017	Occupational level	−.13	−.38	−.17	−.17	.16	1.61						
7. V048A	Self-rated occupational level	.20	.40	.17	.09	−.17	−.69	1.87					
8. V049	Expected changes of standard of living	.06	.16	.03	.08	−.06	−.14	.13	1.01				
9. V050	Changes in standard of living	.11	.25	.13	.06	−.13	−.18	.21	.17	1.25			
10. V109	Fairness relative income position	.07	.22	.30	.20	−.25	−.31	.29	.14	.15	.52		
11. V233	Equalization and work enjoyment	−.19	−.30	−.13	−.06	.12	.15	−.20	−.02	−.10	−.08	.60	
12. CLASS2	Dummy perception of class	.17	.23	.06	.01	−.12	−.07	.08	.03	.09	.04	−.09	
13. V221	Social security and mobility	.15	.14	.05	−.15	−.03	.06	−.01	−.02	.08	−.05	−.04	
14. V122	Expected changes inequality	.20	.22	.12	.05	−.11	−.14	.17	.10	.18	.16	−.07	
15. EMPL	Dummy employer	−.16	−.22	−.00	−.01	.10	.41	−.43	−.11	−.11	−.10	.13	
16. EDMOB	Intergenerational educational mobility	−.05	−.18	−.14	−.14	.10	.37	−.37	−.05	−.11	−.18	.13	
17. DGEREF	Dummy "gereformeerde kerk"	−.14	−.09	−.09	.03	.00	.07	−.06	.02	−.04	.01	.02	
18. V239	Equalization and unemployment	−.21	−.24	−.12	.00	.05	.03	−.04	.04	.02	.08	.25	
19. V011	Educational level	−.15	−.37	−.20	−.23	.14	.70	−.60	−.15	−.18	−.31	.15	
20. V119	Perceived change inequality	.21	.37	.22	.12	−.16	−.28	.28	.12	.14	.20	−.17	
21. V038	Salience of income comparison	−.13	−.10	−.15	.04	.19	−.02	.02	−.05	−.01	−.18	−.01	
22. POL	Political preference	.30	.40	.14	−.09	−.13	−.24	.28	.02	.20	.07	−.18	
23. TEST	Estimated Inequality	.11	.05	.22	−.02	−.05	−.07	.08	.05	.11	.01	−.02	
24. TESTLOW	TEST for bottom 40%	.17	.25	.24	.11	−.25	−.40	.41	.01	.18	.30	−.18	
25. DISCON	Discontent with equalization	−.28	−.38	−.03	.13	.11	−.03	−.04	.06	.01	.07	.27	
26. V005	Year of birth	.11	.04	.06	−.11	−.07	−.01	.07	−.27	−.05	−.01	−.03	
27. V246	Union membership	−.08	−.09	−.08	.01	.04	−.02	.03	−.16	.01	.00	.03	
28. V373	Income	−.22	−.29	−.26	−.12	.18	.46	−.50	−.02	−.15	−.29	.19	
29. DV018	Dummy self-employment	−.04	−.06	.15	.03	−.03	.15	−.35	.03	−.10	.14	.05	
30. V214	Income satisfaction	.18	.22	.36	.12	−.30	−.26	.25	.15	.17	.51	−.15	

[a]Pairwise deletion of cases with missing variables.

13	14	15	16	17	18	19	20	21	22	23	24	25	26	27	28	29	30
.77																	
.07	1.40																
−.03	−.12	.33															
.08	−.06	.18	1.78														
−.05	−.03	.05	.09	.28													
−.03	.06	.04	.01	−.06	.73												
.14	−.14	.26	.56	.03	.04	1.96											
−.02	.34	−.14	−.19	−.01	−.09	−.33	1.50										
−.05	−.01	−.03	−.07	−.04	.04	−.04	.01	.74									
.24	.19	−.20	−.05	−.19	−.08	−.14	.17	−.08	1.58								
−.02	.10	−.03	−.08	.00	−.03	−.08	.11	.01	.01	.13							
.04	.12	−.17	−.23	−.08	−.03	−.34	.16	−.06	.18	.32	.19						
−.19	−.08	.14	.01	−.04	.32	−.01	−.13	.10	−.27	.01	−.06	5.06					
.10	.01	−.09	−.04	−.12	−.08	.09	−.04	−.06	.22	−.05	.11	−.07	10.8				
−.03	−.04	−.02	−.07	−.11	.06	−.03	−.06	.06	−.02	.06	.16	.07	.13	.50			
.01	−.16	.38	.23	.03	.10	.42	−.26	.04	−.24	−.12	−.50	.09	−.20	−.10	14.5		
−.11	−.02	.36	.02	.06	−.00	−.05	.06	−.00	−.23	−.04	−.04	.10	−.14	−.09	.09	.31	
.03	.15	−.10	−.17	−.08	.04	−.25	.15	−.21	.12	.04	.34	.04	.02	.01	−.29	.05	1.45

Lenski, G. (1966). Power and privilege. New York : McGraw-Hill.
Mustert, G. R. (1976) Van dubbeltjes en kwartjes [Of Nickels and Dimes]. Den Haag: WRR.
Mustert, G. R. (1977). Meten met mate(n) [Measurement with measure(s)]. ESB, 331–335.
Nie, N. H. et. al. (1975). Statistical package for the social sciences (2nd ed.). New York: McGraw-Hill.
Overlaet, B., & Lagrou L. (1981). Attitude toward a redistribution of income. Journal of Economic Psychology, I, 197–215.
Robinson, R. V., Bell, W. (1978). Equality, success and social justice in England and the U.S., American Sociological Review, 43, 125–143.
Robinson, R. V., Kelley, J. (1979). Class as conceived of by Marx and Dahrendorf: Effects on income inequality and politics in the United States and Great Britain. American Sociological Review, 44, 38–58.
Runciman, W. G. (1966). Relative deprivation and social justice, A study of attitudes to social inequality in twentieth century England Routledge Kegan Paul.
Schokkaert E., Lagrou L. (1983). An empirical approach to distributive Justice London: Journal of Public Economics, 21, 33–52.
Social and Cultural Planning Bureau. (1986). Social and cultural report 1986. Den Haag: Staatsuitgeverij.
Szirmai, A. (1982). Matigingsbereidheid en nivelleringsgeneigheid [Acceptance of income restraint and preference for income equalization]. Onderzoeks-memorandum 119. Groningen: Instituut voor Economisch Onderzoek.
Szirmai, A. (1982b) Nivelleringsethos [The Ethic of Equalization]. In J. J. Godschalk P. L. J. Hermkens (eds.): Sociologie en Inkomensbeleid (pp. 119–160) [Sociology and incomes policy], Rotterdam: NSAV.
Szirmai, A., (1984) How do we really feel about income equalization. The Netherlands Journal of Sociology, 20, 115–133.
Szirmai, A., (1988). Inequality observed. A study of attitudes toward income inequality. Aldershot: Avebury.
Tazelaar, F., Wippler R., (1981). Die Theorie mentaler Inkongruenzen und Ihre Anwendung in der empirische Sozialforschung, Paper, Sociological Institute, State University of Utrecht, 1981.
Tazelaar, F. (1981). Mentale incongruenties—sociale restricties—gedrag: een onderzoek naar beroepsparticipatie van gehuwde vrouwelijke academici [Mental incongruities—social restrictions—behavior: A study of labor market participation of married female university graduates]. Dissertation, Utrecht.
Vermaat, A. J. (1975). Het meten van ongelijkheid [The measurement of inequality]. In J. van den Doel, A. Hoogerwerf (eds.), Gelijkheid en ongelijkheid in Nederland [Equality and inequality in the Netherlands], Alphen a/d Rijn: Samsom.
Wonnacott, R., & Wonnacott Th. J. (1970). Econometrics. New York: Wiley & Sons.
Wright, E. O., Perrone, L. (1977). Marxist class categories and income inequality American Sociological Review, 42, 32–55.

12

Future Trends in the Study of Social Justice

Herman Steensma and Riël Vermunt

Introduction

All justice is social justice. In all societies, rules and norms determine who gets what, and how much, of what there is. In this case, we speak of distributive justice. Rules and norms also guide the process of making these distributions. In that case, we speak of procedural justice.

Not everyone is equally sensitive to these norms and rules. And in some situations, people seem to be more sensitive than in other situations. On some occasions, people are willing to suffer to promote justice. But there is also evidence that people can be very opportunistic and egotistical. Frequently, it is assumed that people are motivated by the desire to maximize their outcomes. However, it is also clear that principles of justice play a central role in the way people treat one another. This paradox is solved by most theorists by assuming that in the course of human history social rules have been developed about how to engage in mutually profitable endeavors, rules that prevent a war of all against all. So, these "social contract" theorists maintain the image of a "rational man": Rules of justice are followed because they guarantee more profits, at least in the long run.

There are large differences between the theories of those who see justice as a principle adopted by rational human beings. But essen-

Herman Steensma and Riël Vermunt • Department of Social and Organizational Psychology, University of Leiden, P.O. Box 9555, 2333 AK Leiden, The Netherlands.

tially, they all conceptualize justice as an instrumental device for maximizing desired outcomes. And they agree that institutions have been created, both formal and informal, to ensure that people will follow the rules.

This view of justice as instrumental device may be challenged. And it has been challenged in recent years especially by Melvin Lerner. Lerner (1981) believes that justice functions as a guide of its own. Central to his model is that the outcome-maximizing motivations of children may be radically altered in their developmental process. He suggests the development of a "personal contract," that is, a child makes a personal contract with himself or herself based on the assumption that delay of gratification eventually will be rewarded. Who is right, the "social contract" theorists, or Lerner and others? Empirical research might give the answer.

In any case, we may observe that everyone agrees that there are rules of justice, and that these rules and norms are more salient in some situations than in other situations. And that considerations of justice play a central role, both for the functioning of individuals and for the functioning of society.

Here, then, are some of the most important issues and problems that researchers have to face:

- What are the most important principles of justice?
- What are the origins of justice norms, and how do these norms develop in the course of the life of people?
- When and why are certain principles of justice becoming salient?
- What institutional settings are important and why, and how do they function?
- What are the consequences of (in) justice on the functioning of persons, groups and societies?

Up to now, several methods have been used to collect the answers to these (and other) questions. Not everyone is satisfied with the methods that are most commonly used, however. Edward Sampson is well known as a critic of justice research. According to Sampson (1983), most social scientists studying justice are rather uncritically using terms that reflect the given socioeconomic system of the Western world. For instance, many social psychologists examining justice phenomena appropriate concepts like "exchange value" to describe the "value" of persons who are interacting with each other. Insofar as these terms are employed uncritically, these scientists are in fact reproducing the very society that generates these terms, Sampson says. Our modern society is indeed characterized by price-making marketplace exchanges (however, with increasing interventions by states). But there are other ways to steer exchanges between people. Exchanges may be based on nonprice principles, noneconomic motivations. Many societies are based, or have been based, on other principles. So, social scientists adopting the price-making market form are simply taking a slice from a socioeconomic historical time axis, but most of them assume that the "laws" they discover are valid for all times and all places—a highly questionable assumption (see also Gergen, 1973, on this subject). Sampson also criticizes psychologists for their lack of critical analyses of the inequitable distribution of social products. In fact, social science sometimes seems to be a part of the extensive mechanisms that work to legitimize the existing social order and to prevent potential discontent. Undoubtedly, Sampson has made a point. Still, we think things may not be as gloomy as he sketches. For instance, it is now accepted by most researchers that principles of justice vary with the social group in which allocation takes place: With your children, you use the need principle; among friends, equal divisions of outcomes generally are preferred; and in economic relationships, some form of allocation related to inputs is in force.

Also, especially in studies of macrojustice, researchers frequently seem to be inspired by a wish to challenge the existing unequal allocations of society's products. And several social scientists have contributed in one way or another to the success of emancipation movements, for example, by buttressing the call for "equal opportunities" and "affirmative action" with their research results.

So, though Sampson may be right that most scientists are neglecting socioeconomic and historical constraints, he may be wrong—at least partly—in suggesting that they more or less routinely agree with societal injustice. Some chapters in these volumes demonstrate this clearly (see, for instance, the chapters by Deutsch; Lerner; Allegro, Kruidenier, and Steensma). And we are convinced that future research, too, will testify for the fact that social scientists are perfectly able to combine scientific standards with a critical attitude toward societal problems. Still, in spite of our positive conviction, it must be admitted that much research is done in a more or less "traditional" way. However, some interesting new trends may be discerned.

Trends in Social Justice Research

Is there anything to say about the future of justice research? Is interest in some topics and theories growing, whereas interest in other topics is waning? In this final chapter we present some impressions we have about the directions in which justice research is going. These impressions are based upon a perusal of recent literature; the papers presented at the International Conference of Social Justice in Human Relations in Leiden in 1986 and informal meetings with—and communications from—other researchers. We think, then, that in the near future we might see more cross-cultural and interdisciplinary research. Also, there will be more attention for applied research and for the flexible approach in choosing research methods. Finally, there are some interesting theoretical developments that combine justice research with other dominant research traditions.

Cross-Cultural Research

There are those who believe in the universal presence of a certain principle of justice. Gouldner (1960) believed that there exists a universal norm of reciprocity. The norm consists in the obligation we have to help those who helped us and not to injure them. The amount reciprocated should vary according to the amount and value of the reward previously received.

Walster, Walster, and Berscheid (1978) consider equity theory to be a general theory of social behavior, a theory that can integrate the many specialized minitheories that exist. They believe that the equity principle governs all areas of human interaction and even present us an "updated" definitional formula to calculate whether a relationship is equitable or not. The principle amounts to a principle of proportionality between inputs and outcomes from an interaction.

In contrast to those theorists that believe in only one principle, several authors posit a number of justice principles (for a review, see Schwinger, 1980). The most important principles are the "proportionality (or equity, or contribution) principle," the "equality principle" (equal allocation to all individuals), and the "need principle" (allocation according to individual needs).

So the rules for deciding what is just are not invariant, according to the multiple principles approach. Now research has made it clear that frequently gender differences exist in allocation behavior (for a review, see Major & Deaux, 1981). The equality principle seems to be more popular among women than among male allocators. So the standards for what is to be considered just may differ in groups and social aggregates, even within one nation. We may expect that differences in opinions and norms about just behavior may be even larger when we compare different countries with large differences, in culture and sociohistorical context. This suggests an interesting task for justice researchers. They should systematically describe what differences in justice principles (if any) there are between countries, and they should try to explain the reasons for the differences.

Up till now there have been some studies in which attention was paid to the relation between nationalities and conceptions of justice (to mention only a few: Mikula, 1974, who found no differences in reward allocations by Austrian and American students; Mann, Radford, Kanagawa, 1985, who found differences between Japanese and Australian children; Bond, Leung, Wan, 1982, who found that Chinese students in Hong Kong and American students in California differed in how they distributed rewards; Vermunt & Lerner (personal communication) who found that Canadian subjects differed in reward allocation from Dutch subjects). But we think that the time has come for a more systematic large-scale effort to explore and explain cross-cultural differences in justice conceptions and behavior. Fortunately, the conditions for such a large-scale enterprise are rather good. Partly owing to workshops and conferences, justice researchers from several nations get to know each other better—and they seem to love it! Eventually this may result in combined cross-cultural research efforts. Not being too modest, we think that the International Conference on Social Justice in Human Relations may have contributed to a climate that is favorable to cross-cultural research on justice.

Interdisciplinary Research

Issues concerning justice can be found in various domains of life. Accordingly, several disciplines are concerned with research on justice: philosophy, psychology, sociology, political science, social anthropology, economics, criminology, and, of course, jurisprudence.

All these disciplines are characterized by their own prevalent perspectives and research methods. And all these disciplines have brought valuable contributions to the understanding of justice. However, frequently these contributions were known only by the specialists in the particular discipline. This has not always been the case, however. Piaget, for instance, had a deep knowledge of philosophy, sociology, and psychology. Still, presently most researchers only attend the recent literature of their own disciplines. Partly this may be due to the enormous amount of information that is bombarding the modern scientist. It may be fertile, however, to have knowledge of the contributions to the topic in other disciplines. In this respect, it must be noted that most recent books on justice edited by social scientists contain chapters written by both psychologists and sociologists (e.g.,

Lerner & Lerner, 1981; Messick & Cook, 1983; Bierhoff, Cohen, & Greenberg, 1986; Cohen, 1986). The same is true for the present volumes. Though dominated by psychologists, there are also chapters written by sociologists and economists. Also, there are contributions with a definite sociolegal "flavor" (e.g., the contribution by Lloyd-Bostock and the chapter by Tyler and Lind). Real interdisciplinary research, in which a team is formed consisting of researchers from several backgrounds, still is very scarce.[1] But we believe there is again a growing *willingness* to pay more attention to what is accomplished in other disciplines.

The journal *Social Justice Research* testifies to this willingness. It provides a forum for all (social) scientists investigating justice in human affairs. We welcome it as a major contribution to the field of justice research.

More Applied Research

A few years ago, Miner (1984) apparently demonstrated some disdain for one of the best-known theories of justice, that is, equity theory. In evaluating various theories in organizational psychology according to their usefulness, equity theory was rated in the bottom category ("not so useful") because of its lack of specific applications.

Equity theory is not the only theory on justice. Miner's critique, however, draws attention to the relation between basic and applied research in the field of (social) justice. Until recently, however, there was hardly a relation at all. Basic researchers were busy in their laboratories, doing ingenuous experiments with undergraduate students as subjects, and controlling several conditions, meanwhile manipulating a few experimental variables. However, with a few exceptions they showed no interest in applying their theories in real life. Applied researchers also were very busy doing research in the field by order of central or local government, or in the service of firms, struggling with quite a lot of variables at once, and with relatively little interest in testing specific theories.

Representatives of basic and applied research hardly spoke with each other; sometimes it even seemed that they despised each other. Nowadays, things seem to have been changed. Basic researchers have more interest in nonlaboratory situations; applied researchers show more interest in the possible use of well-developed theories. The net

---

[1]This is not true, however, in some applied settings; for example, a court may seek advice from experts.

result may be a tendency to do more applied research (but with a touch of fundamental theory). This trend can be seen, for instance, in the reader edited by Bierhoff, Cohen, and Greenberg (1986), in which a section was devoted to application of justice research. Also, in the conference on social justice in human relations (1986), there were many papers from the fundamental basic tradition; but also there were quite a number of papers by adherents of more applied research. (And, perhaps still more important, representatives of both approaches had genuine respect for each other.) We think this is a good development that should continue in the future. By using fundamental theory in applied research there is a kind of two-way insemination:

1. Dry theories are filled with lively, vivid real-life examples. In other words, no one can have any doubts about the importance, the relevance of our theories not only for science but also for society.
2. By using theory, it is possible to collect data in a systematic way instead of the more ad-hoc approach that has flourished in the field of applied research.

In this way, a body of knowledge can be accumulated, knowledge that makes sense and that by its firm base in theory allows researchers to predict to other times and other places. Society is confronted with serious problems, for example, unemployment, various forms of discrimination (racial, sexual, class), unanticipated side-effects of new technology, diminishing natural resources, and so forth. Both society and science may profit from the creative use of advanced theories in studying these problems.

Methodological Developments

We noted already the growth of the mixed approach, that is, the integration of fundamental theory and applied research. One of the useful side-effects of this trend is a renewed interest in research methodology. Until recently, most researchers were characterized by a certain one-sidedness. It seems as if researchers only knew how to do laboratory experiments—when they were working in the field of basic research. Or their pet technique was some variation of survey research—when they were working in the applied field. Nowadays, there seems to be a growing interest in being less traditional when choosing research methods. And those researchers that stick with the usual methods recognize the worth of other approaches. The growing interest in the "mixed approach" is not the only reason for the trend of more variety in research methods. Some "internal developments" within a certain research domain also accelerated the interest in new (or better) research methods. For instance, Mikula (1986) pointed out that there was very little evidence on the quality of emotions and on the cognitive processes elicited by the perception of injustice. Methodological difficulties were a major reason for this. As Mikula remarked, however, the bias toward rigorous methodology should not prevent relevant research from being conducted (even if data collected may not be very pure according to strict high-quality standards). Mikula (1986) used two different methodologies to collect data on the experience of injustice: (1)retrospective reports of unjust events people had actually confronted, and (2) a (passive) role-playing technique. Though these methods have their weak spots, some quite interesting results were obtained by using these techniques.

We think that the tendency not to restrict oneself to one technique will grow stronger. Several chapters in these volumes reflect the nonconventional attitude, in this respect, of some researchers (see, e.g., the chapters written by Tyler and Lind; Lloyd-Bostock; and Billig). Personally we welcome this tendency to be nonorthodox in research methods as a means of getting new data that may shed light on complicated issues. As for ourselves, one of us has recently been involved in several action research projects [2] Even in this action research, it was possible to test very fundamental theories.

Summarizing, we may say that the choice of methods should be guided by the problem to be solved and not by what is customary. Of course, we must admit that frequently the conventional methodology is the best methodology for handling the problem! Anyway, there seems to be more interest in a broad spectrum of research methods. Perhaps this will eventually result in solving a problem, repeatedly brought up by Melvin Lerner. Lerner suggests that most present-day research methods are unfit for disclosing what really motivates people. He may be right. Perhaps new methods will support his claim. Perhaps not. But surely they will offer some exciting new insights.

Theoretical Developments

Harry Reis (1986) has constructed a taxonomy of levels of interest in justice phenomena. First, he distinguishes studies concerned with the justice motive from those dealing with specific rules that regulate

---

[2]Some of these projects are mentioned in the final section of the chapter by Allegro, Kruidenier, and Steensma.

interpersonal relations. The next subdivision of his scheme distinguishes principles that focus on procedural justice from those that concern the distribution of outcomes. The final differentiation is made between choice of relevant parameters (called the "determination of value") and the perception of entitling inputs (the evaluation of the level of inputs).

This scheme may have its value, but it is certainly unfit for classifying all justice research (and it should be admitted that Reis does not claim that his taxonomy succeeds in doing that). For instance, the study of emotional reactions to unjust situations is not easy to place in this scheme. Several other problems may arise. We will not elaborate on these problems. Instead we will give our impression about recent theoretical developments. We think, then, that researchers more and more make use of what may be called "bridge theories" (Steensma, 1985). Bridge theories are coupled with another theory to explain difficulties of the latter. Expected utility theory, for instance, may be used to predict which of the several possible reactions to inequity will be chosen by the victim of inequity—a prediction that is not contained in the original set of propositions by Adams (1965). Or, to take another example, attribution theory may be coupled with equity theory to explain variations in the degree of distress produced by inequity (Utne & Kidd, 1980).

In this way, ultimately a network of connected theories may be constructed—a network consisting of the major models and research paradigms of social science (and excluding the many mini theories). Of course, there is still a long way to go. And perhaps there will be some detours. But this is for sure: we will reach some theoretical advance by making clear the connections between theories of justice and theories dominating other research domains.

Conclusion

Modern society is characterized by its rapid changes. These changes offer the opportunity to bring about improvements in social arrangements. Social scientists may contribute to these improvements by furnishing data and theories necessary to guide change in the direction that is desired. Some promising new trends have been discerned in the field of justice research. These trends are helpful, both to answer questions of content (e.g., "what is justice") and of process (e.g., "which procedures must be followed"). The study of justice must have a top priority: Throughout history, reaching justice has been one of the most universal objectives of man.

References

Adams, J. S. (1965). Inequity in social exchange. In L. Berkowitz (Ed.), *Advances in experimental social psychology* (Vol. 2, pp. 267–299). New York: Academic Press.

Bierhoff, H. W., Cohen, R. L., & Greenberg, J. (1986). *Justice in social relations.* New York: Plenum Press.

Bond, M., Leung, K., & Wan, K. C. (1982). How does cultural collectivism operate? The impact of task and maintenance on reward distribution. *Journal of Cross-Cultural Psychology, 13,* 186–200.

Cohen, R. L. (Ed.). (1986). *Justice-views from the social sciences.* New York: Plenum Press.

Gergen, K. J. (1973). Social psychology as history. *Journal of Personality and Social Psychology, 26,* 309–320.

Gouldner, A. W. (1960). The norm of reciprocity: A preliminary statement. *American Sociological Review, 25,* 161–178.

Lerner, M. J. (1981). The justice motive in human relations. In M. J. Lerner & S.C. Lerner (Eds.), *The justice motive in social behavior* (pp. 11–35). New York: Plenum Press.

Lerner, M. J., and Lerner, S.C. (1984). *The justice motive in social behavior.* New York: Plenum Press.

Major, B., & Deaux, K. (1981). Individual differences in equity behavior. In J. Greenberg & R. L. Cohen (Eds.), *Equity and justice in social behavior* (pp. 43–76). New York: Academic Press.

Mann, L., Radford, M., & Kanagawa, C. (1985). Cross-cultural differences in children's use of decision rules: A comparison between Japan and Australia. *Journal of Personality and Social Psychology, 49,* 6, 1557–1564.

Messick, D. M., & Cook, K. S. (Eds.). (1983). *Equity theory—Psychological and sociological perspectives.* New York: Praeger.

Mikula, G. (1974). Nationality, performance, and sex as determinants of reward allocation. *Journal of Personality and Social Psychology, 29,* 4, 435–440.

Mikula, G. (1986). The experience of injustice—Toward a better understanding of its phenomenology. In H. W. Bierhoff *et al.* (Eds.), *Justice in social relations* (pp. 103–123). New York: Plenum Press.

Miner, J. B. (1984). The unpaved road over the mountains: From theory to applications. *The Industrial-Organizational Psychologist, 21,* 2, 9–20.

Reis, H. T. (1986). Levels of interest in the study of interpersonal justice. In H. W. Bierhoff *et al.* (Eds.), *Justice in social relations* (pp. 187–209). New York: Plenum Press.

Sampson, E. E. (1983). *Justice and the critique of pure psychology.* New York: Plenum Press.

Schwinger, T. (1980). Just allocation of goods: Decisions among three principles. In G. Mikula (Eds.), *Justice and social interaction* (pp. 95–125). Bern: Huber.

Steensma, H. O. (1985). De verklaring van werkvoldoening werkmotivatie en werkgedrag. In H. Steensma, R. van der Vlist, J. T. Allegro, *Modern organiseren en menselijker werken* (pp. 19–36). The Hague: Vuga.

Utne, M. K., Kidd, R. F. (1980). Equity and attribution. In G. Mikula (Ed.), *Justice and social interaction* (pp. 63–93). Bern: Huber.

Walster, E., Walster, G. W., & Berscheid, E. (1978). *Equity theory and research.* Boston: Allyn & Bacon.

Author Index

279

Subject Index